Dictatorship in Spanish America

Borzoi Books ON LATIN AMERICA

General Editor
LEWIS HANKE
COLUMBIA UNIVERSITY

Dictatorship
IN
Spanish America

Edited with an Introduction by

HUGH M. HAMILL, JR.

THE UNIVERSITY OF CONNECTICUT

New York: Alfred A. Knopf

1966

L. C. catalog card number: 64–23731

THIS IS A BORZOI BOOK,
PUBLISHED BY ALFRED A. KNOPF, INC.

PUBLISHED MARCH 10, 1965
SECOND PRINTING, APRIL 1966

DEDICATED TO

My Father

And to

The Memory of Jesús de Galíndez

Acknowledgments

My chief debt is to Lewis Hanke, who has made me the fortunate beneficiary of his abiding interest in what he calls "the care and feeding of Latin American dictators." I am, furthermore, indebted to the students of his Colloquium at Columbia University. They read the manuscript during the spring of 1964 and offered valuable suggestions, many of which they will find reflected in the following pages. My wife, Elizabeth Hamill, and my colleague Robert Mead read the Introduction and offered much useful criticism.

Although I am responsible for the translations, I should like to acknowledge the assistance of Celia Lescano of the University of Florida's N.D.E.A. Program in the translation of Raymond Crist's essay. Professor Crist himself gave most kindly of his time to assist this project. Maurice Kohler helped prepare the translation of M. Chevalier's article.

The following deserve my thanks for help in one way or another: George Bernstein, Ronald Cassidento, Robert Gilmore, Charles Hale, Ann Lescoe, John Murra, Carol Raphael, Karen Slaybaugh, Peter H. Smith, and Roberta Smith. The manuscript was skillfully typed by Charlotte Ritchie. The research for the whole project was financed by a grant from the Research Foundation of the University of Connecticut.

Errors, interpretations, and choice of documents can be laid at no other door but mine.

HUGH M. HAMILL, JR.

Storrs, Connecticut
June 1964

Contents

Dictatorship in Spanish America

INTRODUCTION

In romping through the centuries from Pizarro to Perón, both professors and readings in Latin American history survey courses were, until recently, apt to concentrate upon those forceful personalities who played dominant roles in the epoch of conquest, the establishment of viceregal power, and the implementation of Bourbon reforms. The compelling qualities of Hernán Cortés, Pedro de Valdivia, Antonio de Mendoza, and José de Gálvez were followed by the dedicated derring-do of warriors for independence from Bolívar to Hidalgo, and from San Martín to Sucre. Once into the national period, the number of historical personality cults was multiplied. From Santa Anna to Batista, histories of the period since independence were punctuated by accounts of the exploits and atrocities of one dictator after another.

When an instructor essayed the nearly impossible task of treating twenty republics in fifteen weeks, some countries were simply dismissed as having been dominated by a series of strong men: from Páez to Pérez Jiménez in Venezuela, from Francia to Stroessner in Paraguay. Such was the interest in personalist rule that most thoughtful people would have agreed with Prof. J. Fred Rippy in 1937 when he wrote that "Dictators have been so numerous that the history of most of these Latin American countries is to a large extent the biography of these imperious personalities." [1]

Since World War II, however, increasing attention has been paid by writers and teachers to the importance of more impersonal social, economic, intellectual, and, even, psychological forces in the history of Latin America. In one of the most provocative books to emerge in the postwar years, Stanford's Prof. John J. Johnson chose

[1] "Monarchy or Republic?" in *South American Dictators During the First Century of Independence*, ed. by A. Curtis Wilgus (Washington: George Washington University Press, 1937), p. 16.

to "emphasize social groups in a region where, in the view of traditional scholarship, individuals hold the center of the stage. The chief executives, the caudillos, and the colonels who shoot their way into the presidential chair are no longer the effective agents of all political change." [2] Indeed, during the 1930's and 1940's many "traditional" historians had been moved to pessimism and to caudillo interpretations by the widespread reactionary developments which occurred in the wake of the Wall Street collapse of 1929. Most notably Getulio Vargas's advent in Brazil and the Radical Party's loss of power in Argentina appeared to end cautious gropings toward broadly based representative republics. That Venezuela was unable to achieve any durable progress toward democracy after the death of Juan Vicente Gómez in 1935, that Argentina went from oligarchical control to the military coup of June 4, 1943, and eventually to Juan Perón, and that Mexico's one-party rule did not coincide with commonly accepted democratic standards were all factors which kept observers from becoming overly sanguine about the bright future which Costa Rica and Uruguay seemed to augur for Latin America. As late as 1950 a distinguished group of scholars representing the fields of economics, political science, sociology, and history produced a sober clinical report which they entitled "Pathology of Democracy in Latin America." [3]

But by the time Professor Johnson went into print in 1958 to cut down those who persisted in maintaining that Latin America "has no middle class to speak of" and to shift the emphasis away from the individual power-seeker, so many of the Depression–World War II dictators had been ousted that a book by a correspondent for *The New York Times* was already in press entitled *Twi-*

[2] *Political Change in Latin America: the Emergence of the Middle Sectors* (Stanford: Stanford University Press, 1958), p. viii.

[3] W. W. Pierson *et al.*, "Pathology of Democracy in Latin America," *American Political Science Review*, Vol. XLIV (1950), pp. 100-149.

light of the Tyrants.[4] Whether or not the late 1960's and
the 1970's will see such a *Götterdämmerung* is not of
primary concern in this book. On the other hand, if
Spanish American strong men are less ubiquitous than
they once were it is no reason to avoid a serious effort to
understand them, since the caudillo has been one of the
major historical phenomena of the region. The primary
purpose of this book is, then, to explore the nature of
that phenomenon.

The readings which comprise most of this volume have
not been collected in order to provide a complete guide-
book to Spanish American dictators or to emphasize a
particular issue. I have sought no deliberate polarization
which pits the bad tyrant against the forces of democratic
righteousness. Inevitably such critics of dictators as Francisco Bilbao in Chile (Document 7) and Jesús de Galíndez in the Dominican Republic (Document 14)
make plain their distaste for *caudillismo* but their inclusion was not motivated by any effort to moralize. Rather,
most of the selections were made because they suggest
the rich variety of dictatorial types and the multitude of
factors which have conditioned their existence. This is
not to say that the reader is expected to emerge with a
single neatly integrated and compact definition of "The
Spanish American Dictator." On the contrary, it is hoped
that much debate will develop over matters of interpretation and that the suggestions for additional reading in A *Bibliographical Note*, which concludes this
volume, will be an invitation to further study.

The readings have been arranged in a roughly chrono-
logical order beginning with Iberian origins and closing with mid-twentieth century dictatorships. Throughout
the book, descriptive pieces and polemical arguments
have been interspersed with interpretative essays by modern writers. These essays not only develop particular aspects of the phenomenon but also reveal the orientation
of the writers. It is noteworthy that even the most ostensi-

---

[4] Tad Szulc, *Twilight of the Tyrants* (New York: Holt, Rine-
hart and Winston, Inc., 1959).

bly objective treatments of the Spanish American caudillo (of which a nearly endless list might be compiled)
often suggest either personal biases or contemporary influences on the authors. Because interpretations have
been quite as much in flux as dictatorship itself, a secondary or even dual objective in making this book has been
to demonstrate the ways in which different people with
different perspectives have defended or attacked or simply sought to explain Spanish American dictators. The
brief preliminary notes to each of the readings have been
written to suggest something of the origin, philosophy,
and vested interests of the writers.

The Spanish American dictator is but one of the manifestations of political realities in the history of a highly
complex, heterogenous society and cultural area. To concentrate on the phenomenon of the "Man on Horseback" is to invite distortion and a disproportionate emphasis. While the significance of the caudillo may be so
great in some political settings at a given time that one
might say it is only the personality that matters, it would
be wrong to characterize this or any other area of the
world in a single dimension. It is, for instance, difficult
to separate the phenomenon of dictatorship from the
phenomenon of the social revolution which may, as in
the case of Mexico in 1910 and of Cuba in 1956, have begun with the primary intent of getting rid of a strong
man but which, in expanding thereafter to encompass
full-scale revision of the social and economic orders, may
well lead to yet another despotic form of government.
By a concentration on authoritarianism there is, too, the
peril of obscuring the genuine achievement of open
societies, political stability, and security against tyranny
which have come to characterize some Spanish American
countries such as Uruguay.

If the dangers of distortion through concentration are
perceived, however, we may proceed. It might well be
that an intense exploration into the specific nature of
political autocracy will lead to a much wider knowledge
of the society which produces the personalist leader. The

disarray of England's hereditary nobility at the end of the War of the Roses unquestionably conditioned the country for the authoritarian rule of Henry Tudor; the abrupt internal vicissitudes of the First French Republic and the concurrent external War of the First Coalition are in the background of the successful rise of Napoleon Bonaparte; and an absorption in the grisly life of Adolf Hitler is taking scholars ever deeper into the broad historical background of the Weimar Republic and the Third Reich. That an autochthonous American dictator, Huey Long, emerged in Louisiana during the Depression years is also suggestive of the relevance of an autocrat's appeal to immediate social and economic conditions.

The temptation to compare authoritarian figures from age to age and place to place, from Pisistratus to Mao-Tse-Tung, is strong when dealing with New World dictators. Nevertheless, the task of discriminating among the latter is itself so complex that the method of comparative analysis with European and Asiatic models may well be eschewed as less rewarding. Not a few Spanish American leaders in the nineteenth century fancied themselves neo-Napoleons; but do we really learn very much about their countries by knowing the Bonapartist dreams of Agustín de Iturbide in Mexico? Bonapartist dreams offer insight into the characters of the men themselves, but Napoleon is really the exception that proves the rule. Juan Perón may have learned more what *not* to do than to do from his knowledge of Mussolini and Hitler. What makes the comparative approach only incidentally useful is the pressing question of the unique quality of the strong man in Latin America.

To say that the Spanish American dictator is unique is, of course, to say very little if only because "the Spanish American dictator" is a Platonic ideal. A cartoonist's pen may sketch the stereotype of the austere, virile general crushing his horse under him by the combined weight of his sword, his medals, his mustache, and the brass of his absurdly slanted hat; but such lampoons may be as close as we are able to come to any composite ideal. What makes graphic representation difficult is that dictatorship is a dynamic not a static institution. Through time and space real autocrats in Spanish America have ranged from the coarse, bloody tyrant Facundo Quiroga, whom Domingo Sarmiento described in his classic *Civilization and Barbarism* (Document 6), to such principled conservatives as Diego Portales in Chile and the theocratic García Moreno in Ecuador; and from the urbane cosmopolite Rafael Núñez, who was happier writing mediocre poetry than he was ruling Colombia in the 1880's (Document 8), to such modern manipulators of mass psychology as Juan Perón and Fidel Castro. Perhaps terminology is at fault. Perhaps it has trapped us into grouping together too many disparate types of individuals. The word "dictator," meaning "a person exercising absolute power," may be too comprehensive. But what of the Spanish term *"caudillo"*? Is it more useful? This is, after all, the generic term applied freely in Spanish America. With its roots in the Latin *"capitellum,"* which is the diminutive of *"caput"* or "head," "caudillo" is not really more precise than "dictator" except that it does have a resonance which suggests the unique milieu and the conditioning elements of Spanish America. Only through the use of modifying adjectives (or direct application to specific leaders) will it be possible to make the terms "dictator" and "caudillo" refer to anything other than the ideal. The Bolivian social critic Alcides Argüedas (1878-1946), for example, sought to distinguish between the "barbarous caudillos" and the "cultivated caudillos" in two of his books.[5] An endless variety of other modifiers will also be encountered which range from "gaucho" to "military" and from "feudal" to "totalitarian." The friends, enemies, and students of particular caudillos have found descriptive terms for each one which are quite as varied as the leaders themselves. Thus Bolívar was "The Liberator," Arturo Alessandri was "The Lion of Tarapacá," Yrigoyen was *"El Peludo"*—"The Shaggy

---

[5] *Los caudillos bárbaros* (Barcelona, 1929) and *Los caudillos letrados* (Barcelona, 1923).

One," [6] Calles was "The Maximum Chief," Trujillo was "The Benefactor," and almost all were called "The Tyrant" by someone at one time or another. The authors of the analytic and descriptive readings in this volume employ their own terminologies which vary greatly. Finally, the reader may find it advantageous to work out his own classifications which may well be superior to any imposed upon him.

Lest it seem that the only option left is atomistic, it should be said that no matter what the particular variant of dictatorship in Spanish America, no matter what individual caudillo emerges *de carne y hueso*, there is some utility in the idea of caudillismo. That utility lies in the valuable effort to discover common denominators: shared backgrounds of historical antiquity and experience, psychic orientation of peoples, philosophies of government, social stratification, economic dislocation, geographic conditions, and external pressures wherever and whenever they may exist. If there is a common civilization in Spanish America, whatever the regional variations, then the pursuit of knowledge about one institutional element common to the whole area at one time or another may lead to a broader understanding of that civilization.

In the interests of making the pursuit of the meaning of caudillismo more effective, Portuguese American civilization is not directly represented in the readings. The exclusion of Brazil may not seem warranted until it is recalled that the pattern of her history diverges from that of Spanish America at so many points that she does indeed deserve separate treatment as a distinct civilization.[7]

The salutary neglect of Brazil by Portugal in the sixteenth century, the relatively loose colonial governmen-

---

[6] "Peludo" can also mean "tough" and "drunk."

[7] On the subject of her uniqueness as a civilization, see Gilberto Freyre's *New World in the Tropics* (New York: Vintage Books, 1963). John J. Johnson's decision to treat the Brazilian military apart from the collective Spanish American military is pertinent: See *The Military and Society in Latin America* (Stanford: Stanford University Press, 1964), p. vii.

tal organization, the pacific emergence of Brazil into independence, and the nineteenth-century Bragança monarchy most especially set off Brazil's historical emergence from that of Spanish America. For purposes of contrast Brazil's history might help put a study of Spanish American caudillos in relief—but so might the history of France, Germany, or Japan. The twentieth century, to be sure, has produced more common denominators between the two Iberian-rooted civilizations. Getulio Vargas was in part the product of world economic conditions which encouraged the contemporary renascence of caudillismo in Spanish America; he was, also, from Brazil's "gaucho" state, Río Grande do Sul, on the frontier of the Spanish-speaking states of the Río de la Plata. Vargas's manipulation of constitutional provisions to suit his needs was, of course, one of a number of dictatorial techniques which he shared with his Spanish American counterparts. Threats of violence to overthrow him became, on one occasion in 1938, so real that Getulio and his daughter had to defend themselves with firearms against Plinio Salgado's fascistic Integralistas. In spite of Vargas's example, however, comparisons within the Latin American area are more apt to produce statements which begin or end with the phrase "but circumstances were different in Brazil." For this reason, Portuguese America is set aside in this volume.[8]

The generic term "caudillo" has a variant or related term: "cacique." Though less heralded, the *local* cacique, the Spanish American political boss, is as compelling a figure in his own region as the *national* caudillo. In the emergence of the national caudillo it may be argued that the cacique is a *sine qua non*. [This argument is implicit, for instance, in François Chevalier's essay on the dictator's personal ties (Document 2).] The term is New World; the Spaniards early encountered it among the Tainos and Arawaks of the Caribbean. The Arawak term *kassequa* lent itself to Spanish orthography and usage to

---

[8] For one pertinent analysis of Portuguese America, see Alexander Marchant: "Constitutional Dictatorship in Brazil" in *South American Dictators*, pp. 429-469.

mean, at first, local Indian chief, and later any regional strong man, regardless of race. Given geographic isolation and the vastness of the region, the scattered power nuclei, controlled by caciques, were fundamental to the emergence of a national caudillo. Whereas a cacique is a ruler among men, a caudillo is a ruler among caciques. The Mexican Revolution between 1910 and 1920 produced an extraordinary number of examples of this cacique-to-caudillo elevation. This distinction between caudillo and cacique is not universally applied, however, and a given writer may dispense with the term cacique when dealing with sectional leaders and use caudillo. When this happens, the national dictator is usually distinguished as the *"caudillo supremo"* or *"jefe máximo."*

That caudillismo and *caciquismo* are dynamic institutions, subject to change, redefinition, and reappraisal from decade to decade is nowhere more apparent than in the history of Argentina. There is almost a spectrum of caudillo types. It begins with the rude provincial bosses of the *Año Terrible* of 1820 who characterized the littoral and interior provinces for the next several decades; Facundo Quiroga was most notorious among them thanks to Domingo Sarmiento's pen. These quasi-feudal barons achieved and held their power as the old Viceroyalty of La Plata was broken up. A caudillo supremo, Juan Manuel de Rosas, was not long in appearing. For most of the period between 1829 and 1852 Rosas achieved some order, if little progress, in Argentina from his political and economic base in the Province of Buenos Aires. Further yet along the spectrum came the cacique of Entre Rios, Justo José de Urquiza, who possessed a sufficient amount of that imagination which Rosas lacked to transcend his narrow provincial interests and to act as arbiter of an emergent constitutionally based republic. The sophisticated *porteños* of Buenos Aires who gained ascendancy after 1861, in part through the selflessness of Urquiza, produced republican leaders who, in spite of their progressive attitudes, were not totally free of the influence of Quiroga and Rosas. Sarmiento's arbitrary efforts to impose his successor on the country at the end

of his term in 1874 and Bartolomé Mitre's resort to arms
in order to prevent Sarmiento from having his way are
points in evidence. After that, refinements in the manipulation of the constitutional powers of the presidency
had reached such a degree by 1890 that a spokesman for
the opposition Civic Union could say that:

> The President of the republic is exercising *de facto*
> total public power. He has in his hands the reins of
> municipal authority, the keys to the banks, tutelage
> over the provincial governors, control of the voices
> and the votes of the members of congress, and he
> even manages the judicial machinery.[9]

Although the election of the Radical Civic Union's candidate, Hipólito Yrigoyen, to the presidency in 1916 was
acclaimed as a great victory for democratic progress,
Yrigoyen's conduct often bore marked traces of an urban
cacique's approach to national power. It was after the
military *coup d'état* of September 1930 had removed the
aged and, by then, incompetent Yrigoyen from office,
that the train of events began which culminated fifteen
years later in the rise to power of the most skilled caudillo
that Argentina has known, Juan Domingo Perón (Documents 15, 16).

No orderly progression should be imagined, however,
in this apparent continuum from the muscular caudillos
of the era of what Lucas Ayarragaray has called "gau-
chocracy" to the quasi-totalitarian rule of the charismatic
Colonel Perón and his equally charismatic wife, Eva
Duarte de Perón. The urbane Bernardino Rivadavia
brought a cosmopolitan luster and enlightenment to government in Buenos Aires during the 1820's at the very
time that the provincial caciques ruled their fiefs. Constitutional sophistication built on Juan Bautista Alberdi's
Bases orgánicas matured in the century after 1853 simultaneously with the exercise of presidential authoritarianism. Nevertheless, the argument that caudillismo is a

---

[9] Joaquín Castellanos, quoted by José Luis Romero in *A History of Argentine Political Thought*, translated by Thomas F. Mc-
Gann (Stanford: Stanford University Press, 1963), p. 189.

resilient institution of many facets is supported by the Argentine example.

Conditioning elements which effect the institution of caudillismo in Spanish America are as varied as in any society in which there is a complex interaction between the leader and the led. The success of a caudillo is not only measured by the number of years he is able to retain power but also, and more importantly, by the skill with which he weds himself to the patriotic mythology, history, folk customs, religious observances, fraternal and kinship groups, national psychology, and political traditions (even if they are ostensibly republican and constitutional). Rafael Trujillo's sustained effort to be godfather or *compadre* to many newly baptized Dominicans from all strata of society unquestionably contributed to his thirty-year tenure as "Benefactor." When Porfirio Díaz lost his telluric sense and refused to face the social pressures of the early twentieth century in Mexico, his regime faced revolution. The readings develop some of the most consequential conditioners in detail. A suggestive summary here will serve as an introduction.

The ancient Spanish expression *del rey abajo ninguno* ("after the king, no one is superior to me") bespeaks a pride and individualism which is well-rooted in the Iberian past. Spain's twentieth-century Renaissance Man, Salvador de Madariaga, develops the psychological relationship between personal autonomy and dictatorship which emerges from his country's medieval heritage (Document 1). The significance of the *Reconquista*, the eight centuries of intermittent border warfare between Moor and Christian (and just as frequently between Moor and Moor and Christian and Christian!) has been a favorite theme for historians. Military virtues, prowess at arms, and the psychology of the knight-errant were the lodestones of personal ambition. After the reduction of the area of Moorish control to the Kingdom of Granada by 1248, the next two centuries saw an irregular growth, but nonetheless a growth, in the theoretical power of the king and the enlargement of the body of Castillian law based on the *Siete Partidas* of Alfonso X (1252-1284) and the granting of municipal charters or *fueros*. On the one hand, the stress on law gradually became as much a concern for legal forms as a profound respect for the intent of the law. On the other, the theoretical and real power of the monarchy was elaborated by Ferdinand and Isabella along the lines of the Thomistic-Machiavellian dualism which Prof. Richard Morse develops in his essay (Document 3).

The War with Granada (1482-1492) not only ended the Reconquista but also resuscitated the military cult at a crucial time. Had the capture of the Alhambra not been followed by the Columbian voyage later that year, the organic growth of the politico-economic society of the Spanish Kingdoms might have been less conducive to the psychology of caudillismo. As the anthropologist Eric Wolf has pointed out, there were "two tendencies at work" at the end of the fifteenth century. "The first . . . was aristocratic, oriented toward warfare and the gain of riches by warfare." A military nobility and a military peasantry were cooperative agents in the final reconquest and absorption of Moorish territory. Acquisition of loot and "ego enhancement" motivated the knight; the peasant recruit was eager for free land and charters of liberties to protect himself from serfdom. The contrary tendency was based in the Mediterranean capitalist revolution which threatened to end feudal preeminence in Spain as it had done in the commercial centers of the Italian city-states. In the eastern Iberian kingdoms "a prosperous bourgeoisie, long oriented toward maritime trade, controlled the towns." This influence promised to extend itself westward as the frontier was closed in 1492.

As land became scarce, interests which had run parallel up to that time began to conflict; while the soldier-peasant wanted unencumbered land, the aristocrat wanted open range for sheep and cattle or land for dependent cultivators. With the distribution of the fruits of conquest among the conquerors, moreover, readily available wealth became unavailable. How was this new wealth to be produced? To this problem the merchant-entrepreneur of the towns had an answer: capital investment in industry coupled with the reduction of aristocratic power. At this moment, however, the doors to the New World swung wide open to reveal a new frontier: dream cities of gold, endless expanses of land, huge reservoirs of dependent labor. The merchant-entrepreneur receded into obscurity; the knight-adventurer, the visionary of wealth through seizure at sword's point, gained new impetus. . . . In this New World, all men—peasant, merchant, impoverished noble, noble merchant-prince—could dream of becoming lords of land, Indians, and gold. Men who in Spain might have allied themselves politically and economically with the entrepreneurs and traders of the towns against the aristocrat could in this new venture identify themselves with the ideal of the mounted noble.[1]

The searchers after New World utopias, the conquistadores who projected knight-errantry into the rain forests of Middle America and the thin air of the Andes, encountered major Amerindian civilizations which were politically complex. Speculation about the contributions which Meso-American and Andean empires have made to the later emergence of caudillismo are considerable but difficult to substantiate. So much emphasis has been placed upon the cultural achievements of the Aztec, Maya, and Inca civilizations that the easy assumption is that the postconquest influence of these civilizations must have been considerable and at a high level of institutional development. But as the anthropologist George M. Foster has written, "the remarkable thing . . . is not that indigenous culture played such a role in modifying Spanish culture but rather that these powerful

---

[1] Eric R. Wolf, *Sons of the Shaking Earth* (Chicago: The University of Chicago Press, 1959), pp. 157-159. See the provocative discussion of institutional changes in Charles J. Bishko, "The Iberian Background of Latin American History: Recent Progress and Continuing Problems," *The Hispanic American Historical Review*, Vol. XXXVI (1956), pp. 50-81.

native influences should in the long run have been shaped and controlled by even more powerful Iberian forces." [2] It may be argued then that the conquest and colonization of America imposed essentially enduring European institutional patterns on the Amerindian. Deculturation, the destruction of the political, religious, mercantile specialists which accompanied the conquests of Peru and Mexico, definitively broke up the hierarchical political structure of the Incas and Aztecs; the priests, merchants, and all but local governors were replaced by their Spanish counterparts.

The one Amerindian hierarchical group which retained some power after the conquest, in Middle America at least, was the nobility or cacique class. This "nobility was granted tribute exemptions and a number of special privileges, such as permission to ride horses, to wear Spanish clothing, to carry swords, and to use Spanish honorific titles. . . . Much is known of the individual members of this class during the sixteenth and seventeenth centuries; some were wealthy ranchers; a few owned Negro slaves; nearly all seemed to have held municipal offices. . . . [The] location [of the class] was [, however,] almost wholly confined to the towns and cities; its privileges were hereditary; it included both males and females; and royal law accorded it the rank of the *hidalgo* class of the mother country." [3]

Although the caciques retained some power at the municipal level and royal Spanish official bureaucracy was not usually injected into Indian towns below the rank of *corregidor* or *alcalde mayor*, the astute observations of Prof. Charles Gibson of the University of Mich-

---

[2] *Culture and Conquest: America's Spanish Heritage* (Chicago: Quadrangle Books, 1960), p. 2. For a sophisticated statement of the more traditional view of acculturation with attention to variable levels in cultural achievement among Indians of different parts of the hemisphere, see Elman R. Service, "Indian-European Relations in Colonial Latin America," *American Anthropologist*, Vol. LXVII (1955), pp. 411-425.
[3] Charles Gibson, "The Transformation of the Indian Community in New Spain: 1500-1810," *Journal of World History*, Vol. II (1955), pp. 586-587.

igan tend to support Foster's conclusions about the impact of Iberian institutions. In the many facets of local government carried on by caciques as *governadores*, *alcaldes*, *regidores*, and *mayordomos* "the remarkable feature is the degree of municipal Hispanization that Indian officers were able to achieve. The titles and duties, the records kept, the legal forms, the *residencia*, the order of procedure, all were of Spanish origin, and the office-holding Indian class adapted its political behaviour to Spanish norms with regular persistence." [4]

Certain pre-Columbian traditions did remain which had political significance in the eighteenth and nineteenth centuries. A most notable example occurred during the Peruvian revolt begun in 1779 by José Gabriel Condorcanqui. Condorcanqui was educated and well-read. He was particularly impressed with Garcilaso de la Vega's *Royal Commentaries of the Incas*. At the time of his rebellion he claimed to be a direct descendant of the last of the Incas and took the name of Tupac Amaru, that sixteenth-century leader who had been beheaded by Viceroy Francisco de Toledo. Before suffering a fate similar to that of his alleged forebear, Tupac Amaru II promoted a major civil war which eventually led to the death of some 80,000 before the violence was quelled. One important effect was to keep alive the concept of Inca overlordship. At the time of the Argentine declaration of independence in 1816, Manuel Belgrano seriously proposed that an Inca prince be reinstalled in Cuzco as ruler over half of South America. Although San

---

[4] *Ibid.*, pp. 588-589. See this article for a discussion of the relatively uneffected lower orders, *maceguales*, among the Indians. See also Pedro Carrasco, "The Civil-Religious Hierarchy in Mesoamerican Communities: Pre-Spanish Background and Colonial Development," *American Anthropologist*, Vol. LXI (1961), pp. 483-497. For Peru, see especially Gibson's *The Inca Concept of Sovereignty and the Spanish American Administration in Peru* (Austin: University of Texas Institute of Latin American Studies Publication No. 4, 1948). But also see John H. Rowe's evaluation of the Peruvian refusal to succumb to Hispanization in "The Incas Under Spanish Colonial Institutions," *The Hispanic American Historical Review*, Vol. XXXVII (May 1957), pp. 155-199.

Martín was enthusiastic, Belgrano aroused little support for his project. Nevertheless, the idea of substituting the moral authority of a pre-Columbian ruler for that of the Spanish king so as to provide postindependence stability is not without significance.

Perhaps of greater importance than any institutional or symbolic continuity from pre-Columbian times to the postindependence era was the habitual submissive quality of the lower orders in both Peruvian and Mexican society. It is well known that the Spanish conquistadores, once they had reduced the central fortresses and captured the principal political and religious leaders in the major civilizations, had relatively little difficulty in pacifying the empires and harnessing the already available servile labor forces. However, when it came to less sedentary and cultivated peoples like the Yaquis of the Gran Chichimeca and the Araucanians in southern Chile whose authoritarian structures were poorly defined, the Spaniards encountered resistance so strong that in some cases it was not until the nineteenth century that the tribes were overcome.

Even greater than the temptation to overemphasize Amerindian contributions to caudillismo is the temptation to do so with the Spanish conquistadores, though the reasons are more substantial. Dreamers of crusaders' dreams, these veritable men on horseback who commanded the personal loyalty of their followers, held the stage for half a century and were gone. They were replaced by the less imaginative and more loyal bureaucrats of the *audiencias* and by the royal career servants, the viceroys. Our long perspective makes simple the parallel between Francisco Pizarro and Mariano Melgarejo, the *caudillo bárbaro* of Bolivia in the 1860's. However, while it is true that the heroic and epic qualities of the sixteenth-century captains lived on in legend to excite young imaginations, the more subtle institutional development of the colonial era had much more to do with the background of the emergence of the nineteenth-century caudillo. What is especially important to realize about the conquistador who survived what was often a relatively brief period of campaigning is that he and his descendants extended their search for utopia into exploitive but pacific pursuits. As the new masters, they gave themselves easily to a paternalistic squirearchy especially if they were mine operators, hacendados, or encomenderos. As *patrones*, they were in a position to lay the foundations for the social order which would evolve through the next several centuries. Something of the nature of this process and of the particular familial relationships and personal bonds which the new magnates used to extend and secure their power is told by the French scholar François Chevalier in his essay (Document 2). That this emphasis on personal ties was not an isolated colonial phenomenon but had persistent influences on the modern period was suggested by George Foster when he wrote that "*Personalismo*—an effective personal working relationship with the right people— rather than impersonal principle is more often than not the basis on which government, and business as well, functions." [5]

Politically, the colonial order became increasingly structured, Morse would say "Thomistic" (Document 3), especially during and after the reign of Philip II. In the highly complex bureaucracy extending from King and Council of the Indies down to *corregidor* and *cabildo*, two elements of prime significance emerged which bear on caudillismo. The first was intense loyalty to the crown, as symbol, as moral authority, and as source of all bounty. While there were occasional isolated examples of outright rebellion against the king by individuals such as Gonzalo Pizarro in 1544, no widespread revolutions for independence came until after the disappearance of the legitimate monarch from the Spanish throne in 1808. Even then many local movements, such as that of Miguel Hidalgo y Costilla in New Spain, were ostensibly initiated not in the name of independence but rather in order to *preserve* the area for the exiled King Ferdinand. This devotion to the distant symbol of authority should

[5] *Culture and Conquest*, p. 4.

not, however, be confused necessarily with devotion to the immediate agents of the king's government. Tupac Amaru II rebelled not against Charles III but against the venality and corruption of local officials. It was perfectly consistent then and later to go into battle with the cry "Long Live the King and Death to Bad Government!" The moral authority of the Crown was, therefore, above reproach; after independence the trick was to find an adequate surrogate. Many caudillos tried—with varying degrees of success—to fill the moral vacuum themselves.

The second political element of importance in the colonial era was flexibility. The myth of rigid paternalism within the "system" has been dispelled, as may be seen in the writings of Prof. John L. Phelan of the University of Wisconsin. Far more autonomy was left to the Spanish bureaucrat to choose among conflicting legislation, to satisfy the standards of one hierarchical authority rather than another, and to send back undesirable or impractical decrees by employing the famous formula: "I obey, but I do not execute." The longevity of Spanish power in the New World is undoubtedly related to this flexibility.[6] The development of a self-perpetuating bureaucracy, the respect for legal *forms*, and the relative degree of local autonomy are all elements which later eased the task of creating dictatorships that worked behind the mask of democratic constitutional fronts.

What has been called "the crisis of colonialism" and the subsequent wars for Spanish American independence had immediate effects on the development of caudillismo, as the readings by Profs. Raymond Crist and J. Fred Rippy demonstrate (Documents 4 and 5). It was the later years of the Bourbon century (1700-1808) which saw a deliberate impetus given by Charles III to the emergence of a praetorian tradition in the colonial kingdoms. To be sure, neither the Spanish king nor his advisers intended that the criollos who formed the colo-

---

[6] John L. Phelan, "Authority and Flexibility in the Spanish Imperial Bureaucracy," *Administrative Science Quarterly*, Vol. V (1960), pp. 47-65.

nial militia regiments of the professional army should use their training and experience fighting for independence.[7] As one of the few outlets for the energies and ambitions of capable criollos, it is not surprising that the military leadership during the struggle for independence were receptive to new influences. It has been suggested that these men "represented the most aware, cultivated, and cosmopolitan part of the population, educated in the tradition of the French *Encyclopédistes*." The statesmenlike qualities of some of them and their opposition to monarchic forms of conservatism made them "revered as true fathers of the rising nations, and their successors considered themselves the natural and legitimate heirs of the liberators. Thus a military cast [sic] was formed." [8]

The conclusion that all the heroes of the wars of independence were carbon copies of Simón Bolívar, however, should not be hastily reached. Probably for every insurgent captain who was conversant with the ideas of Pufendorf, Rousseau, and the *Encyclopédistes* there were many more who knew nothing of the Enlightenment. The wars, endemic in some areas like New Spain and Venezuela for a decade or more, were physically devastating and psychologically brutalizing. The distinction between patriot and bandit was not always clear. Motivations were frequently materialistic or based on the opportunity to achieve social mobility upwards. With the breakdown of the moral authority of the crown, lawlessness became widespread and was overcome not necessarily by a substitute moral authority but rather by the personal magnetism of a given charismatic leader. Personalism rather than principle tended to prevail. Some indication of this is found in the writings of conservatives, such as Mexico's Lucas Alamán who was frequently

---

[7] The development of a military elite with special privileges is explored in Lyle N. McAlister, *The "Fuero Militar" in New Spain, 1764-1800* (Gainesville: University of Florida Press, 1957).

[8] Victor Alba, "The Stages of Militarism in Latin America," in John J. Johnson (ed.), *The Role of the Military in Underdeveloped Countries* (Princeton: The Rand Corporation, 1962), p. 167.

nostalgic about the order and stability which he felt had
characterized the prerevolutionary *Pax Hispanica*.[9]

Just as an orderly progression from crude to mature
caudillismo is unrealistic to imagine in Argentina, so too
the century and a half since the achievement of independence has seen a most irregular development of
caudillo types throughout Spanish America. Modern tech-
nology, the decline of geographic isolation, and the increase of education have been factors which have altered
the face of Spanish American dictatorship most universally. But many elements which have conditioned caudillismo in one country are lacking in another or may
appear as crucial a generation after they have ceased to be
vital in the first country. Generalizations which depend
upon specific conditioners, then, should be examined
critically. Likewise, categorization of natural and social
forces which have affected the history of caudillismo
must be accomplished with the full awareness that what
applies to Guatemala may not apply at all to Chile in
the same year or the same decade. Various readings in
this volume concentrate upon causative forces; sometimes specific cases in specific places are called into play
and at other times the authors are more general.

In addition to the historical forces prior to 1825, certain domestic conditioners should be mentioned. Among
these is geography. An important study of the interaction between the seminomadic peoples of the Venezuelan Llanos or plains, the emergence of Bolívar's lieutenant José Antonio Páez as a telluric caudillo, and the
nature of the Llanos themselves is provided by the geog-
rapher Crist (Document 4). Closely related are the social anthropological kinship groups which M. Chevalier
explores in depth as a major element of personalism
(Document 2). Students of the phenomenon of caudillismo should inquire closely into the economic and social
structure of each community which produce a strong

[9] See the penetrating analysis of the effects of the separatist wars
by Charles C. Griffin, "Economic and Social Aspects of the Era
of Spanish-American Independence," *The Hispanic American Historical Review*, Vol. XXIX (1949), pp. 170-187.

man in order to relate his power to the existing privileged and depressed groups. The close and mutually advantageous association between caudillos and landed aristocracies is, for example, vitally important. The late Sanford Mosk, an economist from the University of California at Berkeley, has cogently explored this subject:

> In some parts of Latin America estates were enlarged or newly created by depriving Indian villages of lands which they had possessed since before the Conquest, and to which their titles had been confirmed by the Spanish Crown. The most spectacular development of this kind took place in Mexico during the regime of Porfirio Díaz, when the Mexican government gave encouragement and assistance to the *hacendados* in stripping Indian villages of their lands. A variety of methods were used, ranging all the way from technically legal measures to outright robbery. . . . By encouraging the *latifundio*, the course of nineteenth-century economic development in Latin America tended to strengthen and solidify the economic power of the landed aristocracy. Inevitably, political oligarchy was also strengthened. This came about because those who governed were closely connected with the large landowners. Most of the men who were influential in politics came from the landed class, even when the dictator who happened to be at the top was a man from the lower ranks of society. A *caudillo* who held power for any length of time usually became incorporated into the landowning class.[1]

Religious factors may also account for the success of a given caudillo. Indeed the flaming Chilean liberal Francisco Bilbao was so convinced of this that he blamed the worst characteristics of dictatorship on the influence of the Jesuits (Document 7). This may be true when an institutional liaison exists between the caudillo and the Church as a politico-economic power; such was the case

---

[1] "Pathology of Democracy in Latin America: An Economist's Point of View," pp. 133-134.

of Gabriel García Moreno, the arbiter of Ecuador's government along theocratic lines between 1860 and 1875. Religion may also account for a vast popular following when skillfully employed. The use of the Cross and a replica of the Virgin of Guadalupe helped provide the Mexican priest-caudillo, Miguel Hidalgo, with a peasant army in the 1810 rebellion. Most recently, Fidel Castro's resemblance to the bearded image of Jesus Christ has not been overlooked by the Cuban revolutionary's public relations men. By the opposite token, alienation from the Church helped bring down the regimes of at least three military caudillos in the 1950's: Marcos Pérez Jiménez of Venezuela, Juan Perón of Argentina, and Gustavo Rojas Pinilla of Colombia.

The study of psychology suggests other complex ingredients contributing to caudillismo. The cult of virility, *machismo,* is often though not always personified by the Spanish American dictator. The Mexican poet Octavio Paz has sought to explain Mexican temperament in terms of a division between the weak, the followers, the psychically violated and the man who dominates, the *macho,* the *gran chingón.* "One word sums up the aggressiveness, insensitivity, invulnerability, and other attributes of the *macho:* power. It is force without the discipline of any notion of order: arbitrary power, the will without reins and without a set course. . . . [The] caciques, feudal lords, hacienda owners, politicians, generals, captains of industry . . . are all *machos.* . . ." [2] The Mexican variant may not be universally applied without alteration, yet the psychological implications of the cult of masculinity are important for an understanding of the caudillo. Prof. Norman Bailey, a political scientist at Queens College, has made an interesting application of this aspect of caudillo psychology to the influence which the United States has had in the Hemisphere (Document 17).

Influences external to a given country are explored

[2] *The Labyrinth of Solitude: Life and Thought in Mexico* (New York: Grove Press, 1961), pp. 81-82. See the full context of this discussion in Chap. IV, "The Sons of La Malinche."

from several points of view in the readings in addition to Bailey's essay. Professor Johnson, whom we encountered earlier, places emphasis upon the relation between foreign economic and intellectual currents and the growth of caudillismo in his article (Document 10). The concern which United States and European business interests have had for political stability, even though it be dictatorial, is explored briefly by Professor Chevalier (Document 2). And a political scientist, Prof. Russell Fitzgibbon, has suggested the important effect which conditions in one Spanish American country may have on a neighbor in his case study of the associated phenomenon of *continuismo* (Document 12).

Finally, the identifiable qualities and characteristics of the caudillo ideal are multitudinous. The nature of personalism, of the cults and titles which surround the leader, of those instances where political parties are known, at least popularly, by the name of the chieftain rather than by some abstraction; the *planes, pronunciamientos,* and new constitutions which are used to validate violent seizures of power and to perpetuate the new regime; the subsequent role of elections, plebescites, and other manipulations of mass democracy; and the use of intimidation are all explored in the essays, though in none perhaps with more effect than in that by Jesús de Galíndez (Document 14). As the exploration is begun, probably no better suggestion can be made than what is implicit in a recent commentary on the Mexican executive system: "Under a line of civilian 'Party Presidents'—Miguel Alemán, Adolfo Ruíz Cortines, and . . . Adolfo López Mateos—the role of the executive has changed to that of chairman of the board rather than the charismatic hero, the super-*caudillo.*" [3] Whether all Spanish American executives will evolve after the Mexican pattern (or some other open societal organization) is not the point; what is, is that caudillismo, like all other human institutions, is dynamic through history.

---

[3] Howard F. Cline, Mexico: A Matured Latin American Revolution," *Annals of the American Academy of Political and Social Sciences,* Vol. V (1961), p. 87.

I

Theories and Background

◇◇◇◇◇◇◇◇◇◇◇◇◇◇◇◇◇◇◇◇◇◇◇◇◇◇◇◇◇◇◇◇◇◇◇◇◇◇

This first division in the readings provides a sample of the theories which have been used to explain the caudillo. Although the authors of the three essays which follow offer markedly different theoretical views, they agree that knowledge of Spain's medieval development and the emergence of a colonial Spanish civilization in America is requisite for an understanding of dictatorship in the nineteenth and twentieth centuries.

Salvador de Madariaga

MAN AND THE UNIVERSE
IN SPAIN *

The historian, diplomat, novelist, and critic Salvador de Madariaga (1886-   ) has long been absorbed in the psychological traits which differentiate one group or one nation from another. His essay in comparative psychology entitled *Englishmen, Frenchmen, Spaniards* (London: Oxford Press, 1928) is perhaps the best known of his many books. Completely trilingual, Madariaga belongs more to Europe than he does to Spain (where he was born), to France (where he was educated), or to England (where he lives).

In the following selection, which forms part of the background materials in his history of modern Spain, Madariaga emphasizes a common dilemma among the richly diverse population of the Peninsula in its tendency to separatism and dictatorship. His conclusions suggest the Colombian joke that there are in that Andean republic as many political parties as there are people.

* Salvador de Madariaga, *Spain: a Modern History* (New York: Frederick A. Praeger, Inc., 1958), pp. 17-18, 20-23. Reprinted by permission of Frederick A. Praeger, Inc.

Much as the temper of the Spanish people toward the Moors and Jews changed after the eleventh century, until it led them to the wholesale expulsions of a later date, there is no doubt that in their four hundred years of cordial intimacy in peace and war the racial intermixture must have been deep. Not only the Moor but the Jew was bound to become an important element in the Spanish people as at present constituted. The typically Oriental characteristics of the Spaniard, though they may have preexisted, must have been reinforced by these four centuries of familiarity with two typically Oriental races.

The Peninsula acts as a sounding board for Oriental races, who usually give their richest sounds in it. Thus Spain brought to a high degree of excellence no less than three Oriental races: the Arab, the Jew, and the Gypsy. It was in Spain that Arab civilization rose to its highest brilliancy; Spanish Jews were the greatest luminaries of Hebrew civilization since Biblical times; and as for the Gypsy, the superiority of the Spanish type over any other is not to be proved by books, but by the observation of the living specimens which may be found in Andalusia. . . .

A direct observation of [the Spanish] people leads to the same conclusion to which we were led by the survey of the land it inhabits; outward variety and inward unity. . . . The sense of unity under the variety comes from an impression of primitive strength, of all-round synthetic vigor. It may be first observed when dealing with the people. It will be noticed that the people, i.e., the popular classes, north or south, east or west, possess qualities of wisdom, of heart, or manners, which the visitor is used to connect with the cultured or well-to-do levels of society. The usual test—illiteracy—breaks down in Spain. Illiterates speak like Seneca, sing like Blake, and behave like Louis XIV. A composure, a quiet assurance, covered with respect but not oiled with subservience, a genuine fellow feeling, a quick sense of dignity yet free from susceptibility, suggest that the Spanish people are endowed with a natural notion of equality springing from a deep sense of fraternity. A sense rather than a feeling; for rather than a definite movement, or manifestation, or even mood, it is an atmosphere in which moods and movements manifest themselves.

Such a sense of the inherent equality of all men springs from a religious substratum. Whether consciously or not, the Spaniard lives against a background of eternity, and his outlook is more religious than philosophic. Hence it is that the two poles of his psychology are the individual and the universe; the subject and the Whole; and that life for him should consist in the absorbing of the universe by the individual, the *assimilation* of the Whole by the subject.

The individual thus becomes the standard of all life—an individual voluntarily stripped of all but essential tendencies. Instinctively at home in essential things, the Spaniard is therefore apt to evade the grasp of things which are less high up in the scale—things merely necessary or useful or advisable. The Spaniard is therefore unfettered by any sense of social pressure or intellectual standard. He is spontaneous, "all-around," always entirely present and wholly engaged wherever he happens to be. He shuns abstractions as much as any Englishman and is as free from inhibitions as any Frenchman can be. He is neither a citizen of an equalitarian state, nor a partner in a national society, nor a subject in an empire. He is a man.

This individualist is an egoist. His person is the channel through which the life-stream is made to pass, thus acquiring a personality polarized along a definite individual direction. The Spaniard therefore feels patriotism as he feels love—in the form of a passion whereby he absorbs the object of his love and assimilates it; that is to say, makes it his own. He does not belong to his country so much as his country belongs to him, and as his perspective is concrete and individualistic it follows that he is apt to feel his patriotism with an intensity in inverse proportion to the area of the regions which surround him.

Moreover, the instinct for preserving his own liberty

makes him eschew all forms of social cooperation, since all collective work tends to enslave the individual and to reduce him to the status of a piece of machinery. His anti-cooperative instinct comes to reinforce his tendency to dwell on the two poles of his psychology—man and the universe—leaving uncultivated the middle stretches in which social and political communities lie.

These middle stretches are precisely those which can be at best governed by ethical and political principles. But the Spaniard, however interested he may be in such principles, governs his life by an individual sense of direction which works in him precisely by virtue of the passive character of his inward attitude toward life. In what concerns collective, and particularly political, life, the Spaniard is apt to judge events according to a dramatic criterion, singularly free from any practical considerations or intellectual prepossessions. It follows that in Spain, liberty, justice, and free trade matter less than the particular Smith or Jones who is to incarnate them for the time being. Nor, be it said in passing, is such a point of view quite at variance with the experience of countries more politically minded than Spain. In this dramatic criterion of the Spaniard, his sense of man may be observed. His sense of the universe manifests itself in his tendency to found his political institutions on the widest and most universal basis, i.e., the religious basis. Thus his patriotism, considered as a mere manifestation of group consciousness, is weakened both ways: at the individual end, because the individual tends to absorb the nation rather than allow himself to be absorbed by it; at the universal end, because the Spaniard who widens his outlook does not stop at the borders of the nation, and seeks to embrace the whole world.

This oscillation between the two extremes, man and the universe, is the rhythm that underlies the history of Spain.

It is easy to see how these psychological premises lead to the two constant features of Spanish political life which may be symbolized in the words: *dictatorship* and *separatism.* The individual, moved by stronger vertical than horizontal impulses, i.e., by natural forces expressed directly in him rather than by forces transmitted by tradition or absorbed from the environment, tends to assert his personality and (like a bottle already full of its own contents) to refuse other influences. This leads to dictatorship, observable not merely in the public man, statesman, general, cardinal, or king at the head of the state, but in every one of the men at the head (or on the way thereto) of every village, city, region, business firm, or even family in the country.

The dictator is most averse to separatism in others, since it limits the area of his own dictatorship; but he is a separatist himself, for he separates himself from others in what concerns the usual collective functions of study, discussion, give-and-take, and agreement. The strong individual, vertical pattern of the Spaniard and the weakness of his horizontal tendencies, those of course which weave men together in a social tissue, explain the separatism of Spaniards and the ease with which, at the slightest shock, regions, cities, political parties, classes, services of the state, are torn asunder and fall away from each other. Needless to say, there will always be topical causes to determine the cracks in the collective texture of the country; but the facility with which such causes produce the cracks and the depth of the cracks themselves are due to the quality of the texture and not to the circumstances which act upon it. Nothing in fact is more characteristic of the Spanish nature than this *brittle* quality of its collective self which, by the way, we find exemplified in the Disunited States of Spanish America (the fruit of dictatorship and separatism) as opposed to the United States of Anglo-Saxon America.

Separatism and dictatorship, however, are passions of the Spaniard; they are not his sense. When in the realm of sense, the Spaniard is unusually creative and realistic. But for him to attain this plane, he needs a higher passion strong enough to raise him to a unity from the dispersive level in which he is wont to dwell. Such a high passion was the faith which he once attained in the six-teenth and seventeenth centuries and which gave Spain a strength in unity such as she has never known since and may perhaps never know again.

François Chevalier

THE ROOTS OF
PERSONALISMO*

Best known for his monumental study of the creation of the great haciendas in New Spain during the sixteenth and seventeenth centuries (*Land and Society in Colonial Mexico: the Great Hacienda*, Berkeley: University of California Press, 1963), François Chevalier has been director of the Institut des Études Hispaniques of the University of Bordeaux since 1962. His socioeconomic research in Mexico helped him to perceive the importance and varieties of a dictator's reliance on personal support and the limitations which such support has inevitably entailed. Distinguishing clearly between caciquismo and caudillismo, M. Chevalier offers much insight into the personalist aspects of autocracy in the Iberian and colonial past, on the one hand, and into nineteenth and twentieth century history on the other.

---

* François Chevalier, " 'Caudillos' et 'caciques' en Amérique: contribution à l'étude des liens personnels," *Mélanges offerts à Marcel Bataillon par les Hispanistes Français*, a special issue of *Bulletin Hispanique*, Vol. LXIV bis (1962), pp. 30-47. The excerpts given here come from pp. 30-42, 44-47. Translated and printed by permission of the author.

It has been observed that in many countries of Central and South America the local and even national government has often been monopolized by "strong men," "caudillos" and "caciques" who perpetuate themselves in power, sometimes even under cover of constitutional or judicial fictions. There is, also, nothing new in emphasizing the exceptional importance that "personal relations" have had in these countries for the conduct of business affairs and the function of institutions in general. But rarely have these two phenomena been linked so as to delve deeply into their causes and to reveal their mechanisms. . . .

ORIGINS

In times or in countries where life is difficult, where man is placed in a hostile environment constantly menaced by enemies or famine, where a state, if it exists at all, is too weak or too far away to insure the security of individuals, these individuals associate and naturally coalesce into firm groups: at first, into groups of relatives because the ties of blood are fundamental; then into groups of the most faithful, of clients, of friends . . . around an elder, a chief, a powerful man, around a man who has more experience, more initiative, or a man of more material means than the others. Ties of blood and personal bonds are the only ones which have a real importance in societies where written contracts, if they exist at all, play a limited role; where the typical relations of modern societies, and even of certain traditional communities, are found only in the embryonic state.

There are countless examples. In Rome itself the *gens* and the *clientes* survived in spite of the development of a central power having a relatively complex administration and in spite of the birth of the personal property concept under Roman Law, which favors the autonomy of the individual capable of operating independently of a group. With the Germanic invasions, the *clientes* and the group reappear with new vigor, not because of a peculiarly Germanic influence . . . but because of the fact that the newcomers were simply more primitive socially. . . .

In the West during the Middle Ages, the chiefs were surrounded by relatives and retainers who lived and ate with them, who helped them in time of peace as well as in time of war. While in a large part of Europe these faithful received land, at first temporarily and later on in a hereditary manner according to the classic feudal system, in Castille, on the contrary, . . . the *criados* or retainers continued to be rewarded ordinarily by sustenance and by presents, for reasons which doubtless have something to do with the Reconquest of the Peninsula from the Moors and the possible distribution of important spoils of war.

No matter what the causes may be . . . it is noteworthy that in the sixteenth and seventeenth centuries groups of criados around powerful men and high royal functionaries persisted in Spain. They might be hidalgos and nobles; and when it was a question of men of high rank, they did not always live permanently under the same roof as their protector, all the more because they were often charged with missions of confidence, even to foreign countries. Thus Hernán Cortés was a criado of Diego Velázquez. The obligations were clear for each party: protection, help, favors, and presents from one side; of faithfulness and help from the other.

The institution went to America with the conquerors, and it found new forces in the immensity of a continent where the king of Spain had difficulty in making his authority felt in all places. In a case in Mexico in 1602, Guadalajara had only 160 households, but the president of the Audiencia there was surrounded by forty-six relatives and by a quantity of "dependents" who monopolized the offices and the most lucrative jobs of a huge region called New Galicia. Similar cases are by no means rare in the New World. [The Crown], however, reacted against these practices and sought to prohibit the distribution of administrative positions or other advantages to the retainers of Royal bureaucrats. . . . Above all the latter changed posts and could therefore take root in one place with difficulty.

On the other hand, there were few obstacles for the private citizens who had the means, whether Spaniard, creoles, or mestizo, to have permanently the kind of personal following that poverty, insecurity, or the hostility of the environment often rendered natural, and even necessary in many regions of the vast Spanish Empire. . . . Incapable of extending its administration everywhere, at least before the end of the eighteenth century . . . , the government of Madrid sometimes found it advantageous to use powerful men so that order might be kept, even at the cost of abandoning to them a little of its sovereignty. Sometimes contracts of this kind were made with rich proprietors of lands or mines, who took it upon themselves to maintain private armies in exchange for honorary titles. . . . Nevertheless, in a time of monarchic centralization, the king avoided as much as possible the creation of judicial precedents lest his rights be alienated, especially if they were to be hereditarily alienated. There were, therefore, more frequently *de facto* situations, especially in dangerous areas or in troubled times.

It is clear that the mentality of the great proprietors encouraged the proliferation of personal bonds. If they received only a small income from their haciendas, which were, by the way, heavily mortgaged to the Church, they found compensation in the quasi-seignorial prestige that a crowd of men attached to their land and to their person could give to their masters. . . . Employing the authority of their military titles, they occasionally led these followers to fight nomadic Indians and bandits or, during the wars of independence, the party opposed to the one they themselves had chosen. Finally, the haciendas were often entailed estates which belonged to dynasties rather than to individuals; these family lines thus insured the importance and the primitive force of blood ties.

In fact, certain proprietors reigned on their estates somewhat in the manner of lords and seigneurs of ancient time, at least before the reforms of the eighteenth century. Sure of themselves in a world where the hierarchy seemed immutable, their psychology was simple and their authority a tradition. It would not always be so after the earthquakes of independence which seriously shook the established order.

THE NATIONAL PERIOD

In renouncing the presidency of Gran Colombia, Bolívar, in a disillusioned address, foresaw the coming of cruel petty tyrants "of all races and colors" who would divide the continent among themselves. In fact, caudillos, big and small, sprang everywhere from the wars of emancipation. The disappearance of the Spanish state left a void, made larger by the retreat of the traditional aristocracy and soon that of the Church. When a precarious peace returned, the new men often kept the power which audacity and chance had given them. The most energetic—sometimes the most violent—became "the first of his village or the republic, the one who has more authority or power and who because of his pride wants to make himself feared and obeyed by all his inferiors," to employ the definition for "cacique" used by the first Spanish dictionary of the Academy published in 1729.

Where did these chiefs come from? Sometimes they emerged from the old landed aristocracy, but more often from the petite bourgeoisie or from the people. Because it is usually not in his tradition . . . that he commands others, the new man does not feel sure of himself. Therefore he is in urgent need to affirm his power, if necessary by force, and at the same time to distinguish himself from the common man. Thereby we see a new style among these dictators, these caudillos and caciques of the national era, whether they sprang directly or not from the wars of independence.

THE HORSEMEN

In countries where "mounted barbarism" of the gauchos or of the llaneros still ruled, in rural areas of little population, these all powerful caudillos were often primitive beings whose power seemed to be tied to physical force and virility (*hombre macho*). In Argentina the Spanish state abandoned the region to these "kings of the big spurs," to use Sarmiento's expression: a Facundo "courageous almost to boldness, gifted with Herculean strength," an extraordinary knight who imposed himself by violence, and even by terror; a Rosas so overflowing with energy and with life that . . . he could ride a horse almost to death . . . ; in Venezuela a Páez, who became civilized later, Monagas, Zaraza . . . exalted in the popular . . . *corrido*, and also a fictional character taken from life, like Rómulo Gallegos' Doña Bárbara, the terrible female cacique of the boundless wild llano. . . .

It would be easy to make this list of names longer, because in those regions of extensive animal raising which cover vast spaces in almost all the countries of the American continent, it is or was almost impossible to conceive of the chief as other than a man physically stronger than his rivals, a better horseman and a better shot . . . (which, however, did not always prevent him from meeting a violent death . . .).

THE MILITARY MEN

In general, the easiest means for an ambitious man . . . to secure power is, naturally, through a military career. This is true whether he be a man raised by revolution or war to leadership, or whether [he] be a professional soldier, the latter being of particular value in one of the numerous countries where the army is, with the Church, one of the only two solidly organized forces. . . . In fact, almost all dictators have been military men. Those who were not so originally have usually taken the title of "general." . . .

Even in Mexico, a country which has long passed the stage of *pronunciamientos,* and where politics is entirely in the hands of civilians, it is only rather recently that a general changes posts without including in his transfer all those officers who were personally attached to him. This situation, outmoded under the government of Porfirio Díaz, was recreated by the revolution of 1910-1917. Thus in 1919 the psychology of the caudillo and the resort to purely personal ties were still expressed in a manifesto of General Obregón: "I declare myself a candidate for the presidency of the republic, backed by my own pistols without ties with any parties nor offers of any platform. My background as a soldier of the revolution is sufficient guarantee that I know how to insure the well-being of the people and the happiness of the country. He who loves me follow me!"

OTHER STYLES

In the old days the powerful men were great landlords and sometimes captains of private armies. Some of them, who had chosen the party of independence, kept their local power. In Mexico this was reinforced by the renewed incursions of nomadic Indians and by the climate of insecurity which existed in the whole country. The land being the essential source of income and prestige, the generals, caudillos, and caciques had to own haciendas or to acquire some if they had none to start with. Later Porfirio Díaz who favored large holdings . . . integrated the proprietors into his system because they seemed to him the most able to control local governments.

During the nineteenth century, however, ideals change while pressures of the haciendas on the rural communities increase. This brings about an uneasiness among the peasants which is expressed by uprisings of Indians and of village people or peons all anxious to recuperate their land. In Mexico this tendency is clear fifty or eighty years before the agrarian revolution began in 1910-1911. . . . So it was that caudillos of the new style appeared here and there, sensitive to the aspirations of the most humble rural groups from which they sometimes came.

Thus in Mexico General Juan Álvarez emerged all-powerful in the southwest and the state of Guerrero during the decades which followed independence. He is the type of the "good cacique," who lives very simply on his hacienda, and defends the Indian communities and the poor people in these vast regions of arid sierras. . . . In a series of neglected pamphlets, "the patriarch of the south" described the misery of the natives in dramatic fashion, with precise examples, and the methods which the proprietors use in order to despoil them of their water and their lands. . . . He himself quells uprisings by extending justice to the peasants, who are very deeply attached to him at the same time that they express their defiance toward the aloof government of the capital. . . .

Quite different, certainly, was the famous Manuel Lozada, absolute ruler of Nayarit, a little further north, which he dominated through fear and terror for several decades before his death in 1873, first as a bandit chief and then as military commander supported by the conservatives. He was even decorated by order of Napoleon III! This man, once a shepherd on a hacienda and of Cora Indian origin, was a born chief who enjoyed great prestige among all the natives and who did not hesitate, on occasion, to distribute the lands of a hacienda among his soldiers. Finally taken by treason and sent to the firing squad, fifty of Lozada's principal adherents accepted invitations to a great banquet of reconciliation where, at a signal—the host raising his glass—they were all assassinated.

But the chief who wants to stay in power forever— which is the essence of *caciquismo*—must be able to count on the collaboration and unconditional support of forces which he permanently attaches to his person. The popularity, the ascendancy, and the prestige, absolutely necessary to start with, are never sufficient for a prolonged retention of power. To rule by fear or by terror does not last if it is impossible to create a stable community of interest with the men and the groups on which the chief leans. Then, how to succeed? In countries where resources are few, the *primum vivere* is an unavoidable imperative: the chief must first be able to feed his relatives, his dependents . . . and the soldiers who support him. He must be rich.

TO BE RICH

For the caudillo time is pressing. If he is not rich, he must become rich as soon as possible. . . .

Sarmiento in the last century described how Facundo Quiroga, the Argentine caudillo, gathered a large fortune; the means are numerous, from the collection of the tithe to gambling, but the terror he inspires is at the base of all gain. Who would dare bid above the ridiculously small sum which Facundo offers in order to get the right to collect the tithe? Who would dare break up a card game after having won the gold of this frightful chief? It is he alone who can decide when to end the game and it is he who, having unlimited resources at his disposal, will win.

Facundo was, certainly, a kind of a barbarian. Later, in other places, the means may have been more discreet, but especially for those who have nothing to start with influence peddling is a way to acquire some early capital; after which a fortune increases more easily by itself: monopolies on imports or manufacturing, extremely lucrative contracts obtained from the state for public works, contraband . . . and above all the acquisition through intimidation of the best land . . . are but a few of the ways to wealth. . . .

For the ambitious officer or politician during the nineteenth century, all kinds of financial arrangements allowed them to take a cut from the sums borrowed from England or other countries, sums which were generally guaranteed by the income from customs. During the second half of the nineteenth century, the Venezuelan dictator Guzmán Blanco became rich in such a way. . . . Later the increasing commercial relations and the development of foreign capitalistic enterprise in a large part of the continent offered increasing possibilities to the new man thirsty for power and money, a few of whom have made huge fortunes in the twentieth century. The guarantees that the men offered to powerful financial groups were compensated by effective support thanks to which they maintained themselves in power. . . .

There are chiefs of state who still possess large fortunes. For instance, in a country of Central America an open letter to its president has recently been published, a letter which gives in detail all his businesses and properties

—evidently inherited from his low-born father who had governed the country as an absolute master. The list makes quite an impression with its fifty-one stock raising haciendas, forty-six coffee plantations, and eight of sugar cane; thirteen industries; his daily newspaper; his shipping, aviation, trucking, and import-export companies; and finally his interests in almost everything from the monopoly of firearms to gold exports. . . .

If modern capitalism did not color such a system, one would tend to think about the retainers who served their chief, making war or working for him, in exchange for food, presents, and protection. One might even recall the ancient concept of the personal patrimonial state. . . .

THE DEPENDENTS

The men whom caudillos call upon first will naturally be their relatives, because the ties of blood are the surest and the strongest. Familial solidarity often remains very strong in rural and provincial environments, and is sometimes revealed in the form of extreme "vendettas." Spontaneously the relatives, even those living far away, take the side of that member of the family who occupies an important position or who wants to occupy it, and consequently they find themselves fighting with rival factions. These family rivalries, made so famous in the old days in Italy, divided many regions of the American continent, such as the Argentine Rioja at the time of Sarmiento. . . .

The relatives of the strong man expect from him positions, favors, or simply their daily bread. This reaction is so natural that any person receiving a fixed income of any importance would usually feed at his home his cousins and supporters who render him little services in return. For example, in Spain a successful torero may see his whole familial clan move into his house, expecting him to insure their subsistence. By the same token, the caudillo cannot refuse assistance in the form of positions and favors to relatives who, after all, are his surest support. Even the most personally disinterested men sometimes practice nepotism, which seemed natural enough in the old days. Today such practices are severely censured, at least in Mexico where the governor of [Michoacán] recently had to resign under pressure of public opinion. Newspaper readers were shocked to learn that his relatives occupied all the important positions of the state, ranging from treasury and tax collection offices to that of attorney general, including along the way the director of public works, the mayor of the only important city, and the state liquor inspector.

At a much higher level, [Anastasio Somoza of Nicaragua] placed his sons or near relatives at the head of the high command of the army, of the presidential guard, of the bank of issue, and of the presidency of the national assembly. . . . Another and most typical example would be [Trujillo] whose brothers, legitimate and illegitimate sons (the latter in impressive numbers), nephews, relatives, and allies divided among themselves the principal positions of the country in such a manner as to deal with it as with a big business or as a patrimony.

One cannot help but think of the groups of relatives and dependents of ancient Europe when one sees in such Latin American countries the parades of people who accompany, surround, and assist certain chiefs of state, politicians, or important figures when they move from one place to another, or even when they are in their own homes.

To the ties of blood can be added those which create a religious relationship between the *compadres* or godfathers . . . and the relatives of the baptized as well as the child himself. These ties often remain powerful enough to oblige the partners to help each other in all circumstances. Thus [Trujillo] systematically agreed, and even used pressure to become the godfather of thousands of children, obviously in order to create a tie of fidelity toward him with a large number of families, belonging by the way to all social classes including the most humble. There is no doubt that this practice gained [Trujillo] the support of a considerable part of the population, who became thus linked to him as if by a blood relationship. . . .

The local caciques lean so much on these *compadrazgos* that the word itself often takes on a political shade. Among the rural people, the mestizos, and the more advanced Indians, the extraordinary proliferation of these religious relationships even appear, in a spontaneous fashion, to replace and to recreate personal bonds . . . where solidarity among the clan has softened or lost its control. It has been noted that in Maya communities where ancient clannish organizations exist there are neither compadres nor *comadres*. Everywhere else, however, compadrazgo plays an essential role which is perhaps similar to that of the religious brotherhoods of Spain in creating reciprocal obligations of assistance which were, and still are, sometimes necessary in isolated regions where law has little influence and where the individual lacks personal guarantees. Furthermore, the ties of compadrazgo multiply even outside baptism: in some villages this occurs through the acquisition of a religious image to which sponsors or "godfathers" are assigned or through an important event in the life of a child . . . and in other places because all the ancestors and descendants of compadres assume the same title. . . .

The word *amigo* itself implies, especially in the countryside, a solidarity and reciprocal duties which are not evoked to the same degree by the word "friend." . . .

PERSONALITY CULTS

In the political and military phase of the conquest of power, the caudillo lived in a state of quasi-permanent alert. [An Argentine chief] "always had a harnessed horse ready at the door for fighting or for flight at the least sign of attack from his domestic enemies." For the caudillo who has taken power and who retains it for profit, the state of alert, like that of war, leads to a double state of insecurity—first physical, because of the enemy whom he has not been able to eliminate or who rekindles the ambitions of faithless partners, and second, because of that internal sense of insecurity of someone who needs to justify to others, perhaps even to his own kin, the exercise of an unlimited power which has neither the social prestige nor the legitimacy, and certainly not the majesty of an ancient absolute monarchy. Consciously or not, the new chief of state seeks, therefore, to provide a moral and intellectual base for the loyalty of his subjects, for he is well aware that without traditional foundations for fidelity he cannot depend solely on either economic interests or on coercive force.

From this stems the caudillo's propensity to exalt and magnify his personality beyond all limits, especially if his humble origin and total absence of family tradition make him believe in the necessity of convincing others of the transcendental and exceptional character of his own person. From this, also, comes the taste for all which can strike the popular imagination: the theatrical gesture, the sumptuous uniform, the impressive monument, the spectacular performance . . . to engrave the ideal of a superman in the minds of the citizens.

In the Mexico of the first half of the last century a president, Santa Anna, showed such inclinations when he organized the solemn burial of his leg shot away by a cannon ball, or when, after having arranged that he be made dictator for life he organized a whole etiquette according to which his ministers had the obligation to travel in yellow coaches with valets in green livery, while His Most Serene Highness—himself—was escorted by lancers in red uniforms and plumed hats.

Here too it would be easy to give more examples, from the regional cacique who gives the name of his father, of his mother, of himself to markets, to schools, or to avenues of the *pueblos* which he dominates, to the dictator or president with overly ornate and bemedaled uniforms whom it has become such a pleasure to caricature in Mexican newspapers and elsewhere. . . .

THE CAUDILLO AS UNIFIER

If the power of the national dictator is of the same nature as that of the local cacique and they both use similar means, then between them the only difference is one of station; on the other hand, the two authorities may sometimes be at odds, and even at war. According to

circumstances and his personal temperament, the caudillo either will want to destroy the provincial caciques
who limit his power, or else he will cooperate with them
by drawing them into his system of government.

In this regard the Mexican economist Germán Parra
sees in certain Latin American dictatorships a state of social development comparable to that which the emergence of absolute monarchy in Europe represents. In fact,
certain chiefs of state have succeeded in centralizing the
government and in unifying under their authority badly
organized nations which were being exploited to different degrees by local caciques. Thus in Argentina Facundo Quiroga broke the spirit of independence in
eight provinces which he dominated as a semibarbaric
gaucho. He and other tyrants were in turn destroyed by
one of their own, the "federalist" caudillo Rosas, who by
violence and trickery succeeded in what the "unitarian"
parliamentary governments of Buenos Aires had not
been able to obtain: the fusion of the entire country
into one compact unit. . . .

In the same way that the railroad, in replacing the
horse, widened and strengthened the sphere of influence
of the provincial chief, so too the national dictator
tends to replace the local cacique. But because the roots
of personal power were so deep in some more or less
isolated rural areas, it could not be destroyed in a
complete and definitive fashion with one blow. In short,
other caudillos who were not able or who did not want
to choose military means as brutal as those of Rosas
tried to integrate into their system of government those
caciques judged useful and assimilable. Such was the approach of Porfirio Díaz in Mexico. . . .

What General Díaz did was to counteract existing
threats to centralized power and to reinforce the authority and prestige of the state everywhere, which before
him had only little influence beyond the central plateau
except for a small portion of the Atlantic coast. In most
other places "the supreme law was the will of one man
—a cacique." [As Luis Chávez Orozco has written,] "in
order to centralize this power absolutely General Díaz did

not destroy caciquismo, because this would have been impossible even if he had wanted to. What he did, was to give to caciquismo more vigor by placing it under official protection. The result was that all the caciques recognized him as the supreme political authority (the Great Cacique) in exchange for certain economic advantages which he deigned to let them enjoy."

Perhaps geographical reasons obliged Díaz to compromise with certain caciques instead of trying to suppress them. The topography of Mexico presented obstacles to the unification of the country which did not exist in the Argentine pampa: it is only during the last twenty-five or thirty years that the influence of the Mexican capital has been able to penetrate everywhere through the many sierras. This has been due to an important road system, completing on a large scale the work of centralization begun by the Porfirian railways. Moreover, Díaz did not support himself with the army, which never was very large, and he never tried to enrich himself personally.

In a large country with complex structures such as Mexico, no amount of money, distributed as presents, would have been sufficient to win over enough dependents and friends to form solid bases for personal power, which was, as we know, so often managed in isolated provinces or countries with rudimentary economies . . . elsewhere on the American continent. But Díaz let the caciques, governors, and *jefes políticos* get rich under his protective wing, while keeping public opinion opposed to possible rivals and convinced of the advantages and prestige resulting from his personal honesty.

This system, carefully perfected over more than thirty years of rule, left neither perspective nor room for political parties, because everything rested on personal power from the top to the bottom of the ladder. But Díaz felt the need to give to his government the ideological bases which it lacked.

Quite naturally he found these bases in Auguste Comte's Positivism which had been adapted by Mexican thinkers and educators of the second half of the nineteenth century. From a political standpoint, the ideals suited the Porfirian system admirably because they advocated the establishment of an authoritarian regime to fight against any tendency toward anarchy or disintegration, and to maintain social unity at all costs during the transitional phase when theological beliefs were fast disappearing yet before the doctrine of Positivism had definitely triumphed in the minds of the people. This "Order" closely linked as it was to economic "Progress" also represented the goal of the "Científicos," those technocratic friends of Porfirio Díaz. The Científicos and Díaz, however, did not know how to add "Love" for the peasants who had been despoiled of their land, as Comte had finally done. It was this failure which was a fundamental cause of the powerful social revolution of 1910-1911 that caused his downfall.

Especially since the beginning of the century, the influence of powerful economic interests has been and often still is important. Large private companies, most of them foreign, which exploit or sell oil, tropical fruits, sugar, and other export products, are proprietors of large enterprises and huge estates with enormous incomes. Naturally they have feared the demands of their employees, the requests for land from the peasants, the nationalistic and xenophobic tendencies of the mob, and they have also feared popular troubles which might compromise the success of their businesses. Thus their representatives have sometimes shown certain preferences for authoritarian government which seemed to them more capable of insuring order and better disposed to support their interests in exchange for financial and even political support.

The importance of personal and familial ties as a caudillo's means of government may now be somewhat archaic. But as with other American institutions, caudillismo and caciquismo still bear the marks of a long history: the prestige of physical force, of the proud horseman, of the best shot; the semipatriarchal authority of the landed proprietors, once lord and master of extensive domains;

the prowess of the military man who encounters no obstacles . . . ; the ostentation of the new man, who is not quite sure of himself; and finally, the power of the businessman who succeeds in controlling the principal means of production.

Today this boss or that dictator may be maintained and propelled by economic interests in an environment where money retains all the strength and vitality of youth. At the same time he is more and more questioned and threatened; he is often eliminated by societies which have achieved self-awareness and no longer allow themselves to be guided blindly as once they were. However, when the strong man learns how to adapt himself to this new situation, when, instead of representing personal interests and of leaning on clans or families, he becomes the representative of the rural people and the "leader" of masses, then he still may enjoy a long career.

Richard M. Morse

POLITICAL THEORY AND
THE CAUDILLO*

In the wake of M. Chevalier's exploration of personal bonds and the societal relationships of dictatorship, we turn to a provocative and original examination of political theory within the framework of Spain and Spanish America which was first published in 1954. Prof. Richard M. Morse, who teaches Latin American history at Yale, is best known for his work on the history of Latin American urbanization. His examination here of European philosophies which "might be correlated with Spanish American political history" has produced a working polarization of Thomistic medieval values and Machiavellian renaissance values. He associates these with the personal models Isabella of Castile and Ferdinand of Aragón, respectively. The interplay of the concepts of the medieval world order and renaissance statecraft underlies Morse's reconstruction of the Spanish Empire in America and has important implications for an understanding of modern caudillismo.

___

* Richard M. Morse, "Toward a Theory of Spanish American Government," *Journal of the History of Ideas,* Vol. XV (1954), pp. 71-93. The excerpts given here come from pp. 71, 72-74, 75-80, 81-82, 85-90. Reprinted by permission of the author and the *Journal of the History of Ideas.*

1. THE VICEREGAL PERIOD AND ITS ANTECEDENTS

The purpose of this essay is neither fully to analyze the political experience of Spanish America nor to construct a mature theory which will comprehensively illuminate it. The histories of these eighteen countries are, taken singly, too fragmentary and, taken jointly, too uncorrelated to permit of so systematic a project. In this as in most areas of New World studies the elements for conclusive synthesis are still unavailable. Therefore [let us] examine certain formal European notions in the hope, not that they will concisely epitomize Spanish American political experience, but that they may be "played off against" that experience—contrapuntally, perhaps—in a way to evoke corresponding themes. . . .

Spanish American preceded British colonization by more than a century, and thus belongs to an era that antedates not only the Lockean rights of man but also the Bousset- and Hobbes-type apology for the absolutist national state. It is the Catholic kings, Ferdinand and Isabella, who symbolize Spanish America's political heritage.

Isabella in a sense prefigures the divine-right monarch. Her thwarting of the nobles and of the Cortes wherein they formed an estate; her royal agents and administrative reforms that centralized the government; her replacement of feudal levies with a modern army; her use of the faith to further political unity—all have been cited to identify her as a precursor of the Hobbesian autocrat. Yet it must be remembered that for three centuries after Isabella's death the Spanish empire retained, in comparison at least with the burgeoning capitalist countries, many hall marks of the medieval, hierarchical state.

The "common law" of Isabella's Castile was the *Siete Partidas*, drawn up c. 1260 and promulgated in 1348, [which] . . . assumed the nuclear element of society to be, not Lockean atomistic man, but religious, societal man: man with a salvable soul (i.e., in relationship with

God) and man in a station of life (i.e., having mutual
obligations with fellow humans, determinable by principles of Christian justice). The ruler, though not proce-
durally responsible to the people or the estates, was
bound, through his conscience, to be the instrument of
God's immutable, publicly ascertainable law. The *Partidas,* in fact, specifically excoriated the tyrant who strove
to keep his people poor, ignorant and timorous and to
forbid their fellowship and assemblies.

As mistress of the hierarchical Castilian state whose
governance was largely by immanent justice and specially
ceded privileges (*fueros*), Isabella found constant occasion to make inter- as well as intranational assertion of
her spiritual authority. Unlike Aragón—from whose border the Moorish menace had been lifted in the thirteenth
century and whose rulers were therefore indifferent to
the Reconquest—Castile directly confronted Moorish
Granada until 1492. Furthermore, it was Cisneros, the
Queen's confessor, who largely animated the African
campaigns against the infidel Turks and Moslems. And it
was with the Castilian sovereign that the expeditions
which claimed dominion over millions of pagan Amer-
inds were initially associated. In her major foreign ventures, therefore, Isabella's policy reflected not only
politico-military vicissitudes of statecraft but also spiritual
responsibilities in the face of non-Christian multi-
tudes. After Columbus had assigned three hundred Indians to forced labor, it was as the imperious agent of
the Church Universal that Isabella demanded: "By what
authority does the Admiral give my vassals away?"

If Isabella, in her enterprises to the south and overseas
to the west, symbolizes the spiritualist, medieval component of the emergent Spanish empire, then Ferdinand,
whose Aragón was engaged to the east and north, represents a secular, Renaissance counterpart. His holdings
(the Balearics, Sardinia, Sicily, Naples) and his Italian
and Navarrese campaigns confined his problems of rule,
alliance and warfare to the European, Christian community. Isabella presented the unity of spiritually intransi-
gent Christendom to infidel and pagan. Ferdinand was

committed to the shifting, amoral statecraft of competing Christian princes in maintenance and expansion of a domain which, within its Christian context, was diversely composed.

Ferdinand ruled under transitional conditions which precluded resorting for authority to Isabella's Thomistic sanction or to statist apologetics. Managing with sheer personal verve and cunning, he was, in the fullest sense, Machiavellian. . . .

Spanish conquistadors, colonizers and catechizers, then, carried with them to American shores this dual heritage: medieval and Renaissance, Thomistic and Machiavellian. . . . For half a century after Isabella's death in 1504 Spanish New World administration hovered between medieval and Renaissance orientations. . . . [After Philip II came to power in 1556,] the structure of the Spanish American empire assumed the cast which, for purposes of this essay, it kept until c. 1810. That cast I describe as dominantly Thomistic, with recessive Machiavellian characteristics. . . .

In the 1570's, by extending the Inquisition to America and by declaring Church patronage inalienable from the crown, Philip set his governance definitively within a larger framework of divine law, imbuing his own and his agents' directives with spiritual purpose. No entry was left for the atomistic tolerance that England, despite its state religion, had already begun to evince.

The crown considered the political and social hierarchy to be energized at every level and in every department. As Indian peoples were absorbed, for example, they were not indiscriminately reduced to a common stratum. Certain of their leaders retained prestige in the post-conquest society, and many low-born Spaniards raised their own status by marrying caciques' daughters. . . .

To be sure, the social hierarchy had its anomalies. Creoles (American-born whites or near-whites) rarely received the prestige and the economic and political opportunities that were officially assured them. Mestizos, mulattoes, Indians and Negroes, on the contrary, occa-

sionally found a social fluidity that they could not officially have expected. Broadly speaking, however, a man's
status was defined somewhat fixedly by his occupation
and by his place and condition of birth. Transferral from
one status to another (e.g.: an Indian who passed from
mission to *encomienda,* a Negro from slave to free status, or a mestizo to the creole nobility) generally entailed
official sanction and registration.

The multiplicity of judicial systems underscored the
static, functionally compartmented nature of society.
The fact that they—like the several hierarchies of lay
and clerical administrators—constantly disputed each
other's spheres of influence only served to reaffirm the
king's authority as ultimate reconciler. Nuclear elements
—such as municipalities or even individual Indians—as
well as highly placed officers could appeal directly to the
king, or to his proxy, the viceroy, for redress of certain
grievances. The king, even though he might be an inarticulate near-imbecile like Charles II, was symbolic
throughout his realm as the guarantor of status. In
Thomistic idiom, all parts of society were ordered to the
whole as the imperfect to the perfect. This ordering, in-
herently the responsibility of the whole multitude, de-
volved upon the king as a public person acting in their
behalf, for the task of ordering to a given end fell to
the agent best placed and fitted for the specific function. . . .

The Spanish empire, to be sure, could scarcely avert
contagion from the post-medieval world in which it
existed and for which it was in part responsible. The
Jesuits, who had received extensive privileges overseas
for the very purpose of bolstering the empire's moral
and religious base, were outstandingly versed in mod-
ernism. An "enlightened" Bourbon regime expelled
them in 1767 less for their reactionary perversity than for
their shrewd, disciplined commercial activities and their
faith-defying "probabilist" dialectics.

Spanish American bullion was a lodestar for foreign
merchants. Introduced as contraband or else covertly
within the Spanish system itself, the wares of Dutch,

French and English were temptingly cheap, well-made and abundant. They, like the fiscal demands of the mother country, were a constant incentive for creoles to organize local economies from which bullion and exportable surplus might readily be factored out. The calculating acquisitiveness of capitalism, if not its institutions for unlimited accrual, was frequently in evidence.

Moreover, Indian and Negro burden-bearers were, unlike the medieval serf, never fully identified with the historical and cultural ethos of their masters. For this reason they suffered more from the emergent exploitative psychology than, perhaps, post-medieval peasants who remained bound to the land. The African received no comprehensive protective code until 1789. And the very laws that assured the Indian status in return for fixed services could in practice be perverted, rendering him servile to an *encomendero* or a royal agent (*corregidor*). Indeed, the existence of Thomistic guarantees for the common man can be confirmed only by examining Spain's New World experience in selected eras and locales, or by comparing it en bloc with other European ventures in the Antilles and North America.

Yet however strongly such "recessive" Machiavellian, protocapitalist or secularistic traits might erupt, the underpinning of the empire—social, economic, political, intellectual—bore a rubric of the earlier era. Eighteenth-century Bourbon reforms (the notable ones being those of Charles III, 1759-88) did little to alter this generalization. Some reforms—like the intendant system—were superimposed on the old structure, caused added confusion. . . . Others—like the Caracas Company, a more modern and enterprising trade monopoly—found harsh opposition because their services entailed strict enforcement of regulations which a more adaptive, personalistic regime of local control had traditionally winked at.

The hierarchical, multiform, pre-capitalist Spanish America of 1800 was ill prepared for the ways of enlightened despotism, still less for those of Lockean constitutionalism.

2. THE REPUBLICAN PERIOD

That the heterogeneous Spanish American realm was for three centuries relatively free from civil strife and separatist outbreaks must largely be explained by a steadfast loyalty to the politico-spiritual symbol of the crown. Even the sporadic Indian revolts of the eighteenth century were directed not against the Catholic sovereign and imperium but against malfeasance of local agents. . . .

Not until 1809, during Spain's Napoleonic interregnum, did local juntas appear overseas. Yet even then their autonomy, in expectation of a legitimist restoration, was provisional. Only when the ad hoc "liberal" Cortes, established in unoccupied Spain, tried to reduce Spanish America from viceregal to colonial status did the independence campaign, championed by a few firebrands, gather momentum.

Ferdinand VII was restored in 1814. But in the face of the independence movement, his character and policy discredited both himself and the Church, whose support he retained. For Spanish America the Thomistic keystone had been withdrawn. Efforts to supplant it, on a continental basis or even within regional blocs, were vain. No creole caudillo and no prince of European or Inca lineage could command universal fealty or age-old spiritual sanction. A Thomistic sovereign could not be created *ex nihilo*, and Spanish America's centrifugal separatism was for the first time unleashed.

Another idiom than the Thomistic is therefore needed to be played off against the republican experience. Hitherto the most satisfying analyses have been those that attribute Spanish American instability to the imposition of French-, British- and American-type constitutions upon peoples whose illiteracy, poverty, provincialism, political inexperience and social inequalities rendered ineffectual the mechanisms of constitutional democracy. This somewhat negative view, however, does not fully draw one into the fabric of Spanish American politics. If postulates of the Enlightenment were not relevant to that milieu, how, in a positive sense, may we comprehend it?

The answer this essay proposes is that at the moment when the Thomistic component became "recessive," the Machiavellian component, latent since the sixteenth century, became "dominant." . . .

Machiavelli was born into an "Age of Despots." Italian city states had lost their moral base; they no longer shared a common Christian ethos. The pope had become one of many competing temporal rulers. Machiavelli perceived that the mercenary "companies of adventure" of his time, unlike national militias, were undependable since they lacked any larger loyalty. They could be used to further intrigues of statecraft, but not to wage open and steady warfare. The Italian was effective only in duelling and individual combat.

Like Machiavelli, the Spanish American nation-builder of c. 1825 had to contend with nucleated "city states," the rural masses being passive and inarticulate. The absence of any communities intermediate between such nuclei and the erstwhile imperium had been revealed by the autonomous urban juntas of 1809-10. Only the somewhat arbitrary boundaries of colonial administration defined the new nations territorially. Only virulent sectionalism could define them operatively. The Church, once coterminous with the State, had become the intruding handmaiden of a hostile sovereign power (Spain). For lack of a politico-spiritual commonalty, sources and directions of leadership were wholly fortuitous. The consequent emergence of opportunist caudillos—as of Italy's city tyrants—deranged the predictable interplay of hierarchical class interests.

The Spanish American who held to constitutionalism and avowed the existence in fact of a state-community was swept away before winds of personalism. Mexico's Gómez Farías, vice-president under Santa Anna, was a statesman who, despite his energy and dedication, would not infract "the principles of public and private morality," before which, wrote his contemporary, Mora, vanished "his indomitable force of character." Why did he not cast out the treacherous Santa Anna? "Because the step was unconstitutional[:] . . . a famous reason which has kept the reputation of Señor Farías in a very secondary place at best and caused the nation to retrogress half a century."

A similar case was Rivadavia, Argentina's first president and proponent of bourgeois democracy and economic liberalism. His plans and principles had been no match for provincial *caudillismo*. The exiled statesman wrote sadly from Paris in 1830 (shortly before the personalist tyranny of Rosas):

> In my opinion what retards regular and stable advance in those republics stems from the vacillations and doubts that deprive all institutions of that moral force which is indispensable to them and can be given only by conviction and decision. It is evident to me, and would be easy to demonstrate, that the upheavals of our country spring much more immediately from lack of public spirit and of cooperation among responsible men in sustaining order and laws than from attacks of ungovernable, ambitious persons without merit or fitness and of indolent coveters.

Machiavelli's writings are the handbook *par excellence* for the leader who could cope with "lack of public spirit and of cooperation among responsible men." . . .

On nearly every page of Machiavelli appears practical advice which almost seems distilled from the careers of scores of Spanish American caudillos. Of crucial importance is the leader's commanding physical presence. In time of sedition he should:

> . . . present himself before the multitude with all possible grace and dignity, and attired with all the insignia of his rank, so as to inspire more respect. . . . [For] there is no better or safer way of appeasing an excited mob than the presence of some man of imposing appearance and highly respected. [*Discourses*, I, liv]

Among countless leaders and incidents one recalls the moment when Bolivia's ruthless Melgarejo, with six men, entered the palace where his rival, Belzu, was celebrating a coup d'état. The intruder, icily calm, shot the President, then with imperious presence faced and overawed the mob in whose throats the shouts of victory for Belzu had scarcely died away.

The personalist leader must be physically disciplined, skilled in warfare, and "learn the nature of the land, how steep the mountains are, how the valleys debouch, where the plains lie, and understand the nature of rivers and swamps" (*Prince*, XIV; see also *Discourses*, III, xxxix). This is almost a page from the autobiography of Páez, who knew Venezuela's vast *llanos* (inland plains) like the palm of his hand, a knowledge that confounded the royalists in 1817 and later earned respect for him as caudillo of the new republic. Writing of an assault against the Spaniards, Páez recalled:

> Necessity obliged us not only to fight men but to challenge the obstacles opposed by nature. Counting on these, we proposed to turn to our advantage the impediments that gave the enemy surety and trust in his position, for to no one would it occur that in that season cavalry troops could sortie from the lower Apure to cross so much inundated terrain and especially the many streams and five rivers, all at the period of overflow.

This telluric, earthbound quality so vital to Spanish American leaders was matched in Argentina's Quiroga and San Martín, Uruguay's Artigas, Mexico's Pancho Villa, Venezuela's Bolívar, Peru's Santa Cruz and innumerable others. Their guerrilla warfare was a far cry from the chessboard strategy and diplomatic power alignments of Europe. . . .

[But] how is it . . . that Spanish American caudillos or governments have in certain countries and eras, achieved political stability in the face of [the New World's] brand of social and moral centrifugalism? I define three essential modes of stability, which are categorized here merely for schematic purposes and with the understanding that the "pure" type never occurs. By way of further analogy I suggest a correspondence between these types and the three "legitimations of domination" which Max Weber distinguishes in his essay, "Politics as a Vocation." [1]

The first mode of stability is furnished by the Machiavellian leader who asserts himself by dynamic personalism and shrewd self-identification with local "original principles," though without ever relinquishing government, as Machiavelli would have wished, "to the charge of many." The system remains subordinate to the man and unless a suitable "heir" is available, which happens infrequently, it falls with him. Here we perhaps have Weber's charismatic leader with the personal gift of grace, who flouts patriarchal traditionalism and the stable economy, whose justice is Solomonic rather than statutory, who maintains authority "solely by proving his strength in life." One recent writer, Blanksten, holds that the caudillo and charismatic types correspond. George S. Wise, on the other hand, claims that the "stratagem and chicanery" of at least one caudillo (Venezuela's Guzmán Blanco) revealed an insecurity and lack of purpose precluding the oracular, prophetic qualities that he attributes to charismatic legitimacy. Weber's specific consideration of the condottiere type leads me to feel, however, that charisma need not invariably imply "anointment."

The charismatic leader may be dedicated to molding the self-perpetuating traditions of a state-community— for example, Bolívar's vision of federated Andean republics, Morazán's Central American union, the constitutionalism of Mexico's Juárez and perhaps the quasi-theocracy of Ecuador's García Moreno. Or, which is more usual, he may set about exploiting the country as his private fief. In the decades after independence such a caudillo would win the army's allegiance (or create his own plebeian militia), then assert control over the several classes by blandishment, personal magnetism or threat of

---

[1] H. H. Gerth and C. W. Mills (eds.), *From Max Weber: Essays in Sociology* (London, 1947), pp. 78ff.

force—the method depending, in the case of each segment of society, on "original principles" and the leader's
own antecedents. Examples are Argentina's Rosas, Mexico's Santa Anna, Guatemala's Carrera, Paraguay's Francia.

Toward the end of the century the exploitation of
new sources of mineral and agricultural wealth, together with a strong influx of foreign investments,
gave caudillos more dependable leverage for control.
Though force and personalism did not go in the dis-
card, financial resources and the protective favor of
foreigners allowed the leader to govern by "remote control." He adopted bourgeois bon ton and even paid lip
service to constitutionalism. Such men were Venezuela's
Guzmán Blanco, Mexico's Porfirio Díaz, Guatemala's
Barrios.

Intensified economic activity might also give rise to a
second type of state: a modified version of laissez-
faire democracy. This development, which Weber calls
legitimation through bureaucratic competence and public respect for rational legal statutes, has been rare in
Latin America, even in hybrid form. Argentina affords
an example. In that country after 1860, and especially
after 1880, the pampas experienced a torrential land
rush, occasioned by a world demand for meat and grains
and by improved methods of husbandry, transportation
and refrigeration. Though the lion's share of the benefits
accrued to an oligarchy of large proprietors, many immigrants took small homesteads in the northern provinces; moreover, the expanding economy created niches
for articulate, middle-class city dwellers. Argentines were,
relative to Latin America, homogeneous and white. A
growing nucleus identified its interests with the stability
and prosperity of the nation-community, even though
the positions of highest socio-economic authority were
already pre-empted.

Given Argentina's economic direction and momentum, it remained for a series of statesmen-presidents
merely to encourage and guide its development, in tolerable conformance with the Lockean Constitution of 1853.

Eventual malfeasance in high office led, not back to tyranny, but to the emergence in 1890 of the Radical (liberal, middle-class) Party, to free suffrage and the secret ballot, and finally to Radical control of the presidency (1916-1930). Twentieth-century Radical leaders, however, reined back certain socio-economic forces from a natural course by acquiescing in the continued entrenchment of the landowning oligarchy. Only then did thwarted urban classes fall prey to demagoguery of an ominous breed— and to Juan Domingo Perón.

A third solution for anarchy has been a full-scale implementing of the Machiavellian blueprint. A personalist leader emerges (as in the first case), but goes on successfully to create a system, larger than himself, that is faithful to "original principles." In Spanish America such a system is larger than the leader, to frame a paradox, only when it *recognizes* the leader to be larger than itself. This statement has Thomistic implications, and the more successful Spanish American constitutions have translated into modern idiom certain principles under which the viceroyalties enjoyed three centuries of relative stability.

This solution, insofar as it reinvigorates the body social by setting its classes, or "estates," into centrally stabilized equilibrium, is a neo-traditionalism reminiscent of Weber's third category: "the authority of the eternal yesterday." Of Mexico's present Constitution— brought into being in 1917 by Carranza, a shrewd, opportunist caudillo—Frank Tannenbaum has written:

> By implication, the Constitution recognizes that contemporary Mexican society is divided into classes, and that it is the function of the State to protect one class against another. The Constitution is therefore not merely a body of rules equally applicable to all citizens, but also a body of rules specially designed to benefit and protect given groups. The community is not made up of citizens only; it is also made up of classes with special rights within the law. What has in fact happened is that the old idea

of the "estates" has been re-created in Mexican law.
The pattern of the older Spanish State, divided into
clergy, nobility, and commons, has been re-created
in modern dress, with peasants, workers, and capitalists replacing the ancient model. This is not done
formally, but it is done sufficiently well to make
it evident that a very different kind of social structure is envisioned in the law, even if only by implicit
commitment, than that in a liberal democracy. . . .

The Revolution has certainly increased effective
democracy in Mexico. It has also increased, both legally and economically, the dependence of the people and of the communities upon the federal government and the President. The older tradition
that the king rules has survived in modern dress:
the President rules. He rules rather than governs,
and must do so if he is to survive in office and keep
the country at peace.

I have reserved any mention of Chile until now because its history usefully illustrates our three political
types as well as a twentieth-century variant which has
yet to be considered. Like its sister nations, Chile fell
after independence into anarchic factionalism. A revolution of 1829-30, however, brought the conservatives into
power; at their head was Diego Portales who, as a businessman, was atypical among Spanish American nation-
builders. Portales appreciated more keenly than most
the need for disciplined, predictable conditions of life
and was more empirical in perceiving that liberal slogans and mechanisms were meaningless within an aristocratic, agrarian society. His views were reflected in the
centralized, quasi-monarchic Constitution of 1833 which,
by recognizing Chile's hierarchic social anatomy and at
the same time guaranteeing status and justice for the
component members, lent the government a supra-
personalist sanction. Portales himself did not become
president, but wisely designated a military hero, General
Prieto, whose prestige, aristocratic bearing and benevo-
ence, traditionalism and religiosity further enhanced the

office with an aura of legitimacy. None of Chile's presidents was overthrown for sixty years, while the Constitution lasted nearly a century.

Portales, alone among his Spanish American contemporaries, brought to fulfillment the policy of "the compleat Machiavellian." As the century advanced, however, a leavening took place within the system he had fathered. A law of 1852 abolished primogeniture, infusing new blood and interests into the landed oligarchy. Mineral exploitation in the north and the activities of German immigrants in the south posted new directions for economic change and opportunity. The consequent desire for more effective economic competition provided a rallying cry for enthused liberals emerging from the new (1842) University. So too did growing dissatisfaction with the constitutional ban on public exercise of non-Catholic religions.

At length the Chilean élite, larger and more diversely composed than in 1833, revolted against centralized, one-man rule by ejecting President Balmaceda from office in 1891. This élite then governed through its congressional representatives, and the fitfulness of public policy for the next thirty years reflected the jostling of private economic interests.

As in Argentina, however, the modified laissez-faire state could not indefinitely subsist if it was to victimize the increasingly self-aware lower classes, such as, in Chile's case, the copper and nitrate workers. The little man eventually found his champion in President Arturo Alessandri (1920-1925, 1932-1938).[2]

Alessandri's and subsequent administrations repre-

---

[2] The dictatorial interregnum of Carlos Ibáñez (1925-1931) can be considered as Chile's nearest approach to the first, or pure caudillo type of rule. His advent is partially explained by the post-World War I collapse of the world nitrate market, which impaired the mainspring of parliamentary, laissez-faire government and left Chile (since Alessandri had not yet given shape and momentum to his social democracy) in its primordial anarchy. Ibáñez, though sometimes referred to as a "man on horseback," effectively used modern technocratic methods and was not a caudillo of the old stamp—to which his reelection in 1952 bears witness.

sent an attitude toward government that has in this century become universal throughout Spanish America. It has in varying degrees infiltrated the three earlier systems, or combinations thereof, wherever they exist. Essentially, it is a recognition of the need to build into public policies a dynamics for socio-economic change. This need stems from two interrelated phenomena: first, the urbanization and industrialization of hitherto extractive economies; second, the growing self-awareness and articulateness of the citizenry at large.

The Spanish American leader, whether dictator or democrat, is fast adopting a broader, more sophisticated view of how modern political power must be won, maintained and exercised. He also knows that, regardless of any nationalistic rhetoric to which he may be committed, he must import more and more blueprints and technical solutions from abroad. Such solutions, however—whether socialism, fascism, exchange control or river valley authorities—take on a new complexion as they flash into amalgam with conditions of life wholly different from those by which they were engendered. Not only is the receiving ethos broadly speaking *sui generis*, but in a strictly technological sense the particular juxtapositions of ancient and modern in Spanish America are quite beyond the experience of any of the capitalist countries. Therefore slogans of foreign systems ring far differently upon Spanish American ears than their originators imagine.

In fact, Peru's *Aprista* movement and Mexico's forty-year-long "Revolution" attest that Spanish America is starting to generate its own credos. Sometimes, as with Perón's *justicialismo*, they are heartlessly cynical rhetoric. At best they designate, as did our own New Deal, a piecemeal pragmatism, uncommitted to the mysticism or fixed morality prescribed for the New World by Hegel. Yet the fact that Spanish America is by tradition accustomed and by economic necessity forced to rely heavily on official planning, intervention and protection has on occasion led its statesmen to a "total view" (to be distinguished carefully in nature and intent from a to-

talitarian view). From such views flow social, economic
and cultural agenda which, however imperfect of execu-
tion, uniquely contribute to an understanding of man-in-
community.

Co-existent, indeed, with Spanish America's atomism
. . . is a sense of commonalty, however latent, deriving
in large part from its Catholicity (in the ingrained, cultural sense) and from its agrarian, Negro and Indian
heritage. Native to this commonalty is an ethic upon
which the hyper-rationalist logos of the industrial world
seems able to make only limited and conditional en-
croachments. The prediction is sometimes heard among
Spanish Americans that this logos will in the long run
exhaust itself; that their descendants will be freer to
weave certain principles of a pre-Machiavellian age into
the new patterns of an entering one; that the promise
which erractically flashes in the travail of twentieth-
century Mexican democracy is yet to be realized.

II

Caudillismo in the Nineteenth Century

◇◇◇

Centuries are rarely the best dividing lines in any effort at historical periodization unless they are loosely defined. For Spanish America, therefore, the "nineteenth century" cuts through the "seamless web of history" most successfully if the approximate terminal dates 1808-1825 and 1910-1918 are employed. The development of caudillos during the era of independence, their predominance through the middle decades, and the sophisticated pose of some of their number in the generation before World War I are treated in the following division together with an inquiry into the nature of foreign influences on caudillismo throughout the century.

Raymond E. Crist

GEOGRAPHY AND CAUDILLISMO: A CASE STUDY*

Among the elements which have conditioned Spanish civilization in America, the sheer immensity of the plains, the rivers, and the mountains must be assessed no matter what one's personal school of historical interpretation may be. The political and economic phenomenon of regionalism or localism, so much a constant throughout Latin American history, has largely been the product of geographic barriers and distances. The direct relation of geography to the emergence of a specific caudillo, José Antonio Páez, in the Llanos of Venezuela during the wars of indepence is explored in the following article by Raymond E. Crist, Professor of Geography at the University of Florida. Professor Crist's essay suggests something of the spontaneity so frequently associated with the emergence of military leaders during the independence period. As in the case of Páez, the authoritarian leadership exercised in many Spanish American coun-

* Raymond E. Crist: "Desarrollo político y origen de caudillismo en Venezuela," *Revista geográfica americana,* VII (1937), pp. 253-270. The excerpts given here come from pp. 253-255, 257-269. Translated and printed by permission of the author.

tries for half a century thereafter was drawn from among the "Marshals of Ayacucho" and their peers.

The words "Great plains," "Pampas" and "Steppes" conjure up fantastic pictures to the peoples of industrialized communities. We envision vast level regions extending toward infinity, covered by waving grass where millions of head of cattle graze. . . .

Since the beginning of history all big pastoral regions have been the scene of interminable struggles. Attila gathered his hordes in the steppes of Eastern Europe and this big tide of turbulent humanity was able to flood a great part of Western Europe before it finally broke on the already tottering bulwark of the Roman Empire.

Since the European races began their systematic penetration of the whole world, we have witnessed the struggles of the native peoples against the white aggressor in the Great Plains of North America and in the Pampas—from the Quechua word which means open space or country—of South America, as well as in the Australian plains and in the steppes of South Africa.

The Venezuelan Plains or *Llanos* have for centuries been the scene of warlike activities. The numerous Indian tribes fought among themselves long before the Spaniards' arrival and thus were not able to offer the white invader anything but feeble resistance.

The latter had two important material advantages over the Indian: firearms and horses. Even densely populated regions like Mexico and Peru were unable to stop the conquerors' attack for long. The arrows and lances of the Indians of the plains who did not have horses were of no use against the mounted Spaniards with firearms; later on the lance in the hands of the agile mounted plainsmen or *Llaneros* was a very effective weapon.

Eventually the horse came to be so vital to the plainsman's life that if he were deprived of his faithful animal his feet would be cut off, as he would put it in his own figurative language. It is true that if a horse is stolen by a common thief or taken by the government for State use, the owner is practically unable to work. Thus, in the Llanero's life, as in the life of other pastoral peoples, the horse is of great importance. . . .

There are various reasons why the Llanos have continued to be the scene of struggles and bloodshed. The region has never been densely populated, but the inhabitants were intrepid horsemen, always ready for adventure. . . . The Llanos are almost flat . . . so that the smallest irregularity in the surface, a bank or a slight elevation, a river, a forest or a pond may be important as a boundary line. . . . To those used to living on the Llanos, transportation is not a difficult problem and the lack of distinct natural boundaries caused the Llaneros to be highly mobile elements. Once they go on the warpath, whether for valid reasons or not, it is almost impossible for troops from other districts, unfamiliar with the terrain and the living conditions of the region, to capture them; it matters not what the superiority in numbers. . . .

As livestock herds grew in number, the plains on which they grazed were able to support an increasing population. At the beginning, three different races existed in the Llanos: Indians, whites, and Negroes. During several centuries these three races became fused. By the time of the Wars of Independence a rather pronounced amalgamation had taken place. Few individuals of pure blood existed; on the contrary, there was a lot of mixed blood, formed, in varied proportions, by blood from the three races. But the latter, in their ideas, habits, impulses, and love of fighting, had come to be what could almost be designated as a new race: the Llanero. . . .

The inhabitants of vast pastoral areas have many characteristics in common. The Cossacks, Kurds, Tartars, and Bedouins, like the Gaucho and the Llanero, were born and grew up on completely flat plains. They drank in a love of liberty with their mothers' milk and with the air they breathe. They have a strong desire to be independent, to be free from exploitation, especially from the intangible power superimposed from a distance by a centralized government. However, they are willing, under certain circumstances, to submit to the authority of a "guerrilla" leader, or caudillo, whose power rests on his obviously superior force and on the fact that he lives with his men, his "people"; he represents a tangible incarnation of authority. These men have as profound a dislike for manual work as they have devotion to movement on horseback, which gives to those who get used to it a satisfying sense of activity unaccompanied by great physical fatigue. Pastoral peoples also have a profound disdain for sedentary agriculture and urban populations; they are convinced that strength is the great virtue, and that disputes are best solved by arms. Despising danger, they face it with energy and without any thought of themselves. Before the dawn of history, it is a matter of fact that pastoral peoples have been a terrible menace to cities and to sedentary folk, because of their love of freedom of movement, together with their desire to steal and plunder. . . .

It is well to examine the Llanero's background. Most of the Spaniards who settled in the Llanos came from central Spain, where the influence of the Moors was strong racially as well as with regard to their habits and ideas. The Arabs were excellent horsemen, and under Mohammed's successors they rapidly conquered an Empire. In Spain they became sedentary and achieved a brilliant civilization, but they retained many pastoral characteristics. Above all, good horsemanship remained important in the constant battles with the Spaniards. . . .

When the Spaniards finally reconquered the territory which the Arabs had occupied, the circumstances were more favorable to grazing than to agriculture. During 800 years of endemic war they had lost their sedentary habits; property rights had come to be vague over the huge semidesert prairies controlled by the Mesta, that organization of shepherds who sought to assure the movement of their herd and flocks, frequently at the expense of the farmers who were along the route. The

Mesta was very powerful, a kind of state within a state, which profoundly influenced the psychology and habits of thought of the white ancestors of the Llaneros. The Spanish shepherds were imbued with a proud individualism, together with a deep sense of equality toward all human beings under the sun, whether they were Kings or Sultans. . . .

In time the Llanos came to constitute a refuge where a great number of thieves, criminals, smugglers, and runaway slaves lived beyond the law; they constituted a kind of floating population, they made incursions into the cities and ran off with booty and women. The ranchers who were more or less settled complained continuously about the incursions of these desperados, who were capable of living peaceful lives just long enough to plan and execute attacks on the settled inhabitants and escape unpunished. In 1786 it was estimated that 24,000 persons lived as outlaws in the Llanos. Finally, the ranch owners were authorized by the Audiencia to form highly mobile units of mounted men who could capture cattle thieves and other criminals and kill them without any legal formalities. . . .

As we have seen, the Llaneros were naturally born to love liberty and equality. A vigorous person rarely takes into consideration that he is in good health until he gets sick; the Llaneros were not conscious that they were fanatic lovers of liberty till they were, or thought they were, deprived of it. . . . They cared very little who was in power in distant Caracas. . . . It was almost impossible to subdue them, and since they had absolute liberty they wanted to preserve it at all costs.

There existed among them the most absolute equality, but despite this fact they did not reject the authority which a powerful man has always imposed and will always be able to impose. . . . Yet it was absolutely impossible for those rude plainsmen to have held the concept of a great nation as it is understood today or as it was dreamt of at the time by Simón Bolívar. What moved them were the same ideals that move the extreme nationalists of our times. They were inclined to form clans and feudal groups so that they could be as self-sufficient as possible while under the direct orders of a local dictator or chief. The latter would be in turn under the orders of an even more powerful chief and so on, until all the steps of the hierarchy were occupied up to the effective chief or governor whose power rested on his superior strength and will.

A leader of this sort was José Tomás Boves, a man from Asturias who had been in jail because of smuggling and who was later exiled. He took refuge in the Llanos where he soon became an excellent horseman and learned the habits of the Llaneros. That kind of life suited him well; he had a big and powerful body, he feared absolutely nothing, and in a short while he became an imposing figure. In 1811 he briefly embraced the cause of the patriots, but for reasons unknown he later took the side of the Royalists, and brought his people with him. Boves received help from another adventurer, Francisco Morales, who also imposed respect amongst the people of the Llanos. Together they formed the famous "Infernal Legion" and inflicted serious losses on the patriots on several occasions. . . .

[According to Vallenilla Lanz] the great strength of Boves rested on his cavalry although its organization did not follow strict military rules. It was dictated by the peculiar political situation and by his knowledge of the country. Each squad was formed by the people of a town and its surrounding territory. For this reason the squads were known by the names of the towns whence they came: the Guayabal Squad, the Tiznados Squad, etc. Some had three hundred men, some five hunderd, some six hundred, and, as a result of this classification, there was such competition to excel among the different squads that victory was always theirs.

Boves' personal control over the plainsmen naturally ended with his death, which occurred in an armed encounter with his enemies. Immediately afterwards his followers quietly dispersed; most of them returned to their respective towns or cattle ranches. There they lived peacefully until another great figure was able to surround himself with friends and achieve a personal concentration of power and authority much greater than that which Boves enjoyed.

José Antonio Páez was born in 1790, near the village of Acarigua, of extremely poor parents. Little is known about his ancestors. We do know, however, that his father had the privilege of possessing a firearm, because he had a document which proved that he was a "white of pure blood." A document of this kind, however, was easy to purchase by pure whites as well as by people of mixed white and Indian blood, which means that Páez's father was not necessarily a "white on all four sides."

The existing pictures of young Páez reveal certain characteristic Indian features. But the fact that he had a lighter complexion than most of the plainsmen was shown because all his life he had a nickname ("Catire") which alluded to his white blood. The young man received a very poor education and he early had to help his parents earn a living. When still young he made a long business trip for his father, and, on his return with a sum of money, was attacked by bandits. The young man struggled, and killed one of his assailants. . . . Fearful that the authorities would catch him he fled to the Llanos, where so many other outlaws sought refuge.

Páez was an energetic and intelligent young man, however, and he soon found a job as a laborer, for three dollars a month, on the cattle ranch known as "La Calzada" which belonged to don Manuel Pinto. The living conditions in a cattle ranch are certainly not luxurious, even today, so that they must have been much cruder a century or more ago. Laborers lived in a cabin covered with palm leaves and open on all four sides. During the most active season of the year it was necessary to be on horseback from twelve to fifteen hours a day, shoeing horses, castrating calves, and separating cows with their young from the herd. The men lived entirely on a meat diet; they killed the animals when they needed fresh supplies. . . .

The administrator was a gigantic Negro called Manuelote who made life as hard as possible for young Páez.
He made Páez do the heaviest tasks, such as breaking
wild colts and riding herd under the burning tropical sun.
Besides, he had to take care of the horses during the night
and watch that they would not get lost. . . .

The young man's hands were burned by horsehair
reins while breaking colts, and the fact that he used to
ride shirtless on an unpadded wooden saddle gave him
painful blisters on his thighs. Discipline was as severe as
that of a prison. On one occasion, when Páez was in
doubt whether to spur his horse into the river to herd the
cattle, since he himself could not swim, Manuelote
shouted in rage: "I'm not asking whether you know how
to swim, I'm ordering you to get into that river and herd
the cattle."

Sometimes he had to wash his master's feet and swing
his hammock to help him fall asleep. In this way during
the years of his youth the young man learned to know
intimately the people of the plains and their way of life.
This experience was an excellent training for the guerrilla tactics of the future caudillo. He acquired an Arab's
love for his horse and became an excellent horseman. He
had great personal courage, an alert intelligence, and the
gift of command. The years of constant practice in horseback riding, in exploring, and in the use of the lance gave
him great physical strength and a strong will. His power
of observation was sharpened by his life in the open. He
learned to distinguish and interpret signs such as rising
smoke or dust, the flight of vultures and other birds,
and the way in which pasture is bent by passing horses or
cattle. After several years of this hard life, he was transferred to a cattle ranch along the Paguey River, which
belonged to the same owner. Here he met the owner
who liked this serious and intelligent young man and
gave him a position of responsibility. He was put in
charge of taking young bulls to the market, handling the
money, etc.

In the thirteen original colonies of the United States
the descendants of the white settlers, mostly Anglo-

Saxon, fought against the English armed forces for their right to establish their own government. Very few, if any, Negroes or Indians fought on their side. This was not the case with Latin Americans. Undoubtedly the Creoles, the "criollos"—Americans of Spanish ancestry —constituted the element which precipitated the conflict, but it was impossible for them to fight against the Spanish armed forces alone. They received an enormous amount of help from Negro slaves and Indian peasants who had been long under the oppressive yoke of the whites, whether born in America or in the Iberian Peninsula. Páez himself had first-hand knowledge of the injustice suffered by the laborers on the big farms and had a strong desire to help abolish it long before the idea of breaking the tie with the mother country had taken shape in his mind.

In 1809 the future president and general was on his way from La Calzada to Guarico with a herd of cattle and had reached the Portuguesa River. That was at the beginning of February, which is the dry season. At night he camped in "La Huerfanita," where the slaves from the cattle ranch Banco Largo, located on the right bank of the river and whose owner was Gualberto Rodríguez Montenegro, had their headquarters. Many were the complaints against Gonzalo de Orozco and Miguel López, Montenegro's administrator and partner respectively, for they were guilty of a lot of cruelties to the slaves.

During the night a revolt occurred, and Páez, although having a position of trust with one of the most powerful families, made common cause with the Negroes and the Indians. In the battle Orozco was killed and López fled to Calabozo. Apparently Páez did not think again about the cattle in his custody since on the following morning he organized an expedition of three hundred men from the cattle ranch and its vicinity and headed toward Calabozo. His force had been doubled by the time he reached that city. The attack was repulsed and he retired to Apure.

He did not go back to his job in La Calzada. The Cabildo of Caracas organized an expedition against the plunderers, and a reward of 150 pesos was offered for Páez's head. Nine months later, after staying in Apure during the rainy season, he reappeared along the Portuguesa, with a troop of 2,000 lancers. He became a constant menace to the cattle owners of that area and to the interests of the Guipuzcoana Company that had been established in Calabozo. There a reward of 2,000 pesos was offered to whoever could give information as to his hiding place.

Páez's movement was only the beginning. A series of revolts followed in various parts of the Llanos. In 1812 a "mulatto," José de los Santos Mina, organized a troop of 300 lancers, entered the city of Mangas Boceros at night, and captured and killed all the officials. An expedition under the command of Matías Paz was sent against him, but all its members were captured and the chief hanged. One week later Mina joined forces with Páez. Other uprisings occurred; that of an Indian named Juan Caparo, in Apurito, with 200 mounted men, that of Bonifacio García in Barbacoas, with 150 men, and that of Santos Vargas in Guardatinajas, with the plainsmen of the region. All these groups were finally united under Páez's leadership.

It was not difficult to obtain supplies, because of the large herds of cattle existing in the plains; and for the cavalry the men could easily get fresh animals. Because of the great mobility of the rebels, it was impossible for the central government to have a pitched battle with them and destroy them. It soon became apparent that Páez had a natural gift for leadership. Active military life awakened in him latent powers and he came to be a real tactical genius in the territory which he knew so well.

After the terrible sufferings experienced while he worked as a laborer in La Calzada even the fatigues of the continuous battles were sweet. Besides, the plainsmen felt that he was one of them and not a gachupín (a hated Spaniard or other white foreigner) like Boves. . . . On the battlefield or on the parade ground, to be sure, Páez was the general and absolute leader, but during the hours of relaxation he danced with the people, drank, ate, and smoked with them in a spirit of intimate comradeship.

The plainsman's religious life is hardly rich and his beliefs are surely vague. They are not as pious as other pastoral races, such as the Israelites of the Old Testament and the Boers of our times. Páez himself seemed to have the innocent creed of primitive herdsmen. (In his autobiography Páez narrates how he became enraged with a Spaniard he had captured . . . because the prisoner showed more interest in saving his life than in saying his prayers. Because of this unreligious attitude he plunged his spear into his victim with more energy than usual.)

The more prominent plainsmen, especially during the war with Spain, held the belief that they belonged to a chosen people, chosen to free their country from the Spanish yoke. This is a feeling common to most pastoral races. Something similar to this feeling must have prompted Páez when he ordered the inhabitants of San Fernando de Apure to burn the city to prevent it from falling into [the Spanish General] Morillo's hands. And in this case the people obeyed and did not hesitate to burn their own homes to keep them from the invaders, whereas the Tzar of Russia had to use the Cossacks to burn Moscow and keep it from the French. These plain pastoral folk made the sacrifice without a murmur. Their life was simple. In their houses they used the skulls of horses or alligators as chairs; as beds, untanned hides. They ate to keep alive, and not for the pleasure of eating. Black coffee and chewing tobacco were great luxuries to those who were used to a meat diet, with an occasional banana as dessert.

The knowledge that Páez had of the territory was an incalculable advantage in his campaigns. He was able at any moment to tear up the carefully drawn plans of General Headquarters and to form new ones as unforeseen events and terrain changes demanded them. In one battle, he waited till he was upwind from the Royalists and then ordered fifty men to set fire to the dry grass. The flames, with a terrific roar, rolled over the enemy infantry who were in close ranks and the men were almost suffocated by the smoke. They were saved only because they quickly retreated to a sector where the grass had been burnt off a few days before. They were followed, however, for about a league by Páez' lancers, with whom they engaged in hand to hand combat until they reached the Apure River and took refuge in the woods.

On another occasion, when Morillo had camped near the Apure in San Fernando, Páez ordered that four wild horses be lassoed and that their tails be tied together with dry untanned skin. These horses were taken as near as possible to the enemy camp and released. At the same time a few shots were fired and the frightened horses threw themselves like a hurricane among the sleeping soldiers. Páez asserts that the confusion was as great as that caused by the 2,000 bulls that Hannibal released against the Romans. The astute caudillo knew that only by having a constant and abundant supply of horses for his men could he expect victory. Besides, they made great efforts to prevent horses from falling into the hands of the enemy. In February 1817 Páez told Bolívar that he "had got together all the horses of the Llanos. The enemy lacks this resource and while we have them we will be invincible. . . ."

At the beginning of his struggle against Spain, Páez saw in the movement a civil war rather than a war to get free from an oppressive foreign yoke. The Royalist armies were not composed entirely of Spaniards; they had as many Latin Americans as did Bolívar's forces. The Llaneros, although on the side of the patriots, fought for their leader, and because of their ardent love of "guerrilla" fighting, rather than for an idea. They followed Páez with an enthusiasm even greater than what they had had for Boves because they considered Páez one of themselves because of his superior strength and great horsemanship, and even because of his occasional cruel acts; but they did not follow him because they were fighting on the side of those who were in revolt against the mother country. Supremely loyal, they followed him throughout the long years of war until the decisive battle of Carabobo, where they won their full measure of glory and merited the title of "The Bravos of Apure."

Bolívar had dreamed for a long time of a big state in the northern part of South America, and he thought that this victory would make it possible of realization. But this was not to be. Such a vision could not materialize in a pastoral community isolated and self-sufficient. However, the great Páez, due to his experience in organizing men and in knowing people like Bolívar . . . , had considerably enlarged his political vision. His horizon was now beyond the plains where he had spent his early life. Although he did not share Bolívar's dream of a big federation covering half a continent, he was able to see beyond the Llanos and to plan the political unification of a larger area, in fact, of a big nation: Venezuela. When peace was achieved, he immediately took up the task of consolidating this nation politically, although that meant that he had to break with Bolívar. He had acquired in the twenty years spent in campaigns the techniques of military organization and this helped him greatly to build a new civil administration.

Apparently Páez had a natural sense of human rights and dignity and the fact that a great number of Negroes had fought bravely on the side of the patriots made a great impression upon him. One of the most famous Negro slaves in his army was Camejo, known in history as "The First Negro," who was killed in the battle of Carabobo. This Negro was the general's favorite. While in command of local forces, Páez had abolished slavery in the District of Apure, not at all as a result of extensive reading about the rights of man, but simply because he was sincerely opposed to the injustices which were inherent in slavery, and because he needed all the men he could get to defeat the Royalists. He did not understand why these men who had risked their lives for the cause of liberty should continue to live as slaves after having driven the Spaniards from their own country.

As soon as he was firmly in control of his country he started to advocate the abolition of slavery, but the time was not ripe for total abolition. Páez used his influence over Congress to have a law passed with provisions that decidedly limited the evil. Sale of slaves outside the district where they were living was not permitted; no new slaves could be imported into the country; those slaves who were already in the country would receive some rudimentary education. . . .

Páez was able to assume control of his territory because of the intense personal loyalty of his mounted companions. Once he became the head of a centralized government, however, he could no longer be among them. Their loyalty to him gradually weakened because they had to have as a leader a visible and tangible authority, who would live among them, who could drink and dance with them, and not be a mere President in faraway Caracas.

For this reason revolutions periodically broke out.

For many years the old guerrilla leader could muster his forces, dash across the Llanos in forced marches as in previous years, and defeat his enemies even before they realized he was upon them. Then Páez was again the popular and admired warrior of the plains. After inflicting an astounding defeat on a formidable uprising in San Juan de Payara, he earned the title of "León de Payara," an epithet by which he is still known today by his admirers, the Paecistas. . . . Finally he was overthrown by a rival leader and his unfortunate country went through a disastrous series of revolutions and counterrevolutions. . . .

The destiny of the revolutionary cause in Venezuela was decided on the Llanos, for there the patriots enjoyed natural advantages. Climate was, for example, a major ally for Páez; the rainy season was as disastrous for Spanish troops as winter was for Napoleon's Grand Army in Russia. As a guerrilla leader, a caudillo, Páez was himself a product of the grasslands. Sarmiento once made the penetrating assertion that caudillismo sprouted from the very legs of horses in Venezuela as well as in Argentina. Indeed it was the horse which made swift campaigns on the Llanos possible. Easily incorporated into large mobile cavalry units, horses readily adapted to the climate and to the tumult of battle.

The legend of José Antonio Páez will live in the popular imagination for years to come as each future generation adds something to enrich it. The common people will continue to see in him a reflection of themselves because he was one of them and they will, therefore, assign to him the virtues which they themselves would like to possess. He was flesh of their flesh and blood of their blood; he did not look down on them from Olympian heights as did Bolívar, the intellectual. Páez was certainly among the greatest caudillos, although he was nothing but a guerrilla leader. He had learned nothing about military tactics from books, but he knew his country and he knew his people.

J. Fred Rippy

MONARCHY OR REPUBLIC? *

It is one thing to win a revolution by arms; it is quite
another to establish a stable government in place of
the old regime. J. Fred Rippy (1892-   ), Professor
Emeritus at the University of Chicago and a well-
known Latin American historian, here explores the
basic dilemma of the independence period: what substitute for the moral authority of the Spanish crown
can be fashioned which will provide both freedom
and responsible government? The relation of the almost universal choice of constitutional republic to
the conditions which promoted caudillismo is examined by Professor Rippy.

I

There was much doubt, hesitation, and vacillation among
the leaders of [the newly liberated colonies of Spain]
before the final decision was made in favor of a political
system based, in theory at least, upon the principles of

* J. Fred Rippy: "Monarchy or Republic?" from A. Curtis Wil-
gus (ed.), *South American Dictators During the First Century of
Independence* (Washington, D.C.: George Washington University
Press, 1937), pp. 12-21. The excerpts given here come from pp.
12-19. Reprinted by permission of Russell & Russell, Inc., New
York, publishers of the 1963 reissue of this volume.

freedom and popular rule. If they had followed the sign-posts of custom and tradition, as well as the apparent trend of the age, it is probable that they would have established monarchical and not republican institutions.

At the dawn of last century the trend of the Occidental World hardly appeared to be toward democracy. In 1816, just as the Spanish American movement for independence was passing the futile stage and entering the period of substantial achievement, the Western World contained only one republic, and that republic was not in Europe. It was in America.[1]

In Europe a reaction had swept away the institutions set up by men inspired by the English philosophers of the seventeenth century and the French philosophers of the eighteenth. Absolute monarchs sat upon their thrones almost everywhere save in England, where the king's power was limited by a parliament by no means democratic. Spain, the mother of practically all of the nations of southern America, had known, with the exception of one brief period (1812-1814), no other type of government than absolutism since the days of Ferdinand and the Hapsburgs. . . .

It was into such a world that the nations of Hispanic America were born. The climate of opinion was apparently not favorable to democratic republics when the leaders of a dozen new nations to the south confronted the problem of ascertaining the proper form of government for their constituencies. Their attitude and immediate course was determined by the political literature which they read, by their estimate of the political capacity of the people of Hispanic America, by what they supposed these people would demand, and in part no doubt by the prospect of maintaining special privileges for themselves.

Once freed from the intellectual fetters of the colonial period, their minds became active and politico-centric. Some of them at least were not unacquainted with the

---

[1] In Europe there was the Swiss Confederation, but it was suffering from serious internal disorders as well as because of pressure by France and the Holy Alliance.

political thought and practices of ancient Greece, but they appear to have taken few lessons from the Greeks. Some of them were not without knowledge of the history of Rome, but they were to be impressed mainly by its censors, triumvirs, consuls, and dictators. In the main, they concentrated their attention upon the men who had supplied the dynamic ideas of their heroic struggle for independence; upon the French Encyclopedists, Thomas Jefferson, Thomas Paine, and the framers of the Philadelphia Constitution.

The advice which they received from these authoritative sources was not unreservedly and unanimously in favor of the democratic republic. The Founding Fathers of the United States rejected monarchy, but were divided . . . with reference to the political capacity and reliability of average men. The French *philosophes*, while insisting on liberty, natural rights, equality before the law, and the ultimate sovereignty of the people, were not all flaming evangels of democracy. Montesquieu even idealized the British form of government.

If advice from this source gave rise to doubts, careful observation of their constituency caused further perplexity. The nations with whose political destiny they were so deeply concerned were inhabited for the most part by mixed and primitive peoples with traditions of paternalism, oppression, and servilism, and with no experience in freedom and self-government. They lacked homogeneity in race, culture, and ideals. . . . Everywhere the primitive and mixed inhabitants were largely untutored, and many of the whites themselves were illiterate. Moreover, the long and bloody struggle for independence had left the people impoverished and turbulent. The Spanish yoke had been cast off, but the constructive elements required for a democratic régime were almost totally lacking.

One is not surprised, therefore, to find among the leaders of these incipient nations a sharp division of opinion with reference to the kind of political institutions that should be established. In all of the leading centers of population there were civilian political theorists who were advocates of monarchies as well as republics. It is probable that most men of wealth and social position dreaded the social and economic consequences of placing political power in the hands of the plebeians, and were, therefore, monarchists. The outstanding warriors, with the possible exception of José Artigas, Francisco de Paula Santander, and Simón Bolívar (during his early career), were opposed to republics, at least to democratic republics. José de San Martín, Manuel Belgrano, Marcelo T. Alvear, Agustín Iturbide, Rafael Urdaneta, and many others were frankly in favor of monarchs. Bolívar later advocated life senators and presidents; José Antonio Sucre accepted in part the conservative ideas of his great chief; Iturbide grasped the imperial scepter; Bernardo O'Higgins became the autocrat of Chile; José Antonio Páez offered Bolívar a crown; the Negroes of Haiti became kings and emperors.

However, all monarchial plans eventually failed to be realized in Spanish America; the royalties of Europe and the monarchists of America had difficulty in reaching an agreement, the United States was opposed to American kings, the princes were difficult to find, and the people were not disposed to tolerate them. The emperors of Haiti were soon assassinated or deposed; Iturbide was driven from Mexico in 1823; and the ephemeral Maximilian was shot by the Mexicans in 1867. . . . All Hispanic America was destined to be a land of ostensible democratic republics and of actual anarchy alternating with dictatorships. Plato had predicted centuries before that democracies composed of masses of inexperienced and unenlightened men would end in tyranny.

II

In this vast region there has been an almost perpetual and complete contradiction between practice and theory, between the actual and nominal systems of government. On the one hand their constitutional conventions have everywhere declared that the foundations of state organization should be those conceptions of individual and collective freedom which inspired the political the-

orists of the French Revolution or received practical recognition and application in England and the United
States. The doctrine of popular sovereignty has been
explicitly proclaimed; the right of the citizens to change
their form of government at any time that has suited
them has been expressly admitted. The constitutions
have contained practically all of those guaranties which
customarily have been accorded to the members of a
democratic state: freedom of speech, freedom of the
press, freedom of association for all legitimate purposes,
freedom to move from place to place at will and to en-
gage in any lawful occupation, equality before the law,
the right to a speedy trial, and even a large amount of
religious toleration. Everywhere, in brief, the most complete liberty compatible with social security and the continued existence of the state has been assured, so far as
this result could be attained through the medium of written constitutions. On the other hand a very different
régime has existed in actual practice. Chief executives
have frequently invoked the emergency clause, contained in all, or nearly all, of the constitutions, permit-
ting the head of the state to assume discretionary powers
in times of crisis, while they have disregarded the provision which limited the use of such powers strictly to the
duration of the crisis. And with equal frequency individuals have openly seized the government and ruled with
despotic authority in patent disregard of fundamental
charters. . . .

It is likely that this trend of events may be explained
by physical setting, colonial heritage, and racial composition, which are alike unfavorable to the proper functioning of democracy. Most of the region is characterized
by lofty mountains and tropical jungle, and the centers
of population, native as well as Spanish, were, and are,
located mainly in the highlands of the interior or in
coastal areas made comfortable by the cooling breezes.
The settlements were, therefore, widely scattered and,
owing to Spain's failure to build good roads or to establish an adequate system of fluvial and coastal transportation, were so difficult to reach from the seat of govern-

ment that insurgency could not be suppressed in its incipient stages. The privileged groups—the clergy, the planters, and the owners of the mines—who wished to preserve their favorable status by establishing a monarchy now refused to submit themselves to the leveling processes of democracy. Racial animosities existed; the various ethnic groups did not understand one another; there was no community of ideals or interests. The untutored inhabitants lacked habits of self-restraint and self-direction. The whites and mix-bloods had been accustomed to the absolutism of viceroys, captains-general, and governors; the Indians had been subjected indirectly to these Spanish officials and directly to their own chiefs, who had been allowed to survive as instruments of social control, or to the local Spanish administrators and clergy. Participation of the colonials in government had been confined largely to the whites and almost exclusively to the town councils; and the activities which centered around these councils tended to exaggerate local loyalties.

The long and expensive struggle for independence did not tend to promote democracy and freedom. Spaniards born and reared in the Peninsula, the men who constituted almost the only group with any experience in government, were expelled, and the shackles of militarism were riveted upon the people. The generals refused to accept the obscurity of private life under civilian rule; the common soldiers, accustomed to plunder and adventure, were loath to exchange the camp for the field and the shop; the illiterate masses could not resist the appeal of the brilliant uniform and the seductive slogans of the mounted adventurer. Individualism, always strong among the Spaniards and the Indian chiefs, experienced a renaissance at a period when treasuries were empty and administrative ability extremely scarce.

In short, the new nations confronted a domestic crisis.

It was the crisis of anarchy, the anarchy of atomic, imperious wills operating in a medium where the strong man was admired for his virility and liberty

worshipped as a fetish. In brief hours of ecstasy
fledgling political philosophers had written into virgin constitutions all the idealism of their time, but
it was as if they had attached wings to lead.

The very perfection of these documents caused their
violation and thus called for new struggles and new fundamental charters; for ambitious militarists or aspiring re-
formers could point to the yawning chasm between the
utopias described and the exasperating realities which
were plainly evident around them.

The constitutions served as a mighty stimulus to
individualism, but they were without power to impose restraints. They urged loyalty to the nation,
but the constituency knew only loyalty to a locality
or a leader. They held up the ideal of the general
welfare as the goal of the state, but this ideal was too
impersonal for simple men accustomed to following headstrong individuals. To such men, and to
their chiefs as well, the government was not an instrument to be employed for the benefit of the
whole nation, but rather a trophy to be captured
and used in the interest of the leader and his followers. The fundamental laws offered the ballot as a
means of selecting statesmen and determining policies, but why should mere pieces of paper be endowed with such virtue and power . . . ? Government by the counting of ballots at the polls and in
legislative assemblies appeared inane and absurd. It
was far more heroic to hew one's way to power by
saber and *machete* and to determine policies with
the musket and the pistol. . . .

In addition to domestic crisis, the new nations
were exposed from time to time to external danger
—the menace of foreign invasion and conquest. A
score of boundaries were unmarked and uncertain;
no definite and reliable agreements designated the
number of nations that should be set up in the late
Spanish Empire; ambitious leaders threatened almost constantly to extend their dominions at the

expense of their neighbors or to impose their political programmes on other countries at the point of the sword. . . .[2]

Whatever their origin, crises tend to produce strong governments, and in democracies they often produce dictators. In Spanish America, at any rate, this is what occurred. The restraints of custom, conscience, and a community of ideals were not sufficient to preserve order. Coercion by the armed force of the supreme *caudillo* often appeared to be the only bulwark against anarchy or the only method of achieving social change. And yet it must be admitted that the soaring ambition and intense selfishness of the leaders often drove them to exaggerate the crisis in order to justify their appearance as men of the hour or their retention of the reins of government.

Whether sincere or deliberately deceptive, the documents of the period always employed expressions suggesting a crisis: liberator, restorer, regenerator, vindicator, deliverer, savior of the country, and so on. Somebody was constantly having to "save" these countries, although it was not always clear from what calamity they were to be rescued or what benefits their alleged salvation brought. The language of the time was the language of messianic hope and hyperbole.

The national history of Hispanic America is filled with stark tragedy: poverty, suffering, repression, corruption, sycophancy, nostalgic exile, torture, assassination, and death on the field of battle. Yet the historian will hardly censure the leaders of the area for choosing the democratic republic. For, aside from the fact that monarchies would have been most difficult to establish and maintain, it may be doubted whether they would have been better for the majority of the people of these countries than turbulent republics characterized by the alternation of revolutionary chaos and strong men on horseback. The monarchical regime would have meant a hierarchy

---

[2] J. Fred Rippy, in Guy Stanton Ford (ed.), *Dictatorship in the Modern World* (Minneapolis, 1935), pp. 55-57.

of churchmen, landlords, mine owners, and wealthy merchants, with a following of lawyers, physicians, army officers, and the like. It probably would not have resulted in appreciable benefits for the people, and it is likely that such a system would have closed the doors of opportunity to many a talented son of the masses. . . .

Domingo F. Sarmiento

FACUNDO QUIROGA*

Domingo Sarmiento (1811-1888) wrote *Civilization and Barbarism* from Chilean exile in 1845, more than two decades before he became one of Argentina's best known presidents (1868-1874). His famous polarization of the city of Buenos Aires and the provinces of the Río de la Plata, of *porteño* sophistication and gaucho crudity, was part of Sarmiento's polemical attack on the dictatorship of Juan Manuel de Rosas (1829-1852). In this work he assaulted Rosas not directly but by a skillful comparison. In Sarmiento's hands "Bloody Rosas," the unprogressive master gaucho and *jefe máximo*, is inextricably linked to the writer's model: Juan Facundo Quiroga, the provincial caudillo of La Rioja. The nature and conduct of this most notorious of gaucho chieftains during the generation after independence is revealed in the following selection.

. . . Here ends the history of . . . La Rioja. What follows is the history of Quiroga.

That day of evil omen [when Facundo Quiroga seized

---

* Domingo F. Sarmiento: *Life in the Argentine Republic in the Days of the Tyrants; or Civilization and Barbarism*, translated by Mrs. Horace Mann (New York: Hurd and Houghton, 1868), pp. 101-111.

power in La Rioja] corresponds to April of 1835 in the
history of Buenos Ayres—when its country commandant,
its desert hero [Juan Manuel de Rosas], made himself
master of the city.

I ought not to omit, since it is to Quiroga's honor, a
curious fact which occurred at this time (1823). The
feeblest gleam of light is not to be disregarded in the
blackness of that night.

Facundo, upon his triumphant entry into La Rioja,
stopped the ringing of the bells, and after sending a message of condolence to the widow of the slain General,
directed his ashes to be honored with a stately funeral.
He appointed for governor one Blanco, a Spaniard of
low rank, and with him began the new order of affairs
which was to realize the best ideal of government, as conceived by Facundo Quiroga; for, in his long career
among the various cities which he conquered, he never
took upon himself the charge of organizing governments;
he always left that task to others.

The moment of the grasp of power over the destinies
of a commonwealth by a vigorous hand is ever an important one and deserves attention. Old institutions are
strengthened, or give place to others, newer and more
productive of good results, or better adapted to prevailing ideas. From such a focus often diverge the threads
which, as time weaves them together, change the web of
history.

It is otherwise when the prevailing force is one foreign
to civilization,—when an Attila obtains possession of
Rome, or a Tamerlane traverses the plains of Asia; old
forms remain, but the hand of philosophy would afterwards vainly remove them with the view of finding beneath them plants which had gained vigor from the human blood given them for nourishment. Facundo, a
man imbued with the genius of barbarism, gets control
of his country; the traditions of government disappear,
established forms deteriorate, the law is a plaything in
vile hands; and nothing is maintained, nothing established, amid the destruction thus accomplished by the
trampling feet of horses. Freedom from restraint, occupa-

tion, and care, is the supreme good of the gaucho. If La Rioja had contained statutes, as it contained doctors, they would have had horses tied to them, but they would have served no other purpose.

Facundo wanted to have means at his command, and, as he was incapable of creating a revenue system, he resorted to the ordinary proceeding of dull or weak governments; but in this case the monopoly bears the stamp of South American pastoral life, spoliation, and violence. The tithes of La Rioja were at this time farmed out at ten thousand piastres a year; this was the average rate. Facundo made his appearance at the board, and his presence overawed the shepherds. "I offer two thousand piastres a year," said he, "and one more than the best bid." The committee repeated the proposal three times; no one made a bid; all present left, one by one, reading in Quiroga's sinister glance that it was the last one he would allow. The next year he contented himself with sending to the board the following note:—

"I give two thousand dollars and one more than the best bid.

"*Facundo Quiroga.*"

The third year the ceremony of adjudication was omitted, and in 1831, Quiroga again sent to La Rioja the sum of two thousand dollars, his estimate for the tithes.

But to make his tithes bring in a hundred for one, another step was required, and, after the second year, Facundo refused to receive the tribute of animals otherwise than by giving his mark among the proprietors, so that they might brand with it the animals set apart for the tithe and keep them on the place until he called for them. The creatures multiplied, their number was constantly augmented by new tithes, and, after ten years, it might be reckoned that half the stock of a whole pastoral province belonged to the commanding general of the forces, and bore his mark.

It was the immemorial custom in La Rioja that the *estrays*, or the animals that were not marked at a certain age, should become the lawful property of the treasury,

which sent its agents to collect these gleanings, and derived no contemptible revenue from them, but the an-
noyance to the proprietors was intolerable. Facundo demanded the adjudication to himself of these animals, to
meet the expenses he had incurred for the invasion of
the city; expenses which were reducible to the summons
of irregular forces, who assembled, mounted on horses of
their own, and lived constantly on what came in their
way. Already the proprietor of herds which brought him
six thousand bullocks a year, he sent his agents to supply
the city markets, and woe to any competitor who
should appear! This business of supplying meat for the
markets was one which he carried on wherever he ruled,
in San Juan, Mendoza, or Tucumán; and he was always
careful to secure the monopoly of it by proclamation or
simple notification. It is with shame and disgust that I
mention these disgraceful transactions, but the truth
must be told.

The general's first order, after a bloody battle which
had laid a city open to him, was that no one should supply the markets with meat! In Tucumán he learned that
a resident of the place was killing cattle in his house, in
spite of this order. The general of the army of the Andes,
the conqueror of the Citadel, thought the investigation
of so dreadful a crime should be entrusted only to himself. He went in person, and knocked lustily at the door
of the house, which refused to yield, and which the in-
mates, taken by surprise, did not open. A kick from the
illustrious general broke it in, and exposed to his view a
dead ox, whose hide was in process of removal by the
master of the house, who also fell dead in his turn at the
terrible sight of the offended general.

I do not intentionally dwell upon these things. How
many I omit! How many misdeeds I pass over in silence
which are fully proved and known to all! But I am writing the history of government by barbarians, and I am
forced to state its methods.

Mehemet Ali, who became master of Egypt by means
identical with those of Facundo, delivers himself up to
a rapacity unexampled even in Turkey; he establishes

monopolies in every occupation and turns them to his
own profit; but Mehemet Ali, though he springs from a
barbarous nation, rises above his condition so far as to
wish to acquire European civilization for himself and for
the people he oppresses. Facundo, on the contrary, not
only rejects all recognized civilization, but destroys and
disorganizes. Facundo, who does not govern, because any
government implies labour for others' good, gives himself
up to the instincts of an immoderate and unscrupulous
avarice. Selfishness is the foundation of almost all the
great characters of history; selfishness is the chief spring
of all great deeds. Quiroga had this political gift in an
eminent degree and made everything around him contribute to his advantage; wealth, power, authority, all
centered in him; whatever he could not acquire,—polish,
learning, true respectability,—he hated and persecuted
in all those who possessed them.

His hostility to the respectable classes and to the re-
finement of the cities was every day more perceptible,
and the governor of La Rioja, whom he had himself appointed, finally was forced, by daily annoyances, to resign his place. One day, Quiroga, feeling inclined to
pleasantry, was amusing himself with a young man as a
cat sports with a frightened mouse; he liked to play at
killing; the terror of the victim was so ludicrous, that the
executioner was highly diverted, and laughed immoder-
ately, contrary to his habit. He must have sympathy in
his mirth, and he at once ordered the *general* [1] to be beat
throughout the city of Rioja, which called out the citizens
under arms. Facundo, who had given the summons for
diversion's sake, drew up the inhabitants in the principal
square at eleven o'clock at night, dismissed the populace
and retained only the well-to-do householders and the
young men who still had some appearance of culture.
All night he kept them marching and countermarching,
halting, forming line, marching by front or by flank. It
was like a drill-sergeant teaching recruits, and the ser-
geant's stick travelled over the heads of the stupid, and

---

[1] A certain call to arms. [trans.]

the chests of those who were out of line; "What would you have? this is the way to teach!" Morning came, and the pallor, weariness, and exhaustion of the recruits showed what a night they had passed. Their instructor finally sent them to rest, and extended his generosity to the purchase and distribution of pastry, each recipient made in haste to eat his share, for that was part of the sport.

Lessons of such a kind are not lost upon cities, and the skillful politician who has raised similar proceedings to a system in Buenos Ayres, has refined upon them and made them wonderfully effective. For example: during the periods between 1835 and 1840 almost the whole population of Buenos Ayres has passed through the prisons. Sometimes a hundred and fifty citizens would be imprisoned for two or three months, to be then replaced by two hundred who would be kept, perhaps half the year. Wherefore? What had they done? What had they said? Idiots! Do you not see that this is good discipline for the city? Do you not remember the saying of Rosas to Quiroga, that no republic could be established because the people were not prepared for it! This is his way of teaching the city how to obey; he will finish his work, and in 1844, he will be able to show the world a people with but one thought, one opinion, one voice, and that a boundless enthusiasm for the person and will of Rosas! Then, indeed, they will be ready for a republic!

But we will return to La Rioja. A feverish excitement on the subject of investments in the mines of the new States of Spanish America had arisen in England; powerful companies were proposing to draw profit from those of Mexico and Peru; and Rivadavia, who was then residing in London, urged speculators to invest their capital in the Argentine Republic. The mines of Famatina offered an opening for a great enterprise. At the same time, speculators from Buenos Ayres obtained the exclusive right to work those mines, meaning to sell it for an enormous sum to the English companies. These two speculations, one started in England and the other in

Buenos Ayres, conflicted with each other, and were ir-reconcilable. Finally, a bargain was made with another English house, which was to supply funds, and in fact, sent out English superintendents and miners. Later, a speculation was got up to establish a bank at La Rioja, which was to be sold at a high price to the national gov-ernment when it should be organized. On being solicited, Facundo took a large number of shares, making payment with the Jesuits' College, which had been assigned to him, on his demand, in payment of his salary as general. A party of Buenos Ayres stockholders came to La Rioja to carry out the project, and soon asked to be presented to Quiroga, whose name had begun to exercise every-where a mysterious and terrific power. Facundo received them in his lodgings, in very fine silk stockings, ill-made pantaloons, and a common linen poncho.

The grotesque appearance of this figure was not pro-vocative of any smiles from the elegant citizens of Bue-nos Ayres. They were too sagacious not to read the riddle. The man before them meant to humilitate his polished guests, and show them what account he made of their European dresses.

The administrative system established in his province was finally completed by exorbitant duties on the ex-portation of cattle which did not belong to him. But in addition to these direct methods of acquiring wealth, he had one which embraced his whole public career,—gambling! He had a rage for play as some men have for strong drink, and others for tobacco. His mind, though a powerful one, had not the capacity of embracing a large sphere of ideas, and stood in need of this factitious oc-cupation, in which a passion of the soul is in constant exercise, as it is crossed, appeased, provoked, excited, and kept upon the rack. I have always thought that the pas-sion for gambling was some useful faculty that organized society has perverted or left in inaction. The will, self-control, and steadfastness which it requires, are the same which advance the fortunes of the enterprising merchant, the banker, and the conqueror who plays for empires with battles. Facundo had habitually gambled since his childhood; play had been the only pleasure, the only relaxation of his life. But what an agreeable partner he must be who controls the terrors and the lives of the whole party! No one can conceive such a state of things without having had it before his eyes for twenty years. Facundo played unfairly, say his enemies. I do not believe the charge, for cheating at play was unnecessary in his case, and he had been known to pursue to the death, others who were guilty of it. But he played with unlimited means; he never let any one carry from the table the money he used for stakes; the game could not be stopped till he chose; he would play forty hours or more at a time; he feared no one, and if his fellow gamblers annoyed him, he could have them whipped or shot at pleasure. This was the secret of his good luck. Few men ever won much money from him, although, at some periods of the game, heaps of coin lost by him lay upon the table; the game would go on, for the winner did not dare to rise, and in the end he would have nothing but the glory of reckoning that his winnings, afterwards lost, had once been so large.

Gambling, then, was to Quiroga a system of plunder as well as a favorite amusement. No one in La Rioja received money from him, no one possessed any, without being at once invited to a game, or, in other words, to leave his funds in the chieftain's hands. Most of the tradesmen of La Rioja failed and vanished, their money having taken up its quarters in the general's purse; and it was not for want of lessons in prudence from him. A young hand had won four thousand dollars from Facundo, and Facundo declined to play longer. His opponent thought that a snare was in readiness for him, and that his life was in danger. Facundo repeated that he had finished playing; the stupid fellow insisted on another game, and Facundo, complying with the demand, won the four thousand dollars from the other, who then received two hundred lashes for his uncivil pertinacity. . . .

What consequences to La Rioja were occasioned by the destruction of all civil order? Reasonings and discussions are here out of place. A visit to the scene of these occurrences will be sufficient to answer the query. The Llanos of La Rioja are now deserted; their population has emigrated to San Juan; the cisterns are dry which once gave drink to thousands of flocks. Those Llanos which fed those flocks twenty years ago, are now the home of the tiger who has reconquered his former empire, and of a few families of beggars who live upon the fruit of the carob-tree. This is the retribution the Llanos have suffered for the evils which they let loose upon the Republic. "Woe to ye, Bethsaida and Chorazin! Verily I say unto you, that the lot of Sodom and Gomorrah was more tolerable than that which was reserved for you!"

Francisco Bilbao

AMERICA IN DANGER*

The description "fiery liberal" fits no one better than
it does Francisco Bilbao (1823-1865). Influenced by
the ideas and educational theories of the great Venezuelan grammarian Andrés Bello (1781-1865), Bilbao
became one of a new generation of outspoken Chilean
liberals who dated their movement from the founding
of the University of Chile by Bello in 1842. Banished
for his iconoclastic views, Bilbao traveled in Europe
(1844-1850) where he absorbed the Utopian Socialist theories in vogue and witnessed some of the Revolutions of 1848. On his return to Chile his radical
associations soon forced him again into exile, this
time in Peru; he never was able to come home again,
yet his influence was felt inside Chile during and
after his short life.

America in Danger, from which the following selection is taken, was published in 1863 as Bilbao's angry
lament at the weakness of America before the French
invasion of Mexico. In it he notes the failure of Spanish American countries to establish free institutions
and the corresponding growth of caudillismo in the
years since independence. Seeking to explain these
sorry conditions, Bilbao blamed Spain's colonial rule
and most especially, Spanish Catholicism. (It was his
first vigorous attack on what he considered "thought

* Francisco Bilbao: *La América en peligro* (Santiago de Chile:
Ed. Ercilla, 1941). The excerpt given here comes from pp. 32-37.
Translated and printed by permission of Empresa Editora Zig-Zag,
S. A., Santiago.

chained to the text, intelligence bound to dogma" which had led to his exile in 1844.) In this orientation, Bilbao was influenced by the writings of the French cleric Lamennais (1782-1854). Lamennais had attacked Gallicanism, was later rebuffed by Pope Gregory XVI for his democratic leanings, and then abandoned the Church to support the Second French Republic as a deputy.

Though abstract, where *Civilization and Barbarism* is rooted in description and anecdote, Bilbao's attack on dictatorship is as forceful as that of his contemporary Sarmiento. What is, perhaps, especially noteworthy is Bilbao's scathing denunciation of the means by which dictators are apt to circumvent fundamental laws while appearing to observe them scrupulously. The essay is, also, characteristic of the anticlericalism in vogue among mid-nineteenth-century Spanish American liberals.

Catholics profess the dogma of "blind obedience" and they obey an authority which they hold to be infallible. Such an affirmation produces, as we shall see, the monstrous consequences which destroy American society.

The Catholic who holds power or whose authority is fundamentally based in God . . . is naturally inclined to believe himself infallible, and since the Church will support him . . . he is strengthened in his assumption and cloaks himself in pontifical majesty. Such infallibility produces a leader who is irreproachable.

Imagine if you will the fury of such an authority upon seeing himself criticized, contradicted, and refuted! Political opposition is almost equated to heresy and must be exterminated at all cost (*"ad majorem Dei gloriam"*). . . .

Law disappears. What are constitutions, individual guarantees, and free institutions when they depend upon masses educated to blind obedience? What are they before the strong man whose knife is the law and whose supreme authority is anointed? They are nothing. So it is that there are no principles, no justice, no institutions which can resist the pressure or the threat of pressure from the authority. And politics, which ought to free the republic, provides the legal forms which only confirm the farce of elections, delegation of powers and representation and disguise the contaminating despotism.

The triumph of deception and of lies is all consuming; the pretense of truth and legitimacy consecrate the prostitution of the republic.

Happily these tactics are known; yet indifference spreads and political life dies out, suffocated by disillusionment. Then the first consequence of the dualism, or the opposition of politics and dogma, is the logical tendency of authority to invest itself with infallibility. The Catholic republic produces the requisite dictatorship. Machiavellianism reigns. . . .

This tendency toward infallibility, so contrary to our legitimate ideas, emotions, and actions as selfish and partisan men, produces an unrestrained appetite for power. The achievement of power is, then, the primary goal. From this principle is born the immoral rationale that "the ends justify the means."

The contest for power in America is for some a fight for wealth; for others moral superiority, vengeance and despotism over their rivals who suffer the humiliation of defeat; others, perhaps the minority, want power to enact reforms. What is more, one must find absolution and justification to condone ones injustices.

But since there are constitutional provisions which are designed to guarantee everyone his rights, and which I may not violate, I resort to obeying the "letter of the law."

The constitution says: "Thought is Free," to which I add "within the limits established by law"—and since the "law" to which reference is made is statute rather than constitutional, I write into it these exceptions:

"Thought is free," but dogmas may not be disputed, nor may systems be expounded which attack morality. And who is to judge? A commission or jury which is named in the final analysis by my authority. And so we have censorship reestablished under the name of that freest of institutions: the jury. A sublime victory of duplicity. "But the letter of the law has been observed."

The electoral power is the only power which the "sovereign people" exercise, and, indeed, the people do vote—not, however, in order to legislate, directly, but rather to select their delegates who will legislate. Well enough. The majority of voters, then, express the will of the people (according to the system of delegation). This is the basis for republican authority, and it is to this end that the liberty and legality of elections consecrate the legitimacy of power.

Elections, therefore, are free. But suppose I control the election returns? Since I am the established power and have appointed the inspector of elections, what does it matter if the law is ambiguous enough to permit the same person to vote twenty times for a single candidate . . . ? What does it matter if I intimidate the opposition at the polls and control the election? What is the result? My party is perpetuated in power in spite of the swindled popular will. But "the forms have been preserved"; long live the freedom to vote!

"The home is inviolable," but I violate it, adding, "saving in those cases determined by law." In the final analysis it is my power which determines the "cases."

"The death penalty is abolished for political cases," but I shoot prisoners because I decide that these are not "political cases" and since I am the infallible authority I declare that these political prisoners are bandits; thus the "letter of the law is preserved."

The "Executive" may be indicted in the Chamber of Deputies and obliged to submit to a *residencia* [i.e., be subject to impeachment] for one year after retiring from office. But the Chamber was appointed by me, and it remains in office for the year after my retirement. These men who must judge me are my employees, my favorites,

my creatures, my accomplices. Are they going to condemn me? No. They do not even dare accuse me. I am,
therefore, vindicated, and the "letter of the law" has
protected me. . . .

"The press is free." But since I select the jury, I
can, with the authority of the freest of institutions, accuse, harass, persecute, and throttle freedom of the press
within the very structure of liberty. The voice and opinion of a single party then reigns supreme. Infamy en-
shrouds the corpse of the vanquished, and I shout, "The
press is free!"

It is commonly held . . . that the doctrine of the
"separation of powers" is indispensable for the liberty of
the Republic. But suppose that the Executive has the
power to name the judges; that the Executive takes part
in the legislative process; and that the Executive can
employ the electoral laws to name the members of Congress, then what, in the final analysis, has become of the
celebrated separation of powers?

"The guarantees which this Constitution established
may not be suspended." But if I have the power to declare a state of siege in a given province or in the Republic with the authorization, as in Chile, of the "Council of State," whose members are nominated by the president himself, then what security is there for the citizen?

This miserable Machiavellianism, employing the crutch
of the "letter of the law," has resulted in retrogression
and bloodshed in Chile over the past thirty years. There
is debate, the press is free; citizens gather freely, for freedom of assembly is a right; an almost unanimous enlightened public opinion clamors for reform; preparations
are made for the elections which will carry the representatives of reform to power; and, just then, the Executive
Power declares the province or the Republic in a state
of siege, and the suspended constitutional guarantees
blossom over the abyss of "legal" dictatorship and constitutional despotism!

And then? Either resignation or despair or civil war,
etc., etc. The frightful banners of revolution are raised

and blood flows on the battlefield and the scaffold. All respect for law and authority evaporates, and only force remains to proclaim its triumph in the name of liberty and justice. This is Jesuitical dictatorship.

Rafael Núñez

SCIENTIFIC PEACE*

The Church-state relationship was a central problem which many nineteenth-century leaders confronted.[1] Some of them took a strong partisan stand in favor of close association with the Church as a means to achieve order. Most noteworthy was the quasi-theocratic dictator of Ecuador, Gabriel García Moreno. At the opposite pole were the avowed enemies of clericalism, among whom Mexico's Benito Juárez is best remembered.

Between these extremes other leaders took intermediate positions on the knotty problem of centralism versus federalism as well as on the Church-state question. Some of these leaders shifted their ground on both matters according to the political demands made upon them. Among these was Rafael Núñez (1823-1894) of Colombia. Núñez is, moreover, a prime example of those well-educated, sophisticated statesmen whom Spanish America produced in the nineteenth century whose political vision and high principles were not always sufficient to prevent them from becoming dictatorial.

Entering politics in the wake of the European revo-

---

* Rafael Núñez, "La paz científica," in *La reforma política en Colombia* (Bogotá, 1885). The excerpts given here are translated from pp. 97-104.

[1] The nature and importance of this problem is explored in a companion volume in this series: Frederick B. Pike (ed.), *The Conflict Between Church and State in Latin America* (New York: Alfred A. Knopf, Inc., 1964).

lutions of 1848, Núñez was first associated with the liberal anticlerical faction. In 1853, as the thirty-year-old vice-president of the House of Representatives, he signed the federalist constitution of that year which provided for separation of Church and state. After ten years, Núñez grew disillusioned with the extreme liberal elements because of their failure to bring unity and order to the country. He did not, however, openly oppose the extreme liberal Constitution of 1863 though he managed to be absent for the signing of the document. For the next eleven years Núñez was abroad in New York, Le Havre, and Liverpool holding minor diplomatic posts and living in part by his pen. In Europe he was influenced by Spencer and the Social Darwinists and became a frank admirer of the stable English political system. On his return to Colombia in 1874 he associated himself with the moderate or Independent wing of the Liberal party, ran for the presidency in 1875, and was defeated by the Radical candidate. In 1879, however, he won the presidency (1880-1882) and began to work for a constitutional reform, called by him "*La Regeneración*," which would counter the decentralized federalism of the 1863 Constitution. His campaign was conducted largely through an impressive series of over a hundred newspaper articles published between 1881 and 1884 and collected into one volume entitled *Political Reform in Colombia* in 1885.

Núñez believed that peace and internal security were requisite conditions for the nation's social, cultural, economic, and political progress. He attributed the relative backwardness of Colombia to the fact that political order within the country had been an exception and not the rule. He underscored this opinion with vigor in his article entitled "Scientific Peace," published in 1882 and reprinted below, which made clear his belief that unbridled federalism was chiefly to blame. The rest of his essays ranged over the whole economic, social, political, and cultural life of the nation. Together they reveal Rafael

Núñez as a moderate and as a statesman with perceptive abilities of a high order. How then did he become a caudillo?

In 1883, after waiting out the two year term from which he was constitutionally barred, Núñez took his Independent Liberals into a coalition with the Conservatives and was nominated again for the presidency. Successful in the election for the 1884-1886 term, he was determined to achieve for Colombia the program he had sketched over the past three years. Núñez's shift to the right and the threat of centralization through constitutional revision provoked the Radical Liberals to revolt late in 1884. It was this brief and abortive rebellion which put in motion the events which turned President Núñez from constitutional statesman to arbitrary dictator. Impatient to enact his program, and with the revolt as a pretext, he hurried to cut the Gordian knot of slow but legal constitutional reform by supervising the abrogation of the 1863 Constitution. This act did, indeed, make possible the rapid substitution of the centralist Constitution of 1886, but it also destroyed the legitimate authority on which Núñez's office was based. In addition to this, when the constituent assembly was called to draft the new constitution, the Radical Liberals were excluded. As will be noted in the essay which follows, the elimination of an opposition party had been one of the major complaints which Núñez had had with the Radicals during the 1860's and 1870's. "To reduce a political adversary to impotence is . . . to eliminate a cohesive element. . . ."

These twin decisions cost Núñez the achievement of the moderate regeneration he had hoped to obtain. Without an effective opposition, the Conservatives won firm control of the nation and worked a sharp reaction. The Constitution of 1886[2] demonstrates this fully: the formerly sovereign states were shorn

[2] For the complete text, see William M. Gibson, *The Constitutions of Colombia* (Durham: Duke University Press, 1948), pp. 314-349.

completely of their power even to the point of being redesignated "departments"; the four year term Núñez had suggested earlier to replace the two year presidency was stretched to six and the incumbent was provided with extraordinary powers including the right of appointment and removal of department governors; Núñez's early interest in the separation of Church and state was ignored for the new charter proclaimed that "the Apostolic Roman Catholic Church is that of the Nation" and provided for the negotiation of a concordat with the Papacy.

A sensitive and articulate man, a fair poet, an effective prose stylist, and a capable politician, Rafael Núñez became a caudillo in spite of himself. He acquiesced in a reaction which ran well beyond the politically moderate program he had proposed. Although nominal head of the state for most of the time until his death in 1894 and cloaked with enormous political authority, Núñez found the mantle of dictatorship uncomfortable. He retired frequently from the exercise of his office to leave the high altitude of Bogotá for his native coastal Cartagena. Age and ill health were clearly factors, but his ambition to retain power was also undercut by a nagging awareness that he had compromised his ideals to become a caudillo.

———

Since 1860, when the struggle between the old national parties began, a struggle which by 1863 . . . resulted in the complete triumph of liberalism, the Republic has not until now enjoyed a full presidential term of peace.

Between 1864 and 1866 there were three revolutions: one in Cundinamarca, another in Cauca, and one in Panama.

Between 1866 and 1868 there was the *coup d'état* of General Mosquera, the counterrevolution led by General

Acosta, and various local uprisings related to these two events.

Between 1868 and 1870 there was a revolution in Cundinamarca and another in Panama.

Between 1870 and 1872 there were one or two revolts in Boyacá and another in Cundinamarca.

Between 1872 and 1874 there was a series of insurrections in Panama and much unrest in Boyacá.

Between 1874 and 1876 there were disturbances and tumults throughout the Republic.

Between 1876 and 1878 there was a general civil war.

And from 1878 to 1880 there were upheavals in Panama, Antioquia, Cauca, Magdalena, and Tolima and widespread unrest.

It is only since 1880 that the country has experienced an atmosphere of perfect calm.

During the epoch between the dissolution of the old Colombia and 1860 there were six constitutional terms of four years each. Of those six terms peace prevailed only from 1845 to 1849 and . . . from 1855 to 1857.

In the course of our forty odd years of political life since 1832, the maintenance of domestic order has been the exception and civil war, the rule. In the meantime, various Constitutions have prevailed, to wit:

The moderately centralized Constitution of 1832;

The rigidly authoritarian Constitution of 1843;

The nearly federal Constitution of 1853;

The completely federal Constitution of 1858; and

The Constitution of 1863 that went so far along the path of decentralization as to embrace the fundamental principle of state sovereignty.

In undertaking the reform of each existing system, all parties doubtless believed that they were working effectively to secure [civil] order; however, to judge from the obvious results this happy *desideratum* has not been realized since the days of the rigorously centralized Constitution of 1843.

But this Constitution was too alien to the country's dominant political feeling and to its topographic conditions for it to deserve credit as the only pacifying ingredient during the relatively long period that it was in effect. In fact it is my opinion that the intensity of the liberal reaction of . . . 1849 was due in part to the nature of the document.

If we set aside written institutions, however, in order to focus upon the effects of administrative policy assayed by the rulers, we discover that those men established policies in keeping with the national character so well that peace was maintained as a result.

The conservative administration of General Mosquera from 1845 to 1849 committed errors; but it was distinguished by the liberality with which it treated the vanquished and prostrate liberal party and by the practical guarantees which it accorded to popular suffrage.

The conservative administration of [Manuel María] Mallarino [1855-1857] went further yet and with better faith along this road of generosity and foresight.

In both periods, as I have said, utter peace reigned from one end of the country to the other. The administrations following those two were not characterized as tolerant and disorders occurred which were more or less general, deep-seated, and destructive.

The present administration was met by the animosities resulting from the continuous conflicts of the years 1878 to 1880; but the guarantees openly made to the conservative party, defeated in 1877 and powerless as Poland, have surely produced, for the third time, that yet rare phenomenon of a peaceful presidential term; and this without sacrificing any principles or political power.

Politics is an experimental science, like all the sciences of its kind; and if the same methods of governing, tried three times under different circumstances, have produced identical results in the preservation of order, we ought rightly to deduce that these methods of governing precisely suit the Republic and ought to be the norm for all governmental agents who wish not to release the maleficent spirit of armed discord.

But it is not only experience which counsels the adop-

tion of a policy of conciliation to which we refer. There
are, in short, ample reasons which explain the fruitfulness
of such a course.

Our principal parties are roughly balanced when it
comes to numbers of supporters. The liberal party might
be less in number but, on the other hand, it is more
resolute and active. The proportion of our population
which boasts some culture is slight, and the numbers of
bureaucrats which that portion can supply is severely
limited. The total exclusion of one party is, therefore, a
major administrative error which borders upon immoral-
ity.

What is the result of such exclusion? In the first place,
public service suffers from a deficiency of aptitudes. Second, many of the benefits of the competition of ideas
and of healthy emulation in the conduct of public business are lost. Third, it is a fact that the domination of
an oligarch results, which gradually undermines the fundamental principles of the established constitutional political system. Fourth, the political atmosphere becomes
perverted by the spectacle of such illegitimate domination and individual consciences suffer the effects of this
moral poisoning. The injustices practiced on high necessarily have their repercussions and reflections at the base
of the pyramid. And finally, the leaders fall to quarreling
among themselves for lack of a counterpoise and behave
ultimately like the soldiers of Cadmus who cut each
other to pieces. Under such adverse circumstances . . .
only a spark is necessary to produce an explosion in a
society so disposed to experimentation.

It is especially important to note that since 1863 the
greater part of our battles have been between members
of the liberal party itself. Conflicts between liberals and
conservatives have occurred only occasionally during the
last eighteen years. It would seem, then, that the neutral-
ization of our old adversaries is, in many ways, far from
being a safety valve for us.

The desirable and necessary reorganization of the liberal party cannot be realized through speeches and osten-
tatious displays; and even less yet when everyone knows

the artificial quality of the movement which is really quite opposed to the attainment of the stated objectives. . . . Some of our politicians fall frequently into the grave error of supposing that the national audience lacks the discernment to tell false notes from true ones; but the fact is that such discernment exists and the concord which so many legitimate interests demand, will not come unless a course of rectitude is sincerely adopted. Bile may be useful for something, but surely it is inadequate for the conciliation of our divergent wills.

The reorganization of a political party must begin with the unification of beliefs and with the frank pursuit in practice of the principles which compose the party creed; otherwise the simple pursuit of physical domination of the country is certain to corrupt and lead, sooner or later, to dissolution and anarchy. The reason for this is clear. Raw domination is, in essence, a business enterprise like any other, and since it does not offer tangible advantages for all partisans, those excluded from the fruits of exploitation will raise the banner of dissidence. By the nature of things men fall out as the magnetism of material benefits wanes unless, and only if, ideas unite them.

The fear of a common danger is another, though less durable, agent of party harmony. To reduce a political adversary to impotence is, then, to eliminate a cohesive element which might replace absent or diminishing moral bonds.

These are not paradoxes, but realities which have been encountered frequently throughout our agitated contemporary political history.

Whenever we or our closest friends express ourselves in these terms, others immediately try to suggest that we are bent upon turning down the road to conservatism. With like reasoning, the French revolutionaries . . . guillotined each other until the Empire came and concluded everything in a horrible Olympian carnival of blood. The conservatives know perfectly well that profound philosophical convictions separate them from us, yet for that very reason we must show only the most careful respect for their religious creed. What does unite us to their political community today is our sterling liberalism. This brand of liberalism leads us frequently to shield the conservatives against the intransigence [of the radical liberals] which threatens and persecutes us as well because of the plain fact . . . that we replaced them in running the government in response to the persistent will of a people long fatigued by years of violence. Such intransigence born of the lamentable wedding of overweening vanity and ambition would seem, to put it bluntly, the legacy of the Zipas [who ruled the Chibchas] and of the Kings of Spain.

The administrative policy of the present administration has been the result of serious reflection and of experience. Far from wishing to destroy the community to which men of good faith adhere, that policy would save it following the counsel of a rigorous and abundant logic. The evidence of our progress along the path of salvation is already manifest everywhere. If shortsighted men would only compare 1873, 1875, and 1879 with 1881 they must realize that the harsh mountain of hatred has been reduced to a negotiable hill. Still the drums of revolt beat again and from time to time new alarms run the spectrum of absurdity; but the battalions do not respond, only a few professional rebels and small squads of *caudillos* heed the call to arms. The mass of the people remain confident and tranquil.

Carlos Octavio Bunge

CACIQUISMO
IN OUR AMERICA*

Written in the late nineteenth century (as we have
defined it), the Argentine sociologist, novelist, and
educator Carlos Octavio Bunge (1875-1918) first
published *Our America* in 1903. The book went
through many editions; the following selection is
from the sixth edition, to which Bunge's brilliant
contemporary José Ingenieros contributed a long introduction. Influential and popular because of its
stormy attack upon Spanish character and because it
evoked the Social Darwinist and Positivist thought
then in vogue, *Our America* suggests an important
fin de siècle pattern by which the phenomenon of
caudillismo was explained. The Spaniard is for Bunge
chiefly to blame for the "cacicability" of the Latin
American, but the Indian and Negro admixtures have
produced resignation, sadness, laziness, and deca-
dence to go with Spanish arrogance. Bunge, however,
was confident that Argentina could expect a bright
future based on energy and progress because so many
European immigrants were flooding into the country.
On the other hand, he hurled no moral anathemas at
such a contemporary dictatorship as that of Porfirio
Díaz (1876-1911) which he held to be a relatively

---

* Carlos Octavio Bunge, *Nuestra América: ensayo de psicología
social*, 6th ed. (Buenos Aires: Casa Vaccaro, 1918). The excerpts
included here are translated from pp. 246-248, 224-225, 242.

successful attempt to bring order and progress to an
innately slothful mestizo society.

———

The politico-philosophical conception of the republic,
understood as a democratic society whose citizens possess not only the right but also the duty of governing
the *res publica* by means of representatives elected for
that purpose, is essentially European. It was born in
Greece from whence it passed to Rome. It was the great
innovation which Europe contributed to ancient history,
reacting to the autocracies of the Orient; it was some sort
of *prechristian Christianity* since it advanced the principle of equality, if not for all men at least for those citizens who composed the nation. The republic is, therefore, neither Asiatic nor African but rather a severely
European institution belonging only to the purest of
European races. . . . Even though in the Middle Ages
monarchic forms were adopted, these monarchies were
more republican than they were autocratic; the republican principle remained latent in the people, and was revealed in communal liberties, parliaments, guilds, and so
forth. England was always a monarchic republic; she
forced her kings to agree to the Magna Carta and she
executed Charles I. . . . Switzerland is a typical republic. In the Germanic states and the countries of the
North, the most absolute princes respect certain popular
liberties. In France, the Revolution demonstrates that
beneath monarchic despotism there throbbed profound
republican sentiments. Even in Italy certain aristocratic
republics, which were *sui generis*, persisted through the
medieval centuries.

It is only just to note that neither in Spain nor in
Portugal was absolutism confused with tyranny. The
caesarist principle of the *princeps legibus solutus* had
few defenders, and was generally fought by theologians

and canonists who sustained the opposite doctrine, accepted by canon law: *Princeps tenentur et ipsi vivere legisbus suis.* The decline of the admirably democratic organization of the twelfth and thirteenth century councils was the result of multiple causation. Among these causes ought to be weighed the influence of Moorish blood which *Africanized* the population of the Peninsula to a certain point. Alexander Dumas, a mulatto who well understood the character of the Africans because of his own psychological affinity, once coined a graphic phrase when he said, with that insolence and exaggeration common to his ethnic bastardy, "Europe ends at the foot of the Pyrenees." In spite of this, Charles I and Philip II contrived to reduce communal freedoms and privileges only after extensive bloody fighting. . . .

On the other hand, we know that the [pre-Columbian] indigenous Americans were quite as absolute as the most powerful Oriental autocracies; and we know that the African Negroes bore their servility to their fierce petty kings to such a degree as to speak to them only when prostrate, to kiss their footsteps, and to eat their excrement!

Adding together the Afro-hispanic antecedents (although these were not of decisive importance) and the Indian experience, it is difficult if not impossible to suppose that democracies might have been improvised with success in Latin America after independence. The Cabildos were the only bastions of the ancient Spanish communal liberties, and they were most certainly shabby bastions! On the other hand, the North American people at the time of independence possessed a certain republican individualism in their ideas, in their customs, in their institutions, and in their blood dating back to Caesar and Hamilcar, even to prehistoric times! For them, the republic is natural, original, and pertinent; among the Spanish Americans it must be perforce imitative, conventional, and hybrid . . . and so it is that "no people can be great unless it cultivates its own character"; I almost prefer for "Our America" the satrapies of caciques which are open, honest, and unmasked. Were it possible, I would even use ancient Indian names! . . . Let us be true to ourselves . . . !

The *cacicability* of each Spanish American nation is in inverse proportion to its degree of European blood. For this reason the tyranny of Rosas over Buenos Aires, which was the most European of the Spanish American states, was also the bloodiest in Hispanic American history. . . . Mexico, in contrast to Buenos Aires, is perhaps the most Indian country in America and there the despotism of Porfirio Díaz has been the most pacific and most prolonged. Blessed despotism!

One would suppose that the cacique, in order to possess the requisite psychology, ought always to be either mestizo or mulatto. A pessimist might think that the position would be repugnant to a pure European; that political success in the Spanish American countries is dependent upon being more or less swarthy. Such is not the case! The strong race is always the white race. And, given the human vanity of the European, the white man is tempted to play the cacique quite as much as any Mandingo, which explains well enough why some thoroughly pure Goths have disguised themselves and, crowned with brilliant plumes, have grasped a lance bloody to the hilt in order to rule. . . .

I find [a related] key to the curious Hispanic American phenomenon of caudillismo or caciquismo in collective sloth. Among indolent people it is easy for the most active to be outstanding. Then the rabble, composed of those citizens who are too apathetic to think and to act for themselves and take responsibilities, gladly abrogate their sovereignty . . . to whom? To him whose qualities best inspire confidence and who knows best how to capture the sympathy of everyone. . . . Is he the most able? One presumes so; but he need not be as long as he is the most feared and beloved.

Although it is in the best interests of everyone to entrust the plumed spear of symbolic authority to the most competent, it is in the best interest of the individual, who wishes to thrive in the shadow of power, to have a close personal friend for governor. It is for this reason that caciquismo sometimes produces regimes of the most shameful compliance. A cacique must have friendships before personal merits and he must maintain them in order to maintain himself in power. But what about such things as laws, the national wealth, progress? They matter little if there is no social pressure to combat degeneration and injustice! . . .

In the career of a cacique there is always an initial stage in which he deceives the mob with feigned and superficial virtues. . . . Once securely in power, it is customary to strip himself of such appearances as one might remove an uncomfortable suit of clothes which restrains one's movements. Once the first praiseworthy and virtuous impression is made, the verdict is in and it is irreversible because the public will no longer take the trouble to revise the first impression. . . . Why bother to investigate, to revise judgment, perhaps to condemn? It would be a great deal of work; it is much easier for one to be quiet; and, far better yet, to serve and to flatter the cacique . . . because the reward, at once received, would recompense his whole clan, man by man. . . . There is no concern for independence or individual strife! Such implies individual effort which is so often arduous and really the province of commerce, industry, the arts and sciences; the object of life is, after all, rest and relaxation. . . . The gods have created men that they might watch them repose in elegance. If the sheep rest more than the shepherd, let us be sheep not shepherds! . . .

It would be a great error to suppose that caciquismo must always be a retrograde and tumultuous system. Caciquismo is not anarchy, nor tyranny, nor reaction; it is simply laziness, nothing more than laziness. Only in abnormal times has the cacique appeared, as in the eyes of Sarmiento, like a spectre enveloped in a tattered red poncho brandishing his lance as if it were a scythe.

It may be that the genesis of caciquismo was in anarchy; but, in the course of the evolution of American history, it has acquired a pacific form, perhaps the most

pacific of demagogic and even democratic governments.
. . . By "pacific" I mean that the conflict of ideas and
of parties is avoided; whatever agitation there is, is reduced to personal feuds between one cacique and another. The people, restrained by their incurable native
indolence, will leave them to fight it out, unperturbed,
as simple spectators who do not commit themselves in
advance to the triumph of one or the other. Such is the
nature of the *civilized caciquismo* of our modern age, so
thoroughly in contrast to that of our medieval period.
It is a long distance from Facundo Quiroga to Porfirio
Díaz!

John J. Johnson

FOREIGN FACTORS IN DICTATORSHIP IN LATIN AMERICA*

Stanford University's Prof. John J. Johnson is best known for his analysis of the emergent "middle sectors" in Latin American society (published in 1958 under the title *Political Change in Latin America*) and his more recent studies of the military's role in politics. In the following article Professor Johnson applies himself to some of the foreign influences which he believes have affected caudillismo, with particular attention to the nineteenth century. By "foreign" he means "nondomestic or nonnational as opposed to nonregional" or non-Latin American. Stressing the roles which immediate neighbors as well as more distant powers (European and North American) have played in the continuum of dictatorial absolutism in particular Latin American countries, the author suggests that subtle external influences, such as educational models and philosophical systems, may have been quite as important as more direct pressures.

* John J. Johnson, "Foreign Factors in Dictatorship in Latin America," *The Pacific Historical Review*, Vol. XX (May 1951), pp. 127-141. The excerpts given here come from pp. 128-137. Reprinted by permission of the author and *The Pacific Historical Review*.

[Among the] explanations for the phenomena of almost constant unrest and tyranny in Latin America [are] foreign pressures. . . . Before investigating the subject it will be necessary to make a few observations and do some delimiting.

The first observation is that writers, when dealing with the foreign factor in Latin American dictatorship, too often limit themselves to intervention, economic imperialism, the Monroe Doctrine, and recognition. A half-century of dictatorship in the Caribbean bears witness to the importance of the first three. While the responsibility of recognition is equally well established, there is a division of opinion as to what type of recognition policy would least contribute to the possibilities of dictatorship in Latin America.

Second, it could be noted that many of what we call representative thinkers of Latin America, and not a few of those in the United States, who put the finger of guilt on the imperialism and materialism of the United States citizenry and the lack of a consistent State Department policy, are sometimes amazingly blind to such weaknesses in Latin America. If the purpose of this survey were to discuss the "treatment" that the United States has given Latin America over the years, without in any way trying to defend it, it would not be unreasonable to compare the seizure of Panama with the taking of Tarapacá by Chile[1]; to draw parallels between the expansive attitude of the United States following the Mexican War with the thinking of Brazil around 1900 when her boundaries were notably extended, and again in the

---

[1] In each case the aggressor, among other things, argued that the area upon which he had designs was important to his national development as well as to world commerce, and maintained that a nonprogressive, bickering state, playing the role of "a dog in the manger," should not be permitted to impede the forward march.

1920's when she sought to establish Brazilian hegemony over South America; and to conclude that the materialism of the United States seldom has been carried to any greater extreme than that of the Argentines, agriculturally satiated as they were, who, following the conclusion of World War II, forced a starving Europe to pay five dollars and more a bushel for wheat.

Third, among an important segment of Latin Americans who concern themselves with the problem of dictatorship, foreign factors, when considered, are most often those originating outside Latin America, rather than those foreign to any one given nation. In this study the term foreign will be considered as nondomestic or nonnational, as opposed simply to nonregional. The aforementioned obvious pressures will be by-passed for several less publicized ones, and two types of factors will be considered—those emanating from the outside and over which the peoples of the individual nations were more or less helpless in controlling, and those coming from the outside but which were or are due to the practices and thinking of the peoples who go to make up the separate states.

Much has been made of the failure of certain European countries and the United States to give adequate material and moral support to the cause of Latin American independence between the years 1810 and 1825. Many have lamented the misfortunes arising from the failure of the idealistic constitutions written during the wars of liberation, the authors of which, having become so imbued with the political forms of more advanced peoples, paid only slight heed to realities.

On the other hand, the British loans of the mid-1820's have received relatively little attention. Actually, it would appear that those loans did as much to promote the cause of dictatorship in Latin America as any single factor originating outside the area up to that time. And in retrospect it is perhaps not too harsh to say that England did several of the new republics a gross injustice by making funds available to them—an injustice on at least three counts. The loans were made because there was a vast surplus of investment capital resulting in lower interest rates in England and not because the investors were misinformed as to conditions in South America; in fact a number of volumes and articles in English had appeared which objectively presented the situation and pointed out the inherent dangers. A greater injustice stemmed from the fact that at the very time when the chief executives in the various nations, personalists by nature and representatives of minority groups, should have been forced to go to their own peoples for support, they were in several instances freed from that responsibility by the British loans. The first crop of strong men quickly comprehended how much easier it would be to grant concessions to foreigners in return for loans than to derive revenue by taxing those who controlled the wealth. That the leaders learned the lesson well is evidenced by the number who came to power and retained it by means of hazardous borrowing abroad.

Finally, British merchants followed British pounds—merchants who were anti-Catholic, merchants who were accustomed to English law and who soon wearied of the legal maneuvers of the people with whom they were dealing, merchants who came to disdain the very people with whom they were carrying on commerce. A flourishing trade was the desire of the businessman, and just as the dictator learned the advantage of foreign loans, so the foreign trader quickly appreciated the virtues of authoritarian government.

The British loans did not save the young republics from economic chaos. Payments were soon discontinued on interest as well as on principal. It was not long before there developed in England an unhealthy collective concept: "Latin America." Embittered by financial losses and apparently vastly ignorant regarding the area, they made little effort to distinguish between Argentine and Chilean, between Peruvian and Bolivian. To the Englishman the Latin American peoples were all the same, all anarchic, untrustworthy, and ruled by despots concerned only with their own welfare and that of their coteries.

London investment brokers turned their backs on the struggling nations, not to return in most cases until mid-century. It was a generation later (c. 1880) before British capital was joined by that from the United States. For several decades thereafter English and United States capitalists and technicians, welcomed by the various Latin American government officials who mortgaged the future of their countries in the belief that the problem of communications was to be solved, concentrated on the construction of railroads. Latin America was doomed to be disappointed. Money was raised abroad. Valuable technical knowledge was supplied which made possible some of the great engineering feats of the nineteenth century. But it would be difficult to prove that funds or technical advice were utilized in the best interests of the recipients. At the end of the fifty-year railroad building spree, Latin America awoke to the fact that proffered assistance from Europe and the United States had contributed little to the developmental pattern. Each nation had railroad lines, with varying gauges, in most cases leading from the interior to the nearest port, so that raw materials could be shipped more easily to Europe and the United States. Not a single country in Latin America had a railroad system.

Mexico's predicament is illustrative. Under the dictator Porfirio Díaz a series of north-south lines was constructed which directed the wealth of Mexico away from the political center and served primarily as feeders for the east-west lines across the United States.

If economic dislocation is a factor conducive to dictatorship, as it surely is, then the responsibility of the foreigner concerned with railroad building is large, how large it is impossible to say. Certainly there is plenty of evidence that the foreigners who shared in the program regarded the various nations as economic colonies of Europe and the United States rather than as sovereign powers.

Of the foreign factors accounting for dictatorship and for which the several Latin American countries themselves must assume a considerable degree of responsibility the most obvious is perhaps diplomatic asylum and its corollary, exile. Diplomatic asylum, in a sense a form of extra-territoriality, by the eighteenth century played a decreasingly important role in the relations of nations with a Western European background. However, with the rise of the Latin American republics the institution took a new lease on life. A cursory acquaintance with the Latin American mind and the conditions under which the nations came into existence shows why this occurred. The fatalistic acceptance by the majority of mass murder paradoxically has been reconciled with an abhorrence of capital punishment, as evidenced, for example, by the sympathy so often expressed for revolutionaries who have unsuccessfully attempted to shoot their way into the presidencies.

One of the earliest grounds for upholding asylum and exile stemmed from the rigid caste system, carried over from the period of Spanish domination. The jails and prisons—poorly constructed and with few provisions for sanitation and comfort—were unfit, or so it was thought, for the elite of society; and it was this group for whom diplomatic asylum was almost wholly reserved. Tied to this argument was that of the economic plight of the new states. The construction of prisons strong enough to retain a prisoner and at the same time comfortable enough for persons of the upper stratum was beyond the financial means of the embryonic republics.

Coincidental with these considerations was the more widely used defense of saving the most capable man power. In countries that had come into existence with a minimum of political experience there was a dearth of able leaders. In the ensuing struggles for power, diplomatic asylum and exile seemed to offer the surest and most economical means of conserving the ruling class. The loser, whether morally right or wrong, was assured a place of retreat so long as asylum was respected. Protected by a foreign flag, he could await the cooling of tempers, marking time while in most cases arrangements were made for his passage into exile.

Each of the arguments presented above was openly

espoused and had merits, but it would appear from the records that while they were offered to the populace as warrantable reasons for clemency, a self-survival rather than a moral, economic, or social basis ordinarily was the primary cause for tolerating asylum and exile. Each leader was aware that in the next shuffle of the cards the help of the lately defeated statesman or ousted warrior might be needed desperately. Furthermore, the victor was not oblivious to the fact that it paid to set a good example. If he displayed leniency in triumph he might more rightly expect mercy in adversity. Nor was it likely that in an area where political changes came at an amazing pace, the man temporarily on top could forget that it was probably his predecessor who had said, "I have the choice of respecting asylum and eventually letting my enemies go into exile or shooting them."

The step from asylum into exile was short and exile has contributed time and again to dictatorship in the countries to the south. With the opposition perched across the border, the individual commanding at home could see real and imaginary threats to the fatherland. One method commonly seized upon to meet emergencies in Latin America has been to increase the already multiple powers of the chief executive. In more cases than not the person in control thus has been able to meet the menace of political malcontents operating from neighboring states; moreover, in cases of failure, his successors usually found it advisable to assume dictatorial power. That is only part of the story. The chief executive, in preparing to meet the danger from the outside, frequently increased the military strength of his country. Then, if the perils did not materialize, an enlarged armed force was left without a major assignment, reluctant, nevertheless, to be demobilized. This posed a thorny problem for the president. Too often he sought to solve it by stirring up trouble with the neighboring state by accusing it of harboring or giving encouragement to elements hostile to the established order. Impending war or war itself has resulted. In either case the defense of the honor of the country made it possible for the ruler to strengthen his position, while increased tensions served to divert attention from unpleasant realities at home. Nor has it been too unusual for the army to find its own way out of the dilemma by overthrowing the incumbent and seizing power for one of its own leaders.

The extent to which the Latin Americans can be held responsible for dictatorship resulting from asylum and exile can be fairly definitely established. On a slightly different level of responsibility are some factors contributing to dictatorship which have resulted from the inclination of the official and upper-class Latin American to imitate the United States and certain countries of Europe.

Almost everywhere in Latin America one hears that the nations cannot hope for political stability until they have an educated electorate. The point may be well taken, yet there as elsewhere education is confused with literacy. Wherever laws fix an educational qualification for suffrage, the ability to read and write or simply to write is the test applied. One cannot help questioning the assumption that literacy actually makes for a better voter, or if common sense mixed with freedom of expression is not what is needed. But, since it is so commonly accepted that the educational factor must be considered in accounting for dictatorship in Latin America, an examination of some foreign influences on the type and extent of education and thought there is called for.

Throughout the nineteenth century many of the elite of the various republics received their education in Europe, and today that same class is taking advantage of opportunities in the United States. This means that the formative years of many of the leaders of Latin America —political, literary, social, and economic—have been spent away from their home countries.

A considerable number of those who went overseas for their training of simply for travel became imbued with new ideas which they later wanted to see applied in their native lands. It is a truism that much of what they absorbed was not adaptable to the social and political environment of their homelands. Historically speaking, the idealistic constitutions of the 1810-1825 period are our first notable example of the failure of those who had assimilated outside cultures to superimpose what appeared to be good upon a society unprepared to receive it. Decade after decade the influences of foreign education continued to be felt in various ways, until finally no less an authority than the great Argentine thinker, Juan Bautista Alberdi, rose vindictively against scholars trained abroad. Writing in the 1870's he charged a section of them and their disciples with fomenting civil discord and, because of their advocacy of local autonomy, held them largely responsible for the continuance of the federalist-centralist struggle which was plaguing much of the area. In the opinion of Alberdi the Latin American youth who went abroad to study often came almost wholly under the influences of professors who were far removed from the realities of life, who were enthralled by radical theories, and who were often rabid champions of decentralization. After making this observation Alberdi concluded that "the youth whose mind is molded in this school, in these ideas, returns to America a demagogue in every sense of the term, a bachelor in revolutions, a seditionist by principle."

It should be noted that Alberdi's concern is, by implication, primarily with the foreign-trained intellectual as a rabble-rousing idealist eager to reform his fatherland. He does not accuse his villain of being a dictator, because after the first wave of despots, several of whom had European experiences, the foreign-trained scholar ordinarily did not assume that role. Rather he was the "disloyal opposition" who in playing the part of agitator afforded those who opposed him additional grounds for appropriating dictatorial powers.

Through little fault of the people or governments of Europe and the United States their influence is reflected in the general want of sound elementary school systems in Latin America. Until recently when the Latin American leader thought of primary education he ordinarily conceived of it in terms of the way it evolved in England, France, and the United States. In retrospect it is evident that this thinking was extremely unfortunate. The nations which served as educational yardsticks for Latin America lived in a different world. They had put, during the development of their school systems, considerable emphasis on the plant and such equipment as books, blackboards, and desks. It is known today, both in the United States and in Latin America, that education, when necessary, can be imparted with a minimum of these former essentials. But for a century after the winning of independence the Latin American nations wanted facsimiles of the models they chose to copy, and, being unable to afford the costs, they allowed their school systems to languish and generations of youths to go untrained.

Hands were thrown up in despair until José Vasconcelos, as minister of education under President Obregón, led the way in education adapted to the means at hand and designed to prepare the child to live better in his surroundings. Under the imaginative guidance of Vasconcelos and that of his successors . . . Mexico's elementary education program has gone forward, often with a dearth of material aids, and today is meriting the attention of progressive educators in her sister republics. . . . Millions [, however,] remain to be trained so that they may become more productive and responsible members of society. The number of voters who can read and write is increasing, but very few more are educated. So, if the lack of education per se is a major factor contributing to dictatorship—which the author questions—while there are signs for hope, the ground is still fertile for the appearance of tyrants. Nevertheless, the foreign factor will decline in importance as the republics adopt school systems which are more in accord with the realities of their own societies.

Latin America has felt the impact of many philosophies originating in Europe, but of these that have influenced the politics of the republics, the positivism of Auguste Comte seems to have contributed most directly to dictatorship. Of the nations where this philosophy met with acceptance, Mexico and Brazil experienced the most noticeable impact.[2] Brought to Mexico in modified form during the presidency of Benito Juárez, positivism's emphasis on order and progress was construed to serve the ends of the new ruling class that had emerged during the 1850's. Its provision for a type of social Darwinism admirably served the ends of the select and arrogant members of the cult generally referred to as the *científicos*. The self-made materialists comprising the group after the mid-nineties played a prominent role in shaping the thinking of the aging Porfirio Díaz. Order, efficiency, improvement were their slogans, and were to be achieved at any cost to the nation—and the price was high. It is certain that for a decade and a half the *científicos* kept Mexico on the road to material progress, but it is extremely doubtful whether they were fully aware of the social implications of the change from an agricultural to an industrial economy, whether they were at all cognizant of the significance of the shifting of peoples and the bringing of large numbers of laborers together in relatively compact units. The *científicos* not only helped to retain Porfirio in control, but their stranglehold on Mexican politics survived until destroyed by other dictators with their own axes to grind. . . .

---

[2] Francisco García Calderón, Peruvian literary figure and diplomat, writing shortly before the turn of the nineteenth century, stated that positivism was then the dominant political philosophy in Latin America. After emphasizing the appeal of Comte's "law and order" to the political factions, he added that, "Minds formed by Catholicism, even if they have lost their faith, demand secular dogmas, and verities organized in a facile system: in short, a new faith, and the positivist philosophy satisfies that craving. At the same time material progress, based upon scientific development, and the utilitarianism which exaggerates the importance of wealth, find in positivism, which disdains futile ideologies, a system adequate to industrial life." Francisco García Calderón, *Latin America: Its Rise and Progress* (London, 1913), pp. 252-258.

III

Twentieth-Century Dynamics

◇◇

"Caudillo" is frequently used to distinguish the ruder strongmen of the nineteenth century. Nevertheless, as R. A. Humphreys has pointed out, "the dictator of the present age . . . is the heir of the nineteenth-century caudillo." [1] There is, then, perhaps more continuity than division in the history of caudillismo in the nineteenth and twentieth centuries. This is borne out by the similarity between the "new" constitutional gambits of *"continuismo"* (Document 12) and the constitutional tricks which Bilbao attacked over a hundred years ago. Nevertheless, new pressures, new ideologies, and new techniques have unquestionably left their mark on the twentieth-century dictator. If "totalitarianism" suggests the manipulation of every aspect of national life and the control of thoughts as well as actions, then it is well to question the nature of modern caudillismo in the Dominican Republic, Argentina, and Cuba. This final section provides an opportunity to explore the contemporary dynamics of dictatorship in Spanish America.

---

[1] R. A. Humphreys, "Latin America: the Caudillo Tradition," in *Soldiers and Governments: Nine Studies in Civil-Military Relations*, ed. by Michael Howard (Bloomington: Indiana University Press, 1959), p. 162.

Lyle N. McAlister

DICTATORS AND THE

MILITARY *

Among the many facets of caudillismo none has attracted more comment than the role of the military.
Since it is commonly held that he who controls the
army controls the state, a critical examination of the
relationship between dictators and armed forces is in
order. The following selection has been included because it is provocative rather than dogmatic and
because it suggests the variety of ways in which a caudillo and his country's military may interact. Subsequent selections contain evidence of some of the
types of civil-military relations explained here by
Prof. Lyle McAlister, the Director of the Center for
Latin American Studies at the University of Florida
and a noted historian of Mexican military institutions.

It is hardly necessary to assert that the armed forces have
been important factors in the historical development of

* Lyle N. McAlister, "Civil-military Relations in Latin America," *Journal of Inter-American Studies*, Vol. III (July 1961), pp.
341-350. The excerpts given here come from pp. 341-344. Reprinted by permission of the *Journal of Inter-American Studies*.

the nations of Latin America. By bringing into association men from all parts of the national territory, by
posing as the incarnation of the national spirit, and by
teaching patriotism and exalting national virtues, they
have been a significant influence in overcoming regionalism and localism. By providing an avenue for advancement for members of lower social strata, they have encouraged social mobility. In many countries they have
contributed to the transition from traditional to modern
societies through their work in constructing communications systems, their emphasis on general and technical
education within their ranks, and by their demands for
industrialization. In the political sphere they have repeatedly overthrown the governments that created them;
generals have employed the forces entrusted to them to
make themselves heads of state; military factions have
intervened in the political process in support of specific
economic objectives or of broader ideologies. In a less
spectacular fashion, the armed forces acting through political parties as in Mexico, or through officers occupying
cabinet posts have exerted powerful influences on public
policy.

These facts are generally recognized and a great deal
has been written about Latin-American "militarism." Existing literature, however, raises some serious conceptual
and methodological problems. These may be defined by
posing and commenting on a series of questions. In the
first place, do the interrelations between the military and
society at large constitute a discrete sociological and historical problem susceptible to systematic description and
analysis? Some scholars concerned with general principles
of social organization and with the history or sociology of
regions other than Latin America have conceived of
them in this fashion. Max Weber and later Gaetano
Mosca recognized the importance of military factors in
shaping societies and developed concepts and methods
for dealing with the problem. Subsequently historians
and social scientists have refined and expanded the ideas
of Weber and Mosca and produced a substantial body of
literature dealing with these interrelationships in general

and with their manifestations in the United States, Germany, Japan, the Middle East and Southeast Asia.

Perhaps because of their more obvious and immediate nature, the political and administrative aspects of this problem have been stressed; that is, the distribution of power within the state between civil and military elements. This area of study is commonly called "civil-military relations." The range of civil-military relations extends from situations in which civil authority is supreme to the direct and forcible usurpation of power by the military for nonmilitary ends.

The political role of the armed forces has likewise been stressed in Latin America. In general, however, Latin Americanists have been unwilling or unable to face up to the nature of interrelations between the military and civil elements of the state. The recent publications of Edwin Lieuwen, Victor Alba, [John Johnson] and Theodore Wyckoff are exceptions to this generalization. Much of Latin-American history has been written in terms of "Progress toward Democracy" or "The Struggle for Democracy." Within this teleological system the armed forces are regarded as "Obstacles to the Achievement of Democracy." Now no right-thinking person would deny that democracy is a desirable goal and it would be mean-spirited indeed not to wish the Latin-Americans success in their struggle toward it. Yet, this conceptual framework encourages simplistic interpretations and explanations. The military is conceived of as a force external to and interfering with "normal" historical processes rather than as an integral element in them. In this position it can conveniently be regarded as a constant whose importance is recognized and accepted but which need not be described or analyzed systematically.

Second, if the importance of the military as a power factor in Latin America is accepted and the nature of its relations with the civil elements of the state can be regarded as a discrete historical and sociological problem, what is the scope of the problem and how may it be defined? The most commonly used term to describe the role of the armed forces in Latin America is "militarism."

In the sense that it means the use of military force or
threat of force to achieve non-military ends, it is adequate. It has, however, two disadvantages. To many
scholars it has a more specific usage; that is, a system or
way of life which glorifies war, in which the military is a
high-status profession, in which an entire nation is oriented toward military virtues and mores, and which has
strong imperialist overtones. Such a system may have
existed in Paraguay during the dictatorship of Francisco
Solano López, and the G.O.U. in Argentina may have
aspired to it. It has, however, been atypical of Latin America. Also, it does not cover instances in which armed
forces have been nonpolitical and, if the problem is to be
viewed broadly, such instances also require description
and analysis. Another commonly used expression is "the
army in politics," but this term also excludes situations
where the military has been nonpolitical. Moreover, it
seems rather too mild an expression with which to describe the praetorian excesses of some Latin-American armies in the nineteenth century. "Civil-military relations"
is also open to the latter criticism. It is, however, comprehensive enough to cover the range of phenomena involved in the problem and its accepted usage elsewhere
is an argument for its adoption by Latin Americanists.

Third, what is the structure of the problem? As H. Stuart
Hughes remarks, historians are reluctant to make distinc-
tions and tend to view their problems as all of one
piece. Thus *pronunciamientos, cuartelazos, golpes de es-
tado, machetismo,* militarism, praetorianism and all
other instances where armed forces transcend their
purely military functions tend to be viewed as phenomena of the same order and explainable with more or less
the same formula. Sometimes these phenomena are even
confused with military history. This is equivalent to regarding the Assumption of Mary and the exercise of the
ecclesiastical patronage as belonging to the same order
of things or of teaching surgery and medical sociology
in the same course. In fact a diversity of patterns or
systems of civil-military relations has existed in Latin
America and each pattern consists of complex interac-

tions involving the structure, status, and power of groups, both civil and military, and the motivations of individuals, as these several elements are influenced by the political, social and economic environment. Thus the role of the Brazilian officer corps in the overthrow of the Empire, the institutionalized gangsterism prevailing in the contemporary Dominican Republic and the *pronunciamientos* of Antonio López de Santa Anna are sharply different examples of civil-military relations involving different types of civil and military elements interacting in different environmental situations.

At a schematic level several types of civil-military relations in Latin America may be defined. The first might be called the "Praetorian State." It is characterized by the frequent overthrow of governments by military revolutions or *coups d'état* for nonmilitary purposes. It tends to be associated with a high degree of social and political disorganization and a low degree of professionalism within the armed forces. Examples are Mexico during the first thirty years of the republic and Venezuela before and after the dictatorship of Juan Vicente Gómez. The second might be described as the "Gendarmist State." It emerges when a single individual, generally but not always a military man, uses a mercenary army to make himself master of the state, imposes social and political order, tames the army and uses it as a gendarmery to maintain himself in power. The dictatorships of Gómez in Venezuela, and Anastacio Somoza in Nicaragua are examples. The third type, after Harold Lasswell, is the "Garrison State." In it the military not only dominates or strongly influences the political system but it attempts to militarize the state and society at large. It occurs in connection with deep fears of aggression from the outside or strong aggressive tendencies within and is associated with a relatively high degree of political and social stability and a professionalized military establishment. Paraguay under Francisco Solano López might be taken as an example of this type. As noted above, it is atypical of Latin America. Fourth, is the "Civilist State." It is characterized by civil supremacy over the military and exists in relatively stable societies with professionalized armed forces. Examples are Argentina between 1861 and 1930 and Uruguay since the turn of this century. A fifth type may be emerging in Cuba but it is as yet difficult to identify.

It should be added that these are ideal types in the Weberian sense. They do not exist in pure form and may shade or metamorphose into one another. Thus a strong *caudillo* may in certain circumstances transform a praetorian state into a gendarmist state as in the case of Porfirio Díaz and Rafael Trujillo, or the weakening or death of a leader or pressures within a society may turn a gendarmist state into a praetorian state as, for example, Mexico after 1910. Changes in the social or economic structure within praetorian or gendarmist states may result in the emergence of a civilist pattern as in contemporary Mexico, while conversely political, social or economic strains within a civilist state may result in the emergence of praetorian or gendarmist patterns as in the case of Argentina after 1930 or Colombia after 1949. These paradigms, it should be added, are not intended to present conclusions. They are devices to illustrate a point and to encourage the asking of pertinent questions.

Russell H. Fitzgibbon

CONTINUISMO*

One of the most pressing problems which has plagued caudillos ever since independence is the problem of legitimacy. Justification of power has two essential dimensions: the vertical or immediate sort required at the time power is achieved, and the horizontal or long-term justification for indefinite retention of personalist rule. Within the vertical dimension the leader may have achieved power through force or through popular revolutionary support. His power may be based at once upon the military and upon his charismatic appeal as the anointed of his people. Either or both of these supports may be sufficient to sustain him in power through the horizontal time dimension. Most caudillos, however, especially those who may expect to encounter an articulate and educated opposition, soon find the need to cultivate the framework if not the spirit of what Max Weber has called "rational legitimacy," a government based upon fundamental laws. Even in the vertical stage, many power seekers have sought to justify their uprisings by the hallowed pattern of *plan* and *pronunciamiento*. Once in control, the elaboration of new constitutional forms has been standard operating procedure. Though refined in the twentieth century, such constitutional reliance was firmly rooted in

* Russell H. Fitzgibbon, " 'Continuismo' in Central America and the Caribbean," *The Inter-American Quarterly*, Vol. II (July 1940), pp. 56-74. The excerpts given here come from pp. 56-59, 62-64, 68-74. Reprinted by permission of the author.

the ninteenth century as Francisco Bilbao has so vigorously demonstrated (Document 7). Constitutions, however, commonly set limits either upon the length of term of office or upon the re-election of the chief executive or both. A dilemma then presents itself to the new master who would build a life term for himself at the same time that he attempts to acquire rational legitimacy through constitutionalism to add to his other props: military, charismatic, oligarchic, proletarian, or whatever. (The dilemma is the same, if less acute, for the duly elected president who wishes to go beyond his constitutionally limited term.) One solution to his dilemma is called *continuismo;* its nature is explored in the following essay, written in 1939-1940, by a prominent authority on Latin American politics, Prof. Russell H. Fitzgibbon, of the University of California at Santa Barbara.

Continuismo, we may say, is the practice of continuing the administration in power in a Latin American country by the process of a constitutional amendment, or a provision in a new constitution, exempting the president in office, and perhaps other elective officials, from the historic and frequent prohibition against two consecutive terms in office. The precise form of the constitutional change may vary—the general pattern is simple and uniform.

Cuba was easily the dean of experimenters with the device. General Gerardo Machado y Morales was elected president of Cuba in the balloting of 1924, to take office May 20, 1925, under a campaign pledge limiting him to one term in office. Machado, who had resigned a cabinet position years before in protest against the re-electionist plans of his then chief, José Miguel Gómez, declared in his election manifesto in September 1924 that "a Liberal President cannot be re-elected. This is

now a noble tradition—the most noble of this party."
The General seemingly slammed the door shut, locked
it, and threw away the key when he declared in July
1927 that "a man whose lips had never been defiled
by a lie, would lower his dignity, and dishonor himself,
if after a political labor of twenty-five years during which
he opposed the principle of re-election with the word
and the sword in two revolutions, he should now accept
the principle for himself."

If Machado had locked the door upon himself he
proved a skillful locksmith, however, and soon found a
way of opening it. The Machado-dominated Cuban
congress in the spring and summer of 1927 passed
a set of resolutions aimed at a comprehensive amendment of the constitution. Among other changes, the
presidential term was to be lengthened two years. All
went legally until May 9, 1928. The congress submitted
the series of amendments, as was required of it, to a special convention on May 9, 1928 which, the same day,
adopted a resolution asserting that

> the Constituent Assembly does not vacillate in reaf-
> firming that General Gerardo Machado y Morales,
> because of the obligation he has contracted and be-
> cause of his role as founder of the Republic, is un-
> avoidably bound to accept a new presidential pe-
> riod.

The convention concluded its simple task two days
later but with the omission, inadvertent or otherwise, of
the provision regarding the prolongation of Machado's
term for two additional years. It specified instead that
the single, six-year term provision should become opera-
tive with the first subsequent election. The changes
became effective as part of the constitution on publication in the *Gaceta*, May 11, 1928.

With the way constitutionally cleared Machado became the candidate of all three political parties in the
1928 elections, held on November 2, and was chosen
without opposition to succeed himself, "ignoble," "un-
dignified," and "dishonorable" though it was! The

first of the recent attempts at *continuismo* thus became history.

The contagion of *continuismo* spread first in the Caribbean. The Dominican Republic next fell victim to the malady. . . . A symptom of what was to come had manifested itself in the Dominican Republic even before the Cuban changes of 1928. Horacio Vásquez had assumed the presidency in Santo Domingo (as the capital was then named) on July 12, 1924, under a constitution of June 13, 1924, which established a four-year term for the chief executive with ineligibility for an immediately successive term. The fruits of office apparently tasted sweet, for in 1927 a constituent convention revised the basic law to provide, among other changes, a two-year extension of the terms of the president, vice-president, and members of the congress. The change, effective June 16, 1927, legally continued Vásquez in power from 1928 to 1930. Presidential provisions in the constitution again were juggled in 1929 when an additional amendment on June 20 restored the four-year term for the head of the state and at the same time removed the prohibition on re-election. A further political insurance policy for the ruling régime was the revision of the electoral law of 1924 in a manner which convinced the opposition parties that an attempt to win through election was impossible.

With these changes on the statute books, President Vásquez announced in 1929 that he would be a candidate for re-election in May 1930. Political tension increased throughout 1929 and came to a head early in 1930.

Vásquez' refusal to meet the demand for minority representation on the local election boards was the cue for revolution, which broke out in the north on February 23, 1930, and was carried through to success five days later by the ousting of the régime in power. Chief factor in the success of the insurgents was the defection of General Rafael Leónidas Trujillo Molina, commander of the government forces and an erstwhile private in the United States Marine Corps during its occupation of the island republic. A provisional president, General Estrella Ureña, set presidential elections for May 16, 1930, and himself became the candidate for vice-president on the "government ticket" headed by Trujillo. The withdrawal of the opposition nominees two days before the election permitted the choice of the favored candidates without a contest. [Trujillo's skill in the use of *continuismo* during the next three decades is revealed in the next two selections.]

It was not surprising that with these repeated and presumably successful demonstrations of the efficacy of *continuismo* in the Caribbean republics, the contagion should spread to the neighboring mainland governments of Central America. The first to undertake such experimentation was Guatemala, the efforts of which were, indeed, practically concurrent with those of Haiti. Guatemala had had a long unenlightened political history, alternating between despotism and virtual anarchy. After kaleidoscopic changes in the control of the executive branch late in 1930, General Jorge Ubico came to the presidential palace on February 14, 1931, through elections held February 6-8. The constitution promulgated January 1, 1928, established a six-year term for the president and prohibited re-election during the twelve years following the expiration of the term. The whole emphasis of the relevant articles in the 1928 constitution was on the prevention of indefinite continuance in office, nepotism, and allied problems.

Ubico moved quickly to consolidate his position in the presidency. The *Partido Liberal Progresista*, the candidate of which Ubico had been in his campaign for the presidency, soon became a well-knit personal following. Taking time by the forelock, the president on May 5, 1935, won for his Liberal Progressive party, by methods which may be guessed at if not documented, a majority of the seats in an *Asamblea Nacional Constituyente*, created to consider revision of the basic law. The constitutional assembly, which held only seventeen sessions, worked from the basis of a draft constitution submitted to the *Junta Preparatoria* and by the latter to the full assembly. While Ubico's message to the first plenary session of the assembly contained no reference to the possibility of his own re-election to the presidency, it was a foregone conclusion that with the proceedings under full executive control some provision pointing in that direction would be an easy and logical way out.

The constitution retained the 1928 provision (Article 66) that twelve years must elapse from the expiration of an initial term before a president could again occupy the office. The assembly then provided for the holding of a national plebiscite on the question of continuing Ubico's term of office. This step—convenient substitute for a regular presidential election—was consummated on June 22-24, 1935, and resulted in an officially announced vote of 884,703 to 1,144 in favor of the continuance of General Ubico in the presidency until 1943. Following this overwhelming popular mandate the constituent assembly duly decreed certain transitory provisions under date of July 11, 1935, the first of which provided that

> The Constitutional Presidency of General Jorge Ubico shall end on March 15, 1943, and with such an object the purpose of Article 66 of the Constitution remains in suspense until that date. . . .

The Guatemalan nucleus of *continuismo* spread fanwise in Central America, first to Honduras, successively to El Salvador and Nicaragua. . . .

The last country—to date[1]—to attempt *continuismo* was Nicaragua. The prelude was the political campaign by which General Anastasio Somoza, head of the *Guardia Nacional,* became president in 1937. He had in 1934 announced his entry in the 1936 campaign, although he was doubly barred on constitutional grounds by the fact that he was a nephew by marriage of the incumbent president, Dr. Juan Bautista Sacasa, and by his headship of the national guard. The political situation was further complicated by the alleged complicity of General

---

[1] I.e., 1939-1940. [ed.]

Somoza in the assassination by national guard members of General Augusto Sandino, long an opponent of United States marine occupation of Nicaragua, on February 21, 1934. Somoza more formally entered the presidential race with a statement published in September 1935 in *El Cronista* at León, traditional Liberal stronghold, promising that he would "eliminate all other candidates who bar my path" to the presidency. The political situation tightened as the 1936 elections approached, and on June 6 of that year Somoza forced his uncle out of office. A Somoza partisan became provisional president, and on June 15 the Liberal party gave the national guard chieftain its nomination. The elections on December 8, 1936, were farcical: Somoza received approximately 117,000 votes against 1,100 given his exiled coalition opponent.

Continuismo flowered in Nicaragua with less than half of Somoza's term gone. Dr. Carlos A. Morales, a Liberal justice of the Supreme Court, suggested in an article in *La Prensa* at Managua, the capital, on May 14, 1938, that steps be taken for the revision of the constitution. The congress in August passed the necessary legislation for elections to an *Asamblea Constituyente* to convene on December 15. The elections, held on November 6, resulted in the choice of twenty-seven Liberals, eleven Conservative Nationalists (the pro-Somoza wing of the Conservative party), and seven Conservatives. The president on December 8 issued detailed "provisional regulations" for the government of the constituent assembly, and the plenary sessions opened on December 16. The main work of the assembly got under way early in February 1939 when it began consideration of an 18,000-word draft constitution. This task was completed some seven weeks later with publication of the document in the *Gaceta*.

The 1939 constitution contained several provisions bearing on the presidency. In the first place, after specifying a six-year presidential term, it provided flatly (Article 204) that "the immediate re-election of the President is forbidden." Other seemingly rigorous restrictions upon eligibility and succession were included. A "joker" appeared in Article 350, though, in the statement that

> The amendment of the provision which prohibits the re-election of the President of the Republic and those concerning the duration of the presidential term . . . cannot be decreed except for future need, in order that the amendment may not be a detriment or a help to the officials in service at the time of its promulgation.

In the first of several transitory provisions, the constituent assembly arrogated to itself the function of electing "a citizen who is to exercise the Presidency of the Republic during a term . . . from March 30 of the current year [1939] to May 1, 1947." In the article immediately following, the constituent assembly, with the model of its two northern neighbors before it, transformed itself for an eight-year period into the ordinary legislative congress. In compliance with its self-imposed mandate to choose a president for the ensuing term, the assembly voted on March 24, 1939, the prize going to Somoza with forty-six votes as against seven for Fernando Guzmán, a prominent Conservative party leader. In his inaugural address on March 30 Somoza declared that "One of my greatest ambitions was reformation of the Constitution to represent the will of the people"!

One should be extremely cautious in drawing conclusions and moral judgments about *continuismo*. . . . It is in order, however, to raise a few questions and, perhaps, to venture highly tentative answers.

Why has the practice under discussion been so localized? What conditions in the body politic favor the entrance of such an infection? How incompatible is it with what we define as "democracy"? It may even be proper to ask if it is a disease, i.e., an undesirable manifestation. Two explanations may be suggested as possible and partial answers to the first question. The simple fact of geographic nearness encourages an imitation of political trends and techniques which neighbors have adopted. A certain vague common denominator underlies the countries of "the American Mediterranean," variant though their ethnic compositions, their economic interests, their social structures, and other factors are. In the second place, the location of the countries concerned within the sometime international political orbit of the United States induced a certain lip service to constitutional forms as such. . . . The average Latin American constitution has been more symbol than instrument, however, and it is understandable why, with any external examples of this sort seemingly stressing form, the Central American and Caribbean governments should be concerned with such an aspect. The anomaly appears in the willingness and casualness with which on more than one occasion the régimes endeavoring to preserve the appearance of legality have departed from the prescribed legal methods of effecting new constitutions or constitutional amendments. Viewing the whole picture, the question of sheer constitutionalism becomes artificial and dogmatic.

Continuismo has been favored in middle America by just those conditions which nurture dictatorship—and to just the same extent. A high degree of illiteracy, of political inarticulateness and even unconsciousness, of governmental concentration, all make for those expressions of exaggerated personalism of which this legalized perpetuation of control is a form. Dictatorship has been a normal rather than unusual type of executive development in most of the countries under consideration, and *continuismo* is but a natural result of a dictatorship which wishes to give the color of legality, either for domestic or foreign eyes, to its continuance. Costa Rica is a country of greater literacy, more general popular participation in political expression and consciousness of governmental problems; these factors have a very pertinent relationship to the entire absence of any suggestion of the adoption of *continuismo* in that country.

The practice seems to be in direct and immediate contradiction to political democracy as we know the term. It is naïve, of course, to assume that in any of the countries the constitutional perversion has been accomplished in other than the harshest and most arbitrary sort of manner. The exiled opponents of the various régimes have been loud and persistent in their charges of constitutional perversion and violated democracy. Such charges are naturally to be discounted because of the personal elements entering in, but they certainly contain a strong half-truth. . . .

Continuismo cannot be regarded as a problem in and by itself. To detach it from its environment is to consider the image in a mirror as unrelated to the object which causes it. *Continuismo* is simply a reflection, a symptom, and a result of the larger problem of dictatorship.

*Rafael L. Trujillo Molina**

THE EVOLUTION OF
DEMOCRACY IN
SANTO DOMINGO

The most successful practitioner of *continuismo*
in the Caribbean in recent years was Generalissimo
Rafael Leónidas Trujillo Molina, dictator of the Dominican Republic from 1930 until his assassination
in 1961. As notorious for his totalitarian methods as
any caudillo in history, "The Benefactor" developed
his propaganda machine to a high level of efficiency.
He was particularly concerned with the image of
himself and of his regime which was projected abroad.
Laudatory biographies were presented as gifts to li-
braries all over the United States and major metropolitan newspapers ran expensive full-page advertise-
ments praising Trujillo. The following selection is
characteristic of The Benefactor's concern for his
image. It was first given by him as the inaugural address to the Hemisphere's delegates to the Thirteenth
Pan-American Sanitary Conference at Ciudad Trujillo
on October 2, 1950. Revised and published again
five years later, "The Evolution of Democracy in
Santo Domingo" stands as the remarkable rationale

---

* Rafael L. Trujillo Molina, *The Evolution of Democracy in
Santo Domingo*, 2d ed. (Ciudad Trujillo: Dominican Government,
1955), translated by Otto Vega. The excerpts given here come from
pp. 10, 19-21, 27-31, 34-41, 43, 45-55, 58-64.

of a Spanish American dictator who made the trains run on time. The anti-Communist emphasis is particularly revealing. About 30 percent of the speech is reprinted here. It should be closely compared with the next document by Jesús de Galíndez, which was also published in 1955.

Democracy acts according to the needs and characteristics of each particular group, actuated and governed by the objective structure of each particular society. Democracy is action: economic, religious, political, social, human action—in a word, action which evolves and operates in accordance with the traditions, the history, the ethnology, and the geography of each group, provided of course it is primarily directed towards the improvement of the community.

All during the course of my influence in Dominican affairs, the nation has been administered in accordance with this basic and determining criterion. The results speak for themselves and so far I have no reason for regrets in my executive program. . . .

In 1930 . . . after eighty-six years of bloody warfare, social unrest, poverty, and want we had failed to solve any of our problems: there were still no schools, no hospitals, no employment, no boundary, no roads, no currency, no banks, no agriculture, no industry (except the sugar latifundium), no public buildings, no social security, no electric power, no university, no irrigation system, no bridges, no money, no appreciable production. Not a single step had been taken by 1930 toward regaining our financial independence. . . . Before 1930 a national census had never been taken and a statistical system had never existed. Not a single social security law had been enacted and never had a tax reform been attempted.

The Republic was limited to the static maintenance of

a minimum of services wholly dependent on a meager budget essentially designed to meet the overwhelming debt. . . . The spirit of Dominicans dejected by hopeless skepticism. Wealth undeveloped, services paralyzed, trade inactive, the capital city destroyed, creditors demanding payment, public opinion divided into countless individual factions of a primitive nature, local bossism as active as ever and, in the background of the whole picture, "the monster of armed rebellion trying to raise its Hydra head."

Such a picture was enough to discourage even the most enthusiastic and optimistic. But I had confidence in the country's future, in the good faith of my people and in the immanent will of God. I had the patience and the faith to undertake and carry out a program of government which was embodied in a single word: *build!*

As had happened repeatedly before, the financial crisis of 1930 brought about a political crisis. Factious ringleaders plotted revolt and some of them started the nation on the road to civil war. . . . I was convinced that the generalization of a new upheaval would mean final collapse. The Republic could not stand . . . further proof of its unfitness for self-government. Dominicans were not responsible, of course, for many of the fundamental aspects of the situation, which was actually the inevitable upshot of poverty and economic subservience; but surely in the end the tragic balance of chaos would fall upon our shoulders.

The year 1931 passed amid great difficulties. Revolt began to appear everywhere and it became necessary to subdue more than one revolutionary attempt. In a message addressed to the National Congress on February 27, 1932, I had occasion to refer to the most trying effort exerted in order to maintain order in the country. It was impossible to think of a new period of bloodshed, wastefulness and executive irresponsibility at a time when all the energies, the thinking capacity and the self-respect of Dominicans ought to be bound together in a single effort for national regeneration capable of leading us along the righteous path of civility to the only revolution possible: the revolution against the public administration methods hitherto responsible for the wasteful depletion of the sources of our common welfare. That long-coveted revolution could not come from the horse-riding guerrillas or from turmoil, or from anarchy, or from shameful poverty, or from lack of faith, or from the narrow-mindedness of local chieftains, or from foreign intervention, or from subservience. The revolution had to be brought about by way of thoughtful reconstruction, sacrifice, peace and order.

While the government confronted these serious difficulties in maintaining order, I also had to face the financial crisis. I was not willing to maintain peace by dint of subduing the seditious spirit of Dominicans—fundamentally a consequence of profound social inadequacy—simply in order that our creditors might enjoy a maximum guarantee of payment. My purpose was to make of peace an instrument of the revolution itself; to give peace a constructive, positive social meaning. To do that it was necessary to eradicate the basic problems and to perform, under the guidance of government, a thorough transformation of our essential values. . . .

In the course of four dark and anxious years we . . . succeeded not only in surviving and avoiding final collapse but in becoming an example of honesty and efficiency. . . . Notwithstanding this accomplishment, our efforts had only given us a moment of rest. We had rid ourselves of oppressive demands, but nothing had yet been accomplished towards real liberation. Further proof on our part was needed and the people had to be educated and prepared for it.

In August 1934 [I took] the oath of office for a second presidential term. . . . Amidst the serious difficulties encountered during my first term since 1931, I undertook to organize a political force which could join me in carrying out the arduous program I had outlined. However plausible my intentions might have been, they required the support of public opinion and a sense of national responsibility profoundly conscious of our common welfare. Therefore the *Dominican Party* made its

appearance on the nation's political arena. That staunch-
est supporter of my Administration stands today as a
living expression of the constructive ideals of a whole
Dominican generation.

The *Dominican Party* represents a paramount effort of organization against the self-indulgent, factious
methods of policy-lacking groups. Thanks to its disciplined and purposeful existence, the Republic has attained national objectives of far-reaching import. Dominicans of all times and even the foreigners who ruled us
on various occasions struggled vainly in search of those
objectives. The formation of a stable, majority-carrying
political body was one of our major requirements, one
of the basic prerequisites for the desired change. The
principle of authority could not be effective without a co-
herent grouping of the masses around a well-defined program. With public opinion divided into a hundred different interfighting groups unable to find the way to
national unity, it was impossible to take any serious steps
towards regeneration. . . . It was not a case of facing
mere routine difficulties, such as are bound to exist even
in organized and well-established democracies. We were
struggling against veritable organic deficiencies. . . .
Very few Dominicans believed in 1930 that financial reorganization was feasible without foreign control or considered that the free issuance of a sound national currency, or the final cancellation of the foreign debt, or
the establishment of a self-supporting national bank, to
name only a few examples, were at all possible. . . .

The experience of our barren and tormenting past had
driven us into a state of unbelief and self-distrust from
which it was vital to emerge. But first a series of psychological elements had to be created in contrast with
our past background. That was the mission I entrusted
to the *Dominican Party*. As its name suggests, the Party's
activities are carried out on a nationwide basis and the
organization is not incompatible with any other serious
movement aimed at our social and political rehabilitation. . . . Respect for the law, the spirit of cooperation
and association, the sense of collective unrewarded re-

sponsibility, mass subordination to the principle of authority—sum and substance of any stable social organization—were conditions that had not taken root in our national conscience before 1930. It was therefore our duty and responsibility to create this series of intangible and imponderable elements, just as much as it was —but perhaps with greater urgency—our duty and responsibility to build roads and bridges, hospitals and schools. So long as strong foundations were not laid for a new Dominican ethical code, we could not hope for a revision of our frustrated past. The change would have to begin at the very root of our national spirit, at the bottom of our attitude toward life itself.

Without a working institution, without an active organization, without a flexible, disciplined and responsible force identified with the government's constructive aims, the fulfillment of such aims . . . would have never materialized. When I thought of creating the *Dominican Party,* I did not have in mind just another party. I was thinking in terms of a Dominican social substratum capable of carrying out the vital rehabilitation program upon which our life as a nation depended. As an inevitable consequence of our peculiar social conditions, the Party has been an instrument of civilization.

The change in our character is so obvious and the practice of cooperation is now so deeply rooted in our population, that the following data, which I consider of the utmost importance as it points to social events of the first magnitude, will be sufficient to dispel any doubts in this respect: on September 15th, 1947 compulsory military training was established by Act of Congress. . . . By the time the registration deadline provided by the Act was reached, 448,607 citizens had already complied with the requirements of the law—in this case a law dealing with so thorny a subject as military conscription. During 1949, 33,862 citizens received training and only 240 were, for legitimate reason, exempted from the service. There was not a single case of desertion!

Similarly striking are the enthusiasm and spirit of cooperation that prevailed when our last census was taken. The count over the entire territory was completed in only twelve hours and there was not the slightest evidence of confusion or disorder. Nor was there any need of rectifying figures. These experiences bespeak the new kind of nation where we now live, and speak highly of the new social subject which the Dominican now is.

On various occasions criticism has been directed against the *Dominican Party* as constituting a one-party system offering no possibility for opposition. This contention lacks any valid foundation inasmuch as the Party was originally formed with the same contingent of old factions which had eventually disintegrated and become weary owing to their inadequacy and lack of faith. I should like to stress that men from each and every one of the political groups in existence before 1930, as well as others who had nothing to do with those groups, have been active in my Administration. It is apparent that a new partisan school of thought has come into being in this country which will prevent a reversion to the outmoded system of anomalous, subservient factions whose activities were responsible for many a national calamity and to be sure for the failure of Dominican democracy in the past. Independently of the government party's influence, public opinion has evolved freely towards the formation of a well-defined labor movement and towards constitutional recognition of women's political and civil rights. Both actions are of course consistent with contemporary political trends which, while running parallel with governmental action, are wholly independent of it.

Moreover, public education and every cultural activity sponsored by the government have been conducted in a free and purely objective manner and have never been under the influence of interested foreign movements. The same can be said of religious activities and of all other activities inherent to our nationals or to resident aliens, *provided that such activities are not aimed at destroying or hampering the great task of national reconstruction to which we Dominicans are morally com-*

mitted by command of our ruinous past.[1] If a price must be paid for regeneration and revolution, then we must pay that price in order to live under God and according to the standards of present-day civilization. I am well aware that my work, being human, is not perfect. There are shortcomings and deficiencies. But thus far the good results achieved greatly outbalance the expectations and hopes of even the most optimistic of Dominicans of 1930, of the Dominicans of my own generation. . . .

I have pointed out that each and every one of our national problems awaited solution when the government was entrusted to me, and that these problems, at the same time, called for a well-intentioned hand. The question of demographic organization, which was uppermost among our problems in 1935, could not be met successfully without a scientifically conducted census, hitherto lacking, of our population. This task was undertaken immediately and good results were achieved. In 1936 a likewise thoroughly planned scientific statistical system was set up throughout the country as a fundamental prerequisite to the organization of many other essential public services. . . .

Meanwhile far-reaching reforms and innovations were being brought about by sheer dint of effort. No action involved greater urgency, insofar as our domestic affairs were concerned, than that of raising the low stagnant level of our economy and our production. As we are primarily an agricultural country and were at that time devoid of any other immediately accessible source of wealth, no problem was so pressing as the development of the agricultural and livestock industries. . . .

In order to cope with the unfathomed problem of our agriculture, the government adopted a threefold policy comprising irrigation, farm colonization and distribution of lands, water, seeds and implements to farmer, free of charge. The government also undertook an ambi-

---

[1] Trujillo's italics. [ed.]

tious campaign for farm mechanization and improvement of cultivation methods designed to help farmers obtain the greatest possible profit from their work. . . .

The system of land distribution among farmers lacking financial means was begun in 1935 through the establishment of a Board of Agricultural Protection in each of the country's provinces. This action was completely independent of the farm colonization system. Thus far 3,530,057 *tareas*[2] of land have been distributed among 104,707 people. At an average price of $3 per *tarea*, the value of these lands would amount to $10,590,171. The land grants are made outright, with the sole provision that recipients prove that the land is kept under cultivation. The only effective method of combating idleness is by helping everyone to work for himself. The beneficiaries, almost a hundred thousand strong, who are now small landowning farmers, were so many potential idlers whom we have rescued from the pitfalls of indolence and indulgence that they may gain sustenance for their families. Wanton loafing is strictly forbidden by law in this country. Moreover, I should like to point out that none of the large private enterprises, operating in this country, or even several of them combined, including those controlling the largest properties, maintain in production an area of land equaling that which the government has distributed among the small, needy farmers. . . .

From 1908 to 1935 only 857 kilometers of road had been built throughout the country with funds coming from various loans. This road network was insufficient to carry the volume of the nation's trade and agricultural production. So long as production is not accessible to good roads, it can not be considered as a source of wealth. It was therefore necessary to build roads and permanent bridges. During the last 20 years more than 2,929.13 kilometers of highways and 380 bridges have been built throughout the country at a cost of $20,692,-653.97.

---

[2] *Tarea*: Unit of land measure used in the Dominican Republic, approximately equivalent to one-sixth of an acre. [ed.]

The expansion of agricultural production and of our resources in general called for increasing industrialization of raw materials. The government took upon itself the program for industrialization. The first step towards this end was the establishment of the Industrial Slaughterhouse and Refrigeration Plant in 1944, through which development of the livestock industry was begun. Later a cement plant was installed. In 1948 the government purchased the *Chocolatera Sánchez*, one of the best plants for industrialization of cacao in existence in Latin America. In 1948 also a large incinerating plant was installed at the capital for proper disposal of refuse and for utilization of certain residual matter for industrial purposes. This plant is considered by experts as the best of its kind in the West Indies. . . . Likewise, other basic industries representing a total initial investment of $6,671,850 have been established under official sponsorship. . . .

In 1930 the school situation here was quite deficient. Enrollment throughout the country that year included only 50,739 students and attendance was very low. When I became President, there were only 526 educational centers in this country, the University included, and illiteracy was very high because rural schools were practically nonexistent. It was precisely the time, also, when the pressure of conditions under the economic crisis caused the closing of many schools. . . .

This situation was alarming. Anything might have been expected to happen save that so essential a service as public education should become paralyzed. Now then, even amidst the financial crisis, substantial steps were taken not only to forestall the continuation of this evil but to improve the service and insure its normal operation. From then on budget appropriations for education have increased steadily up to $3,661,932.50 in 1949, and up to $8,836,927.27 for 1955.

The change in the field of education can be appreciated from the following data: school enrollment, including the University's, was 250,684 students during 1949 and average attendance was 86 percent. At the present time there are 5,727 schools functioning in this country, with a combined enrollment of 344,560 students.

The University of Santo Domingo, the oldest in the Americas, has a current enrollment of over 3,000 students. In order to house it decorously, the government is building on the capital's outskirts a University City consisting of a number of buildings for the various departments and schools. When completed, this project will represent a $5,000,000 investment. Half of that amount has already been spent for the construction of the five buildings presently housing the Schools of Medicine, Pharmacy and Dentistry, the Institute of Anatomy, and several laboratories. . . .

The pith of the changes that have taken place in administrative methods and in the general way of life of our people must be found in this simple formula of government: the greater the volume of active and productive wealth, the higher the quality and the number of public services. A nation's wealth must be the measure of its inhabitant's welfare.

This sound policy is making it possible for us to invest hundreds of millions of dollars over a short working period for the purpose of raising the standard of living of a people dejected by four centuries of adversity. We do not hold that everything has been done already, but we do believe that what has been accomplished has placed us firmly on the open and definite road to recovery. . . .

The budget of the Department of Health in 1930 amounted to $160,854.75. At the time there were only 30 hospital beds available for maternity cases in the entire country . . . there were 484 beds in general hospitals, 12 medical dispensaries, one in each Province, and a few understaffed sanitary brigades, made up of medical students, to combat endemic diseases in rural areas.

With such meager resources it was practically impossible to make any serious attempt to improve sanitary services in the country. At the same time it was quite difficult, not to say impossible, to launch a program of sanitation such as conditions demand, so long as the Treasury situation remained unchanged. To set up efficient sanitary services and establish social security we needed money and resources which we lacked and which, moreover, I was unwilling to procure abroad under onerous and enslaving conditions.

Progress thus far in the fields of sanitation and social welfare has been attained through our own means invested in relative proportion to the growth of fiscal revenues and with the sole support of the *Dominican Party*. The magnitude of these programs would in itself be a source of pride to my Administration. At the present time there are 29 hospitals operated by the Department of Public Health with 6,000 beds available to patients, 10 maternity hospitals with a total of 1,000 cribs, plus another 1,000 beds belonging to welfare establishments and social security centers supervised by government departments, and 11 hospitals and 1 clinic made available by the Social Security Chest, with a total of 1,088 beds. . . .

But that is not all. Public health is not solely dependent on hospitals and medical services. There are other elements indispensable to the maintenance of good health and the general welfare. . . . To live well one must have decent quarters, eat adequately and sufficiently, drink potable water, bathe every day, drain all wastes, dress properly; in short, it is necessary to possess a series of material elements without which it is impossible to live in good health. To this end we have brought forth a general program of urbanization and a social welfare program. . . .

This long-range program [included] the paving of streets in all cities, construction of sewer and drainage systems, opening of new streets and avenues, building of public markets, race tracks, zoological gardens, installation of electric light throughout the Republic and, last but not least, with the construction of a chain of modern hotels as a basis for the promotion of the tourist trade. . . .

While no binding concordat between the Dominican

Republic and the Holy See existed then, our government took it upon itself to build a goodly number of churches dedicated to the Roman Catholic Faith, which is that professed by the Dominican people. Our far-ranging rehabilitation program could not be considered complete if it failed to take into full account the religious functions and the most intimate spiritual needs of the people. Government relations with the Church have always been very cordial and this circumstance has enabled the two to execute a full-fledged building program in which the Administration has invested very considerable amounts of money. It includes building for seminaries, for churches throughout the country, parochial houses, Catholic colleges for men and women; it includes also the supplying of ornaments as well as direct help and subsidies to congregations. Preferential attention is given to all endeavors aimed at fostering Catholic sentiment. The vicissitudes of the past also cast the shadow of ruin over our religious institutions and lessened religious fervor. Now a government truly concerned over the fate of its people could not look upon such a loss with indifference. Therefore we undertook to make up for it with fully as much enthusiasm and patriotic feeling as we put into our civic improvement. . . .

The establishment of social welfare services was uppermost in my mind from the very earliest days of my Administration and this objective has been consistently pursued. At the outset . . . it was clear that the government was not financially able, at the time, to attend to such services, [so] I decided to organize them under the auspices of the *Dominican Party*. But those early attempts were as mere trickles against the sea of destitution in which our needy classes drifted helplessly.

However, my will to improve conditions was unshakable. In 1933 I sponsored the first Dominican Medical Congress with a view to studying and properly classifying the grave health and social welfare problems that our people had confronted from time immemorial. . . .

[The resulting] program has been completed in all its

phases. The growth of social welfare services called for
the creation of permanent specialized agencies and these
are now operating under the Department of Social Welfare. . . . We have built comfortable dwellings in social betterment districts in various communities throughout the country. These districts are endowed with every
requirement under modern urban development. We have
built shelters for the aged, and farm reformatories for
boys. We have built recreation centers for workers, maternity clubs, nurseries, sewing centers for female workers (with an attendance of over six thousand), and
elementary schools for illiterate adults. Complete medical services are maintained for the care of children and
free milk distribution stations, established throughout
the country, contribute effectively to preserving the
health of needy children.

In closing my remarks bearing upon governmental action on social problems, I should like to refer to the work
done to improve throughout the relations between capital and labor and to raise conditions among the laboring class within the framework of those relations. . . .

In 1932 . . . I submitted to Congress a bill for a
Workmen's Compensation Law to bring labor accident
regulation into line with the practical demands of modern life. In 1938 two bills were enacted, one dealing with
the Dominicanization of labor which provided for a 70
percent minimum participation of native workers in all
commercial, industrial or agricultural enterprises, and the
other pertaining to the Sabbath as a day of rest and to
closing hours. In 1941 a new bill was adopted providing
for the cash payment of the salaries and wages of agricultural workers. . . . In 1942 I sponsored a substantial amendment to our Constitution aimed at bringing
about wider action by the Administration in favor of
the laboring classes.

The time elapsed since 1935 has been industriously
and profitably employed in Santo Domingo. In twenty
years every value in our community, material as well as
moral, has undergone a substantial change. Not a single
feature of our national life has failed to go through

the machinery of sound, progressive action, though the invigorating outcome of this prolific period cannot be appreciated in its true measure while the programs undertaken are still in full process of development. Nonetheless, from a population standpoint, the results have been abundant. The 1950 census shows an increase in population of 700,000 inhabitants over those in the 1935 census; and while our present population does not fill yet our potential capacity, I am certain that it will not be long before the two million Dominicans counted this year will have arrived at a shining goal of plenitude. The elements of security, health and cleanliness now prevailing in this country will doubtless yield results even more gratifying in the days to come. . . .

I have purposely reserved for the latter part of this account reference to our military institutions and their work during the past few years. Without a foundation of individual and collective security, without a definite agent for order and peace, setting the wheels of progress in motion would have been utterly impossible. While it is true that the Republic has had courageous and seasoned fighters to defend its independence on the field of battle, it is no less true that we never had an adequate military organization designed to uphold internal peace and to safeguard freedom for the nation's civil institutions.

To organize this was quite as necessary as establishing other services. A nation cannot fulfill its historic destiny unless it has armed forces and a military spirit. The career of arms, within the framework of its role as a safeguard, is indispensable among national institutions. To create and organize the armed forces of the Republic is as noble and essential a task as is the building of schools, hospitals, ports or banks, provided of course that by their creation and organization the other administrative services will not be impaired. . . .

We Dominicans were in the midst of our efforts at rehabilitation when the hectic period of readjustment following World War II came about. We had fulfilled loyally the obligations imposed on us by that conflict and

far was it from our minds to suspect that we, the loyal
and devoted supporters of Democracy in that struggle,
were to be the victims of the extremist and demagogic
storm that followed the cessation of hostilities. But the
tempest vented its fury upon us and, had our new national spirit not been cast in so solid a mold, we would
have met with disaster.

In 1942 war conditions brought me back to office.
Side by side with the United States we entered the armed
conflict in view of the treacherous Pearl Harbor attack.
Postwar conditions in 1947, which were even more dangerous to us than the actual period of hostilities, com-
pelled me, against my wishes, to continue in office. The
Dominican Party and the people at large would not
consent to shifting the responsibility of government in
the face of the dangerous contingencies prevailing at the
time. By an imperative command of circumstances, I
was and still am the core of that responsibility. Therefore I could not, either as a man or as a leader, turn my
back upon the most elementary duties of one who was
to be tested at a difficult and perilous juncture.

Since the early months of 1946 the existence of a
definite coalition of governments against the prevailing
order in this country made itself apparent. The political
phenomenon of that coalition developed in violation of
both the spirit and the letter of the Inter-American System, was counter to the stanchest juridical principles
governing international relations and went against all
rules of international law. The Dominican Republic was
complying strictly with all obligations incumbent upon
it in the international field and undoubtedly stood as a
positive element of progress and civilization in this geographical area. None of the governments involved in the
plot had cause or reason for ill will toward us. But the
plot subsisted with all its implications and by mid-1947
it had become an outright threat of war.

The conflict involved deep ideological differences.
Here was an advancing nation eagerly seeking the gist of
its own existence; here indeed was a small country on
the road to self-sufficiency, where order and cooperation

were the very essence of institutions. And there were the others, disjointed and misguided, bent on carrying beyond their borders the noxious spirit of the new economic and political system. We represented the national, in terms of democratic advancement; they represented the international—the Marxist revolution—intent on social and economic domination. The actual promoters of the coalition could not have been concerned over the needs of the Dominican people, whom they neither know nor love. . . .

We met the situation with calm and composure but with firmness as well. At the very moment when we were bringing to an end, through a substantial cash payment, the age-old process of the foreign debt—that hotbed of evil in our wasteful past—the haunting specter of a new disintegration hovered over us. The downfall of the government through social and political interference by alien systems, would have given rise to chaos in this country. Therefore we decided to resist, and not merely for our own convenience but also to test the very nature and raison d'être of the Inter-American System. This decision entailed great sacrifices. On one occasion I pointed out that national defense during that period subtracted from our public treasury over $20,000,000 which would have yielded a better harvest had they been devoted to the nonmilitary investments for which they were originally intended.

When I became fully aware of the extent of the political, economic and military forces that were gathering to disrupt the Republic's rehabilitation program, I tried of course to build up adequate defenses. The Communist plotters knew that we lacked arms to face an event of such magnitude as they were readying. Our resources had been channeled toward promoting a production and wealth that served to meet the requirements of other countries during the war years, and were not used for excessive armament which we never considered necessary for our own democratic way of life.

At the end of 1945 we took steps to acquire in the United States certain war matériel—a very limited amount of it. The Department of State flatly refused to approve the necessary licenses, thereby closing all doors for consideration of our security. Had an attitude more akin to understanding prevailed, our subsequent sacrifice for defense would not have been so burdensome and onerous. To show the measure of that sacrifice, suffice it to say that in order to manufacture our own weapons we had to put $5,000,000 into an industrial war plant.

It was contended at the time that the munitions requested by the Dominican government were not necessary for the nation's defense. The Department of State put it bluntly and distinctly that inasmuch as no threat whatsoever existed against the Republic's security, our government could seek to arm itself only for aggressive purposes. We, the friends of law and order, the ones responsible for what stands to this day as the most genuine program of democratic rehabilitation in Latin America, had to endure the bitterness of this unwarranted rebuke while the agent of anarchy and the promoters of disorder and confusion remained free to plot against a loyal country.

Communism found us alone, but indeed not lacking in courage and strength to thwart its designs and ward off its influence in the Caribbean. We did not even receive moral succor from an unbiased press. American newspapers either held off in a frigid, baffling silence favorable to the Communist scheme, or, to go along with the plotting governments, plunged into a foul campaign to discredit our country and its leaders.

Events moved with pressing swiftness. Hardly had a year transpired since our request for war matériel when, with the knowledge and forbearance of all, we found ourselves facing the most dangerous operation for military attack in our history. Responsibility for this operation rested upon several governments. Subsequent investigations by the Organ of Consultation of the Organization of American States evinced the full scope of that responsibility. The event, unparalleled in the Americas, was undeniably a result of the change international relations have undergone. Now extremist ideas and extremist methods militate against all national limitations and seek to extend themselves beyond geographic frontiers to turn these into a mere symbol of independence that will not be a hindrance to the impulsive ways of Marxism.

This far-reaching implication of the Dominican case was not opportunely minded by those who ought to have regarded it and pondered it most carefully. Our efforts to make that state of affairs understood were unavailing, and the blunder cost us treasure and energy untold. But we have no regrets over this because in the end we derived a profitable lesson in solitude. This humble country of the Caribbean anticipated the bewildering, world-shaking events of today and initiated the great battle that will decide the fate of Western civilization.

Jesús de Galíndez

A REPORT ON
SANTO DOMINGO*

How Jesús de Galíndez, a Loyalist in the Spanish
Civil War, came to the Dominican Republic and
what he encountered there during a residence of six
years are described by him in the following essay. As
a teacher in the Dominican School of Diplomatic
Law and legal adviser to the Government's Labor Department, Galíndez ultimately became too sympa-
thetic to the workers' cause to suit Trujillo. He may
also have had ties with the anti-Trujillo underground.
Feeling threatened, he left in 1946 and settled in
New York where he pursued a doctorate in political
science and served on the faculty of Columbia University. Meanwhile, Galíndez devoted much of his
time to a methodical accumulation of information
about Trujillo's dictatorship. The spirited account
here reproduced, first published in one of the Hemisphere's best known and widely circulated journals, is
one of the reasons Professor Galíndez was marked as
a prime enemy of Trujillo's state. His doctoral dis-

* Jesús de Galíndez Suárez, "Un reportaje sobre Santo Domingo," *Cuadernos americanos*, Vol. LXXX (March-April 1955),
pp. 37-56. The excerpts given here come from pp. 37-51. Translated and reprinted by permission of *Cuadernos americanos*.

sertation, completed early in 1956, was a sober and
damning analysis of "The Era of Trujillo." [1] Nego-
tiations for its publication in English had begun
when, on the night of March 12, 1956, Jesús de
Galíndez mysteriously disappeared from his apart-
ment in Manhattan never to be seen again by his
friends. Subsequently, well-publicized investigations
of the mystery indicated that Dominican agents ab-
ducted, drugged, and then smuggled Galíndez out of
the United States as an "invalid" aboard a light plane
piloted by a young American flyer, Gerald Murphy,
who later disappeared. Once in the Dominican Republic, Galíndez was apparently murdered.

Jesús de Galíndez, who "knew more about Trujillo
than anyone else in the whole world" (according to
his Columbia colleague, Frank Tannenbaum), may
have done more to discredit Trujillo after his death
than while alive. No incident in the modern history
of Spanish American dictatorship has been more of
an international *cause célèbre* than his macabre murder. Like the Ecuadorian journalist Juan Montalvo
(1832-1889) who exulted at the assassination of the
dictator Gabriel García Moreno in 1875 by saying,
"My pen killed him," the shade of Jesús de Galíndez
may have taken grim satisfaction over the riddled
body of Rafael Trujillo in 1961.

I arrived in the Dominican Republic at the end of 1939
as a consequence of the Spanish Civil War in which I
had fought as a good Basque in the loyalist army. The
majority of our refugees went to Mexico; but I was only
twenty-four, with an excess of illusions, and reluctant

---

[1] A Spanish version has been published: Jesús de Galíndez
Suárez, *La era de Trujillo; un estudio casuístico de dictadura hispanoamericana* (Santiago de Chile: Editorial del Pacífico, 1956).

to be one of the nameless mass. I wanted a small country where none of my fellows were going, for there
alone would there be opportunities for me to blaze
a trail in the New World. I had visited the Dominican
legation in Madrid during the days of the siege, and the
memory of some favors extended me gave me the inspiration to present myself at the consulate in Bordeaux
where I acquired the visa which narrowly rescued me
from Europe in the last North American ship. I . . .
stayed in the Dominican Republic . . . for more than
six years; six years during which I came to identify myself with the Dominican people as a brother and had
the opportunity to live under one of the most picturesque
political regimes that has ever existed in the world.

The Dominican Republic divides with Haiti the central island of the Antilles. In 1492 Columbus was capti-
vated by its natural beauty, and from its shores later on
departed almost all the great discoverers and conquerors.
In its capital, Santo Domingo de Guzmán, there came to
flourish a small viceregal court at the beginning of the
sixteenth century. . . . Later the first Spanish colony in
the New World fell into decay; and the attacks of Drake
and other meddlesome corsairs preceeded the settlement
of rude pirates on its more inaccessible coasts; these
later gave origin to the French colony whose slaves proclaimed a Negro republic at the beginning of the nineteenth century which took the indigenous name Haiti.
Three dates and two bloody wars led the way to Dominican independence snatched successively from Spain in
1821, from Haiti in 1844, and from Spain again in 1865;
finally to suffer yet again in the twentieth century the
occupation of North American Marines from 1916 to
1924. Innumerable civil wars and more than one dictator
spatter her national history over the last century; but at
the same time she is able to pride herself on the oldest
university[2] and cathedral in America, on her abundance
of illustrious writers beginning with the poetess Leonor

---

[2] A matter of debate. The Universities of Mexico City and San
Marcos in Lima have better claims. [ed.]

de Ovando in the sixteenth century, and on the island's luxuriant natural wonders. . . .

But in the last twenty-five years this exuberant and tragic land has offered the observer a curious phenomenon. . . . For the Dominicans who endure it the Trujillo regime is a daily drama which silences lips and oppresses hearts. For alert foreigners the benefactor and his megalomanias are a treasure of incredible surprises which merit divulgence.

I confess that when I applied for a visa for the Dominican Republic I did not even think about who would be the president, so engrossed was I in carving out a new life for myself. My first knowledge of "Generalissimo" Rafael L. Trujillo Molina was acquired accidentally in that same Dominican consulate in Bordeaux. We were waiting in line for our passports to be countersigned in a room dominated by the portrait of an imposing personage wearing a hat with a white plume. One of my companions asked the consul, "Is that your president?" and the consul replied somewhat strangely, "No, he is not the president; he is the benefactor." My friend and I looked at each other uncomprehendingly; but, we thought, shrugging our shoulders and putting our doubts to rest, bah! American doings.

I would soon discover the mystery of that "benefactor." I believe that my first Dominican political lesson was received near the Caribbean Sea at the Christopher Columbus Institute which the first refugees to arrive in the country opened. . . . One of our daily visitors was a creole journalist named Gimbernar . . . who was accustomed to boast of being one of the most faithful "Trujillistas." With a pride incomprehensible to us he bragged of being the only deputy who had resigned "by word of mouth." A few weeks later I heard some other comments no less incomprehensible from the lips of [the rector] of the University . . . on whose *finca* we who were aspirants to the faculty were accustomed to gather. President Peynado was dying and it seemed natural that Vice President Troncoso de la Concha would fill the vacancy; nevertheless, the rector assured us in language which appeared sibylline, "The chief wants me to be the new President, but I have told him that Pipí ought not to resign."

Only some time after was I able to clear up these puzzling mysteries. In benefactor Trujillo's Dominican Republic there are elections, for what they are worth. . . . According to the official election returns . . . in 1952, 100 percent of the voters cast their votes for all the candidates, from the president to alderman including senators and deputies. But Trujillo—*el "jefe" y "benefactor"*—makes them sign beforehand undated resignations of their elected offices. Afterwards, from time to time, he has only to add the day's date to one of these resignations and publish it simultaneously "suggesting" the name of the new congressman in accordance with Article 16 of the Constitution—for of course the Constitution is always applied to the letter—according to which if there is a vacancy in a popularly elected post the chief of the former incumbent's party presents a slate of three names from which the party caucus selects the substitute. In such a "constitutional" way the wirepulling of deputies and senators is an everyday affair. With reason our journalist friend boasted of being the only one who "resigned" by word of mouth, for there are legislators who learn about their resignations when they arrive in Congress without previously knowing what is going to happen. Even worse was the case of the Minister of Foreign Relations who, in the presence of a European Chief of Mission, ordered his Protocol Officer to find out why the newspaper whistle was blowing, then had to suffer the shame of being told that his own resignation "had been accepted."

Don Pipí Troncoso de la Concha finally became president, but later on he also had to give it up. This was one of the funniest episodes of the political operetta which I witnessed in the Dominican Republic. . . . It happened in the general election year 1942. Trujillo had been President from 1930 to 1934 and from 1934 to 1938; in 1938 he decided to take a little trip through Europe and he therefore saw to the election of his lieutenant Peynado, the president who died shortly after our arrival. At the end of the interim government of Vice President Troncoso, all Trujillo's favorites were in a quandary because with the date approaching there were no signs which clearly revealed the new "President." It was only rumored that in this year of 1942 there would be a "fight"; this was because some months earlier the Dominican Republic had gone to war with the Axis Powers and circumstances requiring that there be at least a democratic façade it would seem that to set up another candidate for defeat would be a simple matter. The only difficulty was that under Trujillo there only existed one party, the Dominican Party, boss: Trujillo. Thus any fight would be difficult no matter how well contrived.

An opposition party had to be organized rapidly. And one morning we breakfasted to sensational news: the awaited opposition party had been created, but it was called . . . the Trujillista Party! What's up? We had the answer the following morning; heavy type in the morning press informed us of the incredible news that the President of the National Directive Council of the Dominican Party had applied for admission to the new Trujillista Party and had been admitted at once. That was the signal; and everyone rushed to join the two parties.

For several months we witnessed a volcanic election campaign during which the public functionaries and the would-be bureaucrats scurried from meeting to meeting of both parties. The difficulty was in distinguishing one party from the other because all the orators had but one subject: the most enthusiastic adulation of Trujillo. And we went on not knowing who would be the triumphant candidate and who the defeated.

The first convention was that of the Dominican Party, the traditional. The emotion of the delegates was uncontainable, for it was suspected with good reason that they would be "the victors." Finally there rose to the podium the President of the National Directive Council, the same one who had applied for admission to the opposition party; at last we were going to know the name of the favorite to be elected. But, what emotion! The name which came from his lips as the nominee was none other than that of Generalissimo Dr. Rafael L. Trujillo Molina, benefactor of the country. The ovation was overwhelming; there was no longer any doubt that "they" would be the winners. Immediately there was a debate as to who should constitute the special commission which would communicate the good news, the surprise, to Trujillo. It is said that when the commission arrived at his estate, San Cristóbal, the Chief was taking his morning horseback ride and received the congratulations of the commissioners with an eloquent gesture of modesty: they could drink in celebration but as for *himself* he would continue his horseback ride without excitement, being above such human emotions. The following day the press presented us with a full page headline which said: "I will go on riding" (*Seguiré a caballo*). . . .

"I will go on riding" was from that point on the slogan of the election campaign; the entire country was filled with posters with the equestrian figure of the Generalissimo; and a composer improvised a *merengue* with the symbolic refrain "And I go on riding, said the general." The pinnacle of adulation was reached in an immense billboard . . . in the principal street of the capital city —Ciudad Trujillo, naturally—painted by an Italian jeweler who had until recently been an enthusiastic supporter of Mussolini . . . ; the poster read without the least shame: "I will go on riding—said the Chief. And we will follow you on foot." It need hardly be said that Trujillo was elected president unanimously, for the Trujillista Party hurried to endorse his candidature. Thus ended that peculiar opposition party.

But the operetta did not end here. The elections were in May and the inauguration was to be celebrated in August; there were too many months of anticipation. The President of the Chamber—"antitrujillista" just a bit earlier—hurried to point out how difficult the situation was with the country at war; the Dominicans needed

Generalissimo Trujillo at the helm at once, so it was necessary to find an immediate solution. This was easy;
again the Constitution was brought into the game. On
Monday we read the news that the Minister of War (incidentally, Trujillo's younger brother) had resigned and
that President Troncoso had named Trujillo the Great
for the post; on Tuesday President Troncoso resigned in
an emotional session before both Houses; and, always in
accord with the Constitution, the Minister of War occupied the vacancy provisionally. The rest of the combination was simple; a little afterwards the president of the
Senate, Porfirio Herrera, "resigned" and don Pipí was
elected Senate president; the president of the Chamber
of Deputies, Peña Batlle, "resigned" in his turn, and
Herrera was elected Deputy President; Peña Batlle was
named Minister of the Interior, his predecessor going on
to occupy some other post which I have forgotten, and so
on successively. What I cannot be precise about is who
was the functionary who resigned from everything and
was left without a job in this beautiful "constitutional"
arrangement. . . .

All these memories which pile up as I write I became
aware of little by little. . . . Already that muddy vision
of the consulate in Bordeaux, the portrait in white plum-
age, seemed far removed. Now I was coming to know
the Trujillo of flesh and blood; and many other things
besides. Since I arrived in the country, I was able to ad-
mire the beautiful, multicolored neon sign which "President" Peynado rushed to have erected on his house the
day he was "elected": "God and Trujillo." Advertise-
ments for the Lottery proclaimed: "Be rid of poverty;
Trujillo forever." The capital city had had its name
changed from that which Columbus had christened it to
that of Ciudad Trujillo; it was located in Trujillo Province, and that which adjoined was named Trujillo Valdés
(in memory of papa); there were also provinces called
Benefactor, Libertador, San Rafael . . . the highest
mountain had been rebaptized Trujillo Peak. It was incredible the notoriety reached by that man. Above all

for me the best continues to be the sign which I saw on
the door of the Nigua insane asylum: "We owe everything to Trujillo."

How did this glorious operatic "generalissimo" appear?
One of his many genial traits was that he won all his
ranks without having fought in any campaigns. . . . His
official history began in the years of the U. S. Marines'
occupation of Santo Domingo; a young man from San
Cristóbal named Rafael L. Trujillo was one of the few
Dominicans who prepared himself to enroll in the ranks
of the National Guard created in order to maintain
order by the Army of Occupation. On retirement in
1924, Trujillo boasted the rank of captain; and in the
Treaty of Evacuation it was stipulated that the officers of
that Guard would go over and become officers in the
new National Police. Captain Trujillo made a rapid
career, with his native intelligence and North American
training; soon he was Chief Colonel of the Police, which
he reorganized completely with officers in whom he had
confidence; and by 1927 he had become General in
Chief of the recently created Army. Then he had his
chance. Since 1924 the President had been the old caudillo of the past civil wars, General Horacio Vásquez,
against whom some forces from Cibao in the north of the
island revolted. . . . General Trujillo hurried to reaffirm
his loyalty to President Vásquez and advanced with his
forces from the capital in order to combat the rebels; but
secretly he had conspired with the latter and may have
been their leader from the beginning, so that the rebels
peacefully occupied the capital while Trujillo's troops
remained inactive "unable to find the enemy"; President
Vásquez had to flee the country. . . . Months later Trujillo was elected president after an electoral campaign in
which the police, whom he had reorganized, were much
more effective than political rallies; and not long afterwards all his collaborators who might have put him in
the shadows were purged: Vice President Estrella Ureña
was lucky enough to end up exiled in the United States;
but another member of the Provisional Cabinet . . .
was simply assassinated.

Thus began in 1930 the "Glorious Era of Trujillo." . . . It is an era which is carefully acknowledged in official documents and public buildings. For instance, a law issued by a ministerial official must be dated on such and such a day in 1955, 112th year of Independence, 89th of the Restoration, and 25th of the Era of Trujillo. . . .

The human side of this political personage is most interesting and worthy of a novel. . . . He has been married three times; the first appears to have occurred before his star had risen high in the zenith, and the light mulatto characteristics of his famous daughter Flor de Oro perpetuate the memory of a wife discarded when General Trujillo judged it necessary to have a more presentable Señora Trujillo. The second did indeed belong to high society, but she did not satisfy the new President's ideal of beauty; whereupon, in order to marry a third time, he did not hesitate to change the divorce laws. . . . Later the law was modified again because Trujillo lacked a male heir. He sought to acknowledge as his the illegitimate boy born to his third wife a little while before her divorce from a Cuban who denied the child's paternity. Years later Doña María de Trujillo wrote a most curious newspaper column on Sundays which bore the title "Moral Meditations."

This son is the famous "Ramfis." . . . At nine years of age he was named Brigadier General, which for a time provoked widespread rejoicing from everyone. When he reached fourteen, the newspapers duly told us that he had renounced his general's commission in order to begin a military career from the beginning. . . . The [subsequent] letters of congratulation from any number of Secretaries of States, senators and deputies . . . sought to proclaim such an act as a model to be imitated by Dominican youth.

Well, the resultant model could not be anything else but encouraging to the youth of whatever country because new cadet Trujillo climbed rapidly, one by one, all the ranks in the army until he became general at twenty-three. . . . At the same time he took his doctorate in law and obtained the highest decorations of the Orders of Christopher Columbus, Juan Pablo Duarte [a hero of Dominican independence in 1844], and even Trujillo. . . .

Trujillo has a third legitimate child, who was baptized Radamés, who was a colonel, I believe, at seven or eight years of age. [The Benefactor's] younger brother, Héctor, is a general in the army and currently President of the Republic; another brother is brigadier general *honoris causa* and owns a radio-television station; another brother who died—a suicide—also had the rank of general. One brother-in-law is a retired major general, another holds high rank in military aviation, and a third administered the Lottery until a short time ago. . . .

Trujillo's enemies are accustomed to speaking of his reign of terror. The cases which they mention are perfectly true, and I have had occasion to know personally some of the most recent victims. But his most powerful weapon is hunger. Nothing can be done in the Dominican Republic without demonstrating not only that one is not an enemy of the Government but also that one is its avid supporter. Any official petition, including passport applications and import declarations, contains a line for the inclusion of the number and date of one's membership in the Dominican Party. Even the closest favorites know they are at the mercy of the merest caprice; and Trujillo enjoys proving that they are dependent upon that caprice. It is as easy to ascend to the highest offices as it is to be left destitute and even end up in prison.

I recall some cases in point. . . . In 1944 the man who had been Ambassador to the United States was transferred back home with the high position of Advisory Ambassador to the Secretariat of Foreign Relations. When this happened, we were about to celebrate the First Centenary of the Republic and all the ambassador's wife's friends knew that she had brought with her all the dresses necessary for the celebration, and the many receptions and parties. Well enough, but just two weeks before the beginning of the celebrations, Ambassador Troncoso was suddenly dismissed from office so devastatingly that there was no doubt that he had suffered total political disgrace, he was not even "elected" deputy as is the custom when the disgrace is partial. It need hardly be said that he remained isolated at home during the weeks of rejoicing and not even his friends dared invite him to private receptions. Ah, but as soon as the celebrations had ended he was named a member of the Cabinet, I believe as Secretary of the Treasury. In short, the ambassador had been punished by missing the Centenary as a naughty child is punished by missing his dessert. The worst of the matter is that he accepted the new position. . . .

Such political disgrace suggests other complications. In Trujillo's Dominican Republic there is a scale of value for disgrace: A [deposed] minister might expect election as a senator, or, further down, a deputy; still worse he might be left with just the automobile and house the Chief had given him in bonanza days or disgraced further by walking on foot through the streets. A major fall from grace meant complete retirement from public life and real difficulty in gaining any sort of living. It is well to remember that but few ended up in jail; it was usually enough to crack the whip.

After so many years, almost everyone has become accustomed to a life of uncertainty. Punishment or promotion is accepted with the same resignation. A member of the Trujillo cabinet told me in a fleeting moment of confidence and of personal irony that the Chief had made "a flock of tame sheep" out of the Dominican people. But from time to time someone blows up and contrives to escape into exile where he joins the ranks of the "revolutionaries." Then the whip descends on his relatives, some of whom hurry to sign all the necessary documents to disavow the traitor, often publishing a statement to that effect in the newspapers; if they do not the vengeance which cannot reach after the exiles reaches them. . . .

[With respect to communism in the Dominican Republic] it is well to give our attention to the eloquent parody on democracy carried out by Trujillo in 1946. World War II had just ended and many dictatorships were toppling; it was *à la mode* to "democratize." In the Dominican Republic this was easy; it was enough for the President to give the order.

The process had actually begun in December 1941 when the Japanese attacked Pearl Harbor. Within a few hours the news spread through the capital that the Dominican Republic was going to declare war on the Japanese Empire. . . . Curious as to how war is declared I went to the Chamber of Deputies where all the lawmakers were gathered ready to vote with their accustomed unanimity. But hours passed and the ceremony was not begun. This was because Don Pipí was president rather than Trujillo and he had to wait for cabled instructions from the benefactor who was in the United States. . . . Finally the cable arrived, the President sent his message to Parliament requesting their approval in order to declare war, the senators and deputies voted "yes" (including those who had been Germanophiles the day before), and the President signed the declaration of war on Japan. But then arose the major problem: to whom should the declaration of war be read? In Ciudad Trujillo there was no Japanese diplomat. It was finally necessary to rout out of bed a poor Dominican merchant who had the bad luck to be an importer of Japanese goods and also, as a courtesy, an honorary consul. This astonished fellow listened to the solemn declaration of war before he was hauled off by the police as a "suspicious person." Two or three days later we were also at war with Germany and Italy.

And the war was won. Trujillo was one of the victors, one of the champions of democracy. It was then that the "democratization" of the regime really began. . . . In 1946, Trujillo sent an agent to Cuba in order to interview the exiled Dominican Communists there, among them Periclito Franco. The Dominican Government of-

fered them guarantees that they could reorganize pub-
lically in the Republic. The Communists accepted, several
of them returned to the country, and the so-called Popular Socialist Party was for a time the only opposition
party whose activities and propaganda were tolerated.
. . . I do not know how fully the Communists took advantage of this opportunity, for I left the Dominican
Republic at the beginning of 1946; but Trujillo's moves
were clear from the beginning: by the eve of the 1947
elections he could confront the country saying that her
only enemies were the Communists and that he was disposed to save the Dominican Republic from the Communist danger. . . .

This time Periclito ended up in jail with all those de-
ceived youngsters, Communists and non-Communists,
who had fallen into the trap. But "democratization"
went right on. The elections of 1947 were the only ones
during the Trujillo era which saw a "struggle" between
three presidential candidates: Trujillo the Great, Don
Fello Espaillat (who was Secretary of Economy before
he was ordered to join the nominal opposition), and
Panchito Prats as representative of a flaming Labor Party.
. . . A few days before the election all of the deputies
published their support for the saviour candidate; . . .
the list included none other than the "labor" candidate
Panchito Prats. It need hardly be said that Trujillo won.
Some time later, Panchito returned as an "elected"
deputy of the official Dominican Party; Don Fello Espaillat simply died.

Today [1954-1955] the Dominican Republic has returned to its normal course. No longer is it necessary to
"democratize." The Dominican Party (chief: Trujillo)
is the only one; its "anti-Communism" is the topic of the
day; the presidency is proudly occupied by the youngest
brother in the dynasty; and Trujillo is again the benefactor . . . as in the days of my arrival in the Dominican Republic.

Germán Arciniegas

IS A CAUDILLA POSSIBLE?
THE CASE OF
EVITA PERÓN*

Although the influence of Eva María Duarte de
Perón (1919-1952) waned almost as suddenly as it
had appeared, her powerful role in Argentine politics
between 1945 and 1952 makes it imperative that we
question the assumption that caudillismo is a man's
prerogative. The following critical biographical sketch
was written by the Colombian cosmopolite historian
diplomat Germán Arciniegas shortly before Eva
Perón died of cancer. Too close in time to render
Olympian judgment on Evita, Arciniegas, nevertheless, has successfully intertwined her story with that
of Colonel Perón's elevation to power in 1945 and
revealed how much she contributed thereafter to the
essence of *Peronismo.*

Like the double eagle on the Hapsburg coat-of-arms, the
two heads of the Argentine dictatorship are joined in a

* Germán Arciniegas, *The State of Latin America*, translated by
Harriet de Onís (New York: Alfred A. Knopf, Inc., 1952), pp. 27-
46. Excerpts given here come from pp. 27-39, 41-46. Reprinted by
permission of Alfred A. Knopf, Inc.

single body. In this case the body is the firm of *Eva-Perón, Incorporated.* Perón is just a name. There is nothing unique about Perón's political personality; he belongs to the genus *dictator.* But Eva, Evita, is *species argentinensis.* She immediately calls to mind Encarnación Ezcurra, the wife of Juan Manuel Rosas. Rosas belonged to the type of Latin-American dictator which flourished in the nineteenth century, and for more than twenty years he ran Argentina, to quote one of his opponents, "as though it were his ranch." Juan Manuel and Encarnación ruled jointly, enjoying all the delights of absolute power and pursuing a policy of terror without let or hindrance.

Rosas considered himself the Number One *gaucho* of Argentina, a role Perón enjoys too. Rosas maintained himself in power by terror. Argentines were either pro-Rosas or "traitors to their country." His picture was placed on the high altar in the churches, and people used to pull his carriage through the streets of Buenos Aires to show the measure of their devotion. Men wore red vests, and women a red rosette in their hair, because red was the dictator's color. It finally reached the point where the fronts of the houses were painted red. A modern admirer of Rosas, one of those who helped to prepare the way for General Perón's seizure of power, wrote a fulsome biography of the "Restorer of the Laws," as Rosas liked to be styled, in which he calls him a genius for having invented the forerunner of the Gestapo and the Ogpu, which was established in Buenos Aires over a century ago under the name of the *mazorca.* The *mazorca* was a highly efficient system of spying, informing, and punitive action. It has to its credit the first use of red pepper enemas to soften up recalcitrant opponents, a Creole formula that anticipated the castor oil of the Fascists. It was Rosas's ambition then, as it is Perón's today, to have a powerful, united Argentina to defy not only its neighbors, but other powers. To achieve this perfect union Rosas hit upon a very simple device: not to leave a single adversary alive.

Rosas's right arm in carrying out and perfecting this

policy was his wife. There are episodes in the career of Doña Encarnación so similar to those in the life of Evita Perón that it almost makes one believe in the theory of reincarnation. It is impossible to consider the distaff side of Argentine politics without recalling Encarnación. Only then does one understand the opposition of any thinking Argentine to the idea of another woman in the driver's seat. No one can fail to shudder at the thought of a repetition of those barbarous incidents of the nineteenth century.

Manuel Gálvez, novelist and biographer of Rosas, an authority on the subject who makes no effort to conceal his admiration for the dictator, has painted Doña Encarnación in the following terms:

> The wife of the governor of Buenos Aires was all-powerful. Two years before, while her husband was on his way back from a campaign against the Indians, she had engineered against the government of [Juan Ramón] Balcarce a revolution that swept him from power. She manipulated generals and politicians, journalists and ward-heelers, distinguished men like Tomás Guido, and rabble-rousers. Determined, aggressive, fearless, shrewd, and possessed of boundless energy, she had accomplished what none of Rosas's friends was able to do. In her own home, ordering this one, upbraiding the other, insulting, goading, and keeping a watchful eye on all, she organized the revolution known as that of the Restorers, and brought down the government of General Juan Ramón Balcarce. This achievement, which, because it was the work of a woman, and moreover, a woman of the upper class, was unique in our history, conferred on Encarnación a renown and prestige without parallel. From then on she was known as "the heroine of the Federation."

At her home in Biblioteca Street, Encarnación gave audience every morning. Men and women came to see her, for the most part those of the upper and middle ranks of society. The lower classes were looked after by her sister María Josefa in her house in Potosí Street, and these gatherings, which were frequented by Negresses, some of whom were fortune-tellers or pretended to have supernatural powers, were known as Witches' Sabbaths. Encarnación's visitors came looking for jobs or trying to ingratiate themselves with the government. They also acted as informers. All those with an axe to grind knew that Encarnación's influence was supreme with Rosas, who loved her passionately, a sentiment she completely requited. Neither his most intimate friends nor his generals, not his brothers, his parents, or even his daughter Manuelita, could get from Rosas what Encarnación could. She was flesh of his flesh and bone of his bone. She was a masculine type of woman and a complete despot. An unquenchable flame burned in her large, beautiful dark eyes. Her strong, firm features reflected the energy of her nature, which flinched from nothing, not even violence. She hated Rosas's enemies with an implacable fury perhaps even greater than his own. . . .

Before October 17, 1945—a hallowed date in the annals of *peronismo*—Evita was only a bit radio actress in Buenos Aires. After that date she became a world figure. Her trip to Europe in 1947 was one of the events of the year. General Franco sent a plane in which a suite befitting royalty had been installed so that she could travel in state on her visit to Spain. There she was cheered at bullfights, in the public squares, in the streets, by crowds larger than those which gathered to greet Franco. She was presented with a collection of costumes from the different regions of Spain which might have graced a museum. Franco was eager to show the world that he had an ally in Argentina, that his doctrine had spread beyond the Atlantic, and that his dream-empire of Hispanidad was on the way to becoming a reality.

At that moment Evita (who is really a beautiful woman), overblown with her new-found power and her sense of triumph, began to behave like a pampered child. She was late wherever she went, keeping ministers, ambassadors, and avid spectators cooling their heels for two or three hours. They were lent patience by the fact that at that moment Argentina was loading wheat for shipment to Europe. On one occasion Evita ordered the special train in which she was traveling held for several hours while her maids put the finishing touches on her toilette.

In Rome the Argentine Embassy spent a quarter of a million dollars furbishing up the house to receive her. The whole world buzzed over her visit to the Pope. All sorts of stories and anecdotes (many of them of the smoking-car variety) were told about her, as always happens with persons in the public eye. Protest meetings were organized, which the police had to put down with a firm hand. Europe was saying that Perón represented a neo-Fascism and that key posts in his government were held by high former Nazis or Fascists. In Switzerland Evita's automobile was pelted with tomatoes. The King and Queen of England used the pretext of a visit to Scotland to avoid receiving her. In Rio de Janeiro, at the meeting of the Foreign Ministers of America, when Evita walked into the assembly the president dismissed the session as a tribute to her and as a way to avert the possibility of her making a speech.

All these are the natural ups and downs of a public career that began by breaking all traditions. The cards seemed stacked against Evita. Argentine society, than which none is more aristocratic or exclusive, would have refused to admit a person of her background if she had attempted to enter it. The men of that country are not in the habit of taking orders from a woman. The president's wife traditionally plays a purely decorative role in the social life of Buenos Aires.

Shortly after Perón's inauguration, a newsreel showing the transfer of power was exhibited in the Argentine Naval Academy. Evita was prominently in the foreground. The students began to cough and clear their throats. The film was halted, the lights were turned up, and the commandant ordered those who had begun the demonstration to come forward. A dozen midshipmen stood up. They were expelled from the school and a number of others were severely disciplined. The cadets of the Military Academy pronounced themselves in complete accord with the midshipmen—a thing hitherto unheard of—and a navy officer's uniform was burned from one of the lamp-posts of the Plaza de Mayo in Buenos Aires. Those police who had not been on the alert to forestall this outrage were dismissed from their posts.

It began to be whispered that the army officers were planning to ask the President to curtail the political activities of his wife. Whereupon Perón announced that he was appointing her Secretary of Labor and Social Welfare. And, as the Spanish proverb goes, "The one who doesn't like soup will be served two plates." At the great military parade to honor the Year of San Martín . . . in the reviewing stand with General Perón to receive the troops' salute was his wife.

To understand Evita's rise to power, it is necessary to see her against her early background in the theater world of Buenos Aires. In this field Buenos Aires can hold its own with Paris, London, or New York. The best Spanish, French, Italian, German, and Yiddish companies visit that city and present plays before crowded houses. The Comédie Française plays to an audience as appreciative as that in Paris. Toscanini has directed the orchestra at the Colón Theater, and the opening of the Buenos Aires opera season is a more sumptuous affair than that of the Metropolitan in New York.

Out of all this a tradition has grown up. There are great Argentine actresses: Camila Quiroga and her company a generation ago, Mecha Ortiz and Libertad Lamarque today, who are famous on both stage and screen throughout Latin America. There are comedy stars like Paulina Singermann. The same is true of radio. Success does not come easily in the Argentine theatrical world.

Evita—her name at that time was Eva Duarte—was born in the little town of Los Toldos in the province of Buenos Aires, and spent her early years in the provincial atmosphere of Junín, a town of about 35,000 people. She went to Buenos Aires with the ambition of becoming a radio and motion picture actress, and she achieved it. But she never quite reached the top. Critics said that she was still very young, that she showed promise, that she had a future. . . . The pictures in which she worked have since been withdrawn from circulation. Her salary in radio was very small, though she received a sudden and substantial raise shortly before she rose to her present position. At that time she was going to work at the studio in an official car.

But if Evita's rise in the theater was slow, she was exploring other avenues with great success. She had been making the acquaintance of army officers and learning a great deal about politics. She was carried away by the ideas of Perón, who was already beginning to stand out as a leader in inner circles. The generals were engaged in a relentless conspiracy against the civilian government. They had been trained in the old Prussian school, and were unreserved admirers of the Nazi doctrine. They were bored with their humdrum existence under the command of leaders who wore no uniform, and they thirsted after power. They were on the alert for the opportune moment to bring off a coup. And they tried it once, and again, and again. The political atmosphere was charged with electricity.

Perón, who was the most powerful person in the dictatorship that General Edelmiro Farrell had set up, and who was fifty-three years old, fell head over heels in love with Evita, who was twenty-seven. So many things were happening off-stage at this point that it is difficult to determine just what role the shrewdness and ambition of Evita played in the establishment of the machinery for tooling the new-model Argentina. But she knew that it was the hour of decision for her, and that her whole future hinged on it. She gave up her career as an actress and plunged into politics.

The reasons for the triumph of *peronismo* are not immediately apparent. Was it that in Buenos Aires industrial evolution had completed its cycle, and that in its wake had come social inequalities capable of engendering a revolution? Did Evita Duarte, soon to become Evita Perón, have real influence in the officers' clubs where the deals for Perón's seizure of power were being made? Did the response of the masses come from an actual situation or was it skillfully incubated by Perón and harnessed at the decisive moment by Evita Duarte? Is she only collecting her rightful share of the spoils?

For years the struggle for power in Argentina had been carried on in the higher echelons of politics. The people had had nothing to do with it, had felt no pressing need to make it their concern. The Radical party, which represented the majority of the country, had had its hands tied by the state of siege imposed by the military dictatorship. The Socialists, very strong in Buenos Aires, were still thinking in terms of the theories that had informed their action during the nineteenth century, and had no working plan. But the liberation of France, the fall of Berlin, and the defeat of Japan encouraged public opinion to voice its protest and demand the restoration of civilian government and the return of the liberties suspended by Farrell's *junta*, dominated by Perón. There were great public demonstrations that the police had to curb, not without a considerable number of dead and wounded. The students were a prime factor in arousing the civic conscience, and the dictatorship cracked down on the universities. Sixty-four professors were dismissed from their posts for having taken part in the mourning ceremonies held by the students for their slain companions. Newspapers were closed, and over one thousand persons were jailed on political charges. But there was such a popular awareness that the triumph of the Allies represented the triumph of democracy and liberty that the people gathered in the streets again to demand the end of the dictatorship, that is to say, the ousting of Perón, the vice-president. The movement seemed so irresistible that Perón had to resign and was confined to the island of Martín García.

This was the triumph of the Radicals, the Socialists, of public opinion at large. The leaders had made no special appeal to labor. At this juncture, with uncanny foresight, Perón's friends—among them Cipriano Reyes, leader of the extreme Left, and at the moment one of Perón's supporters, and, above all, Evita Duarte—saw that *peronismo's* hour had come. They visited the packing-houses, the factories, and the slums and egged the masses on to seize power. "Shoes, yes! Books, no!" and "We want Perón! Perón! Perón!" became the election slogans.

A program of such ambitious scope had never been presented to these people before. Perón had raised their wages. He promised to carry out only the people's will. He was going to strip the oligarchy of its wealth, which he would hand over to the people. Evita was busy day and night stimulating with frenzied vehemence the appetite these promises had aroused. Out of all this came the great march of the "shirtless" on Buenos Aires. This was diabolically superior to the march of Mussolini's Black Shirts on Rome, and recalled certain episodes of the French Revolution. The people were briefed thus: we are going to appear just as we are, without washing our hands, in dirty shirts or no shirts at all, so that they will see us as we are, and we will demand that they release Perón.

Preparations began on October 15, 1945, for the March of the Shirtless, which took place on October 17. It was the first great manifestation of the mob hysteria of *peronismo*. It was an impressive sight, arranged with all the fanfare and showmanship that are part and parcel of totalitarianism: huge portraits, flags, posters, slogans. Perhaps the crowd was not so large as that which had assembled to celebrate the defeat of the Axis or to demand Perón's ouster. But it was vehement, vociferous, almost brutal. One of the newspapers of Buenos Aires—which takes inordinate pride in its cleanliness, where even the lowest classes are always well dressed and the poorest child in the public schools wears an immaculate white smock—published a picture of the rally with a jeering caption about the bare-chested workers, the shirtless. The *peronistas* saw their opportunity and made the phrase their own: "Yes, we are the shirtless [*descamisa-*

dos], the underprivileged, who are demanding justice!"
Since then Evita has never once addressed the people
without beginning: "Dear shirtless ones."

It was Evita who unleashed this revolution. She dupli-
cated the feat of Doña Encarnación Rosas, who carried
out the revolution against Balcarce in favor of her husband. After a lapse of one hundred and twenty years,
history repeated itself. For Perón's sake, Evita went
down to the workers' districts and made the acquaintance
of the local bosses. She visited the factories, and each
visit was a one-man show. It was then that Evita found
herself, discovered her true vocation. It was only a step
from this to her rise to power, which she now exercises
without consideration or scruple, demanding unconditional surrender from those who used to be above her
in the social scale.

The march of these political events synchronized with
the climax of the love affair. The March of the Shirtless
took place on October 17, 1945, and on October 26 Juan
Perón and Evita Duarte were married at a private ceremony.

It was the story of Cinderella in modern dress. The in-
significant little screen and radio actress had become one
of the outstanding women of her day. There is hardly a
popular magazine in the world whose cover she has not
adorned. *Time, Life,* and the magazine section of *The
New York Times* have published feature articles about
her. Even though her trip to Europe was not all a bed of
roses, one fact stood out clear: Eva Perón was God's gift
to news agencies. She even has her place among the
heavenly bodies, for Captain Guillermo Walbrecher, director of the Observatory of La Plata, has given the name
Evita to a new star discovered by his keen scientist's eye
and his even keener sense of which side his bread is but-
tered on.

Evita has been transformed from a poor working girl
into one of the most sumptuously dressed women in the
world. Chartered planes arrive regularly at Buenos Aires
with the output of the best Paris designers to keep her
wardrobe up to date. A photograph in *Life* showed her

proudly displaying her collection of jewelry, which is kept in the drawers of a cabinet similar to those used for letter-filing. When, as a girl, she pored over movie magazines, she undoubtedly dreamed of the luxury life of the Hollywood stars. And suddenly she found that all this and more was hers. Although the salary of the president of Argentina is $576 a month, Evita spends $40,000 a year on Paris clothes. She owns newspapers and is the head of the largest enterprise in Argentina: the Eva Duarte de Perón Foundation. Her brother, secretary to the president, has amassed a large private fortune.

The setting in which this new Cinderella has her being is clearly reflected in the following report published in *La Nación* on August 24, 1950, of the gift presented to her by the members of Congress when Evita conferred diplomas and medals on the *peronista* delegates:

"The committee presented her with an artistic diamond bracelet, adorned with fourteen charms of platinum, sapphires, diamonds, and rubies. The charms represented: the national flag, the *peronista* shield, a flower-trimmed ship with her wedding date, the image of one of the shirtless, the dates of the president's birthday and hers, the dove of peace, Negrita, Señora Perón's cherished dog, the national coat-of-arms, the party emblem, the symbol of union, the insignia of the General Confederation of Labor, the name of the recipient, and the façade of the legislative palace. . . ."

Evita today has her hands on the controls of several of the most important branches of the administration. Her closest contact is with labor. [But she also] has the power to determine changes of a very serious nature in Argentina's foreign policy. She holds no portfolio, but she has in her hands, among other things, what in Hitler's Germany was called the Ministry of Propaganda. And, above all, she completely controls the Eva Duarte de Perón Foundation. This Foundation did not come into being by law, but through a decree issued by General Perón. It is not under any council or directors or subject to controls of any sort. It is in charge of hospitals, low-cost housing projects, university developments, kindergartens, homes for the aged, vacation camps. Everyone must contribute to it, and liberally. The industrialist who fails to do so may find himself obliged to shut up shop, as happened to the Massone Pharmaceutical Company and to the Mu-Mu candy factory. . . .

As for Evita's political ideas, they are very simple, almost rudimentary, but clear-cut, direct, and effective. They have brought about a radical change in the national point of view. The whole thing boils down to substituting for government by institutions the personal rule of her husband and/or herself. Where the term "public welfare" was formerly employed, "Evita" is now used. When a worker receives an increase of salary, a student a book, an old person relief; or when a clinic, a hospital, a gymnasium, or a playground is opened, it must be regarded as something done not by state or law, but by Evita or Perón. When wheat is shipped abroad, it is not sent by Argentina, but by Perón. An earthquake damages the city of Cúcuta in Colombia; Evita's airplanes immediately take off to bring Evita's aid to the stricken city, and the grateful city hangs out flags bearing the name of Evita. Help is to be found not in the law, but in Perón. There is fear not of the law, but of Perón. There is only one legal norm: Perón. Little by little the name of Argentina is falling into disuse; everyone speaks of Perón, of Evita. The task of building a nation, with its legislatures, congress, and executive branches, which involved a century and a half of arduous struggle, has now culminated in a single name. Evita repeats the same words every day to drive the point home. She stamps it on the mind of the party. She has imposed it, rubbed the nation's nose in it. Those who have ventured to oppose her, not doing as she wanted or not giving her what she wanted, have paid dearly for their integrity.

Behind this simple, elementary program there is a seething, dangerous passion and an unlimited capacity for work. Her radio training has stood her in good stead; she makes speeches to the nation in factories, in theaters, at public gatherings, before Congress, at banquets, on the national holiday, on Labor Day. Not a Christmas

Eve goes by without a message from her to her "dear shirtless ones" of the General Confederation of Labor, nor a New Year's Eve without her radio greeting to the republic.

Like Perón, Evita is an early riser, and between seven and nine in the morning she reads her correspondence. Then her office hours begin. Hundreds of people are already waiting for her. There are union representatives, working men, women who have come from far-off provinces, one to tell her that she has not the money to pay her rent, another that she needs help for her children, a poor girl that she wants a new dress. Evita receives them all, shakes hands with them all, and each one receives twenty, fifty, one hundred, two hundred pesos in crisp new bills that rustle "Evita" in their grateful hands.

At other times the queue is made up of army officers, ambassadors, and ministers, who often are made to wait two or three hours. It is not an uncommon experience for them to overhear the First Lady in her office describing them in the most unflattering billingsgate.

Evita's reception room never fails to amaze foreign visitors. Argentines are unpleasantly reminded of the audiences held by Doña Encarnación and her sister María Josefa Ezcurra, in Rosas's day.

At one o'clock Evita lunches with her husband. Then she signs her letters, and maps out her program for the afternoon: visits to factories, to Congress, to schools. She is wholly dedicated to her political career, to *peronismo*, and to the *peronista* republic. And she pulls more weight than a president. . . .

In the month of August 1951 attention everywhere was fixed on the [coming November] elections. Once more biographical sketches of Evita appeared in newspapers and magazines all over the world. The ruling couple had set their gigantic publicity machine in motion to keep their names before the public. In Buenos Aires, in the stadium of Luna Park, a children's party was organized in honor of Evita. She was there to greet the children in person and to give them presents, a doll to the girls, a bicycle to the boys. As might have been expected, a horde of children like that which followed the Pied Piper converged on Luna Park to cheer the lady Santa Claus. In this youthful mob, children were trampled to death, suffocated. Evita's Christmas greeting to her faithful is a cake and a bottle of cider. The mails are clogged with these bulky Christmas cards. Could the Argentine nation withstand such temptation?

During the early weeks of the campaign . . . the Peróns . . . cut the [exports] of meat to have food on hand for the two million Argentines who would be arriving to beg them to run. Everything was settled: Perón would be asked to accept the presidency, Evita the vice-presidency. Trains, busses, boats would give free transportation to the *viveros* (the name given to those who shout "*Viva Perón*," which constitutes a fairly lucrative profession). They would be given their meals in Buenos Aires. The theaters and the movies were reserved for them. Never had such a holiday been seen in Argentina. And this would be the final proof of the efficiency of the Perón method of learning the will of the people.

But the two million *viveros* who were expected failed to show up. Not even one million appeared. Figures vary as to the number; some say 250,000, some, 150,000. 250,000 people make up an impressive group, but compared with what had been expected, this was a mere handful. . .

What happened [just before the demonstration] took place behind closed doors. All that is known is that "Comrade Espejo," Secretary of the General Confederation of Labor, played his part without muffing a line: "You, *señora*," he said in his speech, ". . . you, comrade Evita . . . you have been and are our guide . . . you, who in the program of justicialism are a symbol and for the workers the leader and standard-bearer, should accept this new sacrifice. . . ." Evita, on the balcony, in a choking voice, began: "My dear shirtless ones . . . do not force me to do a thing I have never wanted to do. . . . I implore you, give me at least four days to think it over. . . ." "No! No!" shouted the *viveros*. "Right now!"

What had gone wrong? Why this hesitation, this semi-refusal? . . . The Peróns withdrew to the presidential residence to size up the situation. After due deliberation, it was conceded that Eva would have to be scratched. It was a victory for the military. The superhuman moral and physical effort that Evita had made had ended in this. . . . Soon after this Eva Perón was no longer seen on the balcony. She had been taken to a hospital. . . .

Fernando N. A. Cuevillas

A CASE FOR CAUDILLAJE[*]

On August 20, 1948, President Juan D. Perón of Argentina made a speech in which he said: "Fortunately I am not one of those Presidents who live a life apart, but on the contrary, I live among my people, just as I have always lived; so that I share all the ups and downs, all the successes and all the disappointments of my working class people. I feel an intimate satisfaction when I see a workman who is well dressed or taking his family to the theatre. I feel just as satisfied as I would feel if I were that workman myself." [1]

Perón was adept at projecting an image of himself as a leader closely attuned to the emotional life of his people. In this as well as in a multitude of other ways he fitted within the frame of reference described in the following selection as *"caudillaje"* by Dr. Fernando N. A. Cuevillas, a sociologist on the faculty of the University of Buenos Aires during the Perón era. Trained at the University of Madrid, where he completed his doctoral dissertation on the subject of Caudillaje in Spanish America, Professor Cuevillas reflects the thinking of those academicians who still remained on Argentine social science faculties by 1953, seven years after Juan Perón became president.

---

[*] Fernando N. A. Cuevillas, "El regimen del caudillaje en Hispanoamérica," *Boletín del Instituto de Sociología*, Vol. XI (1953), pp. 59-75. The excerpts included here are translated from pp. 60-68, 70-75.

[1] *Peronist Doctrine* (Buenos Aires: n.p., n.d.), p. 87.

In this address to a gathering of Spanish American sociologists, Professor Cuevillas provides a rationale for dictatorship by composing a mixture of political theory, social psychological analysis, and but faintly concealed sychophancy. While Perón is mentioned only once by name, it is well to recall the Perón regime throughout.

In spite of the dubious quality of the author's search for untarnished truth, the typology which Cuevillas employs to explain caudillos and the rejection of liberal democracy as a suitable political theory for Spanish American countries suggest certain aspects of the nature of caudillismo not explored in the other documents.

Caudillaje, or the leadership of men, is a sociological institution which may be observed in all human associations and societies. It probably exists through the accidental differences which exist among individuals. Some are learned, some ignorant; some are predominantly rational and others thoughtlessly willful. . . . Men behave in such a way, each after his own fashion, that some govern and others follow, naturally and without violence and without the necessity of written laws. . . . In fact, these men do not reflect on the bases of their obedience. Those who do are in the minority. And perhaps then they justify such obedience as a fulfillment of natural law . . . for in the final analysis the natural society of men is explained in terms of temperaments, affinities, and sympathies. The relationship which we call caudillaje . . . the subordination of one and the supremacy of the other, reflects the basic order among men. . . .

The bonds of caudillaje are found in individual relationships . . . the husband who leads his wife through life, and thanks be to God that it seems that among us

the husband still commands his spouse.[1] Among friends
there is always one who insinuates his control over the
other . . . the incubus and the succubus. Families also
demonstrate the bonds of caudillaje. . . .

In effect all associations are interdependent and hierarchical. . . . And in a political sense I would use "caudillaje" to apply to that regime which consists of the
personification or incarnation of authority, where he
who governs acts with an extraordinary charismatic moral
ascendancy over his pepole: advising them, guiding them,
leading them paternally. The power of the caudillo is inspired authority before it is juridical authority. Caudillaje
appears as a social institution full of ethical content (political and military control, the authentic totality of
power, the psychic leadership of the governed, the moral
magnetism of the leader's personality) which makes it
most suitable for those States whose political life is determined by the integration of individual and collective
traditional values. . . .

This view of the essence of what we call caudillaje
may be further pursued by some reflections on the sociological institutions which might be associated with the
term caudillo:

1. *The caudillo is not a public functionary.* He is
not a functionary in the modern sense of the official who
must confine himself to the strict fulfillment of this or
that provision of such and such an article of a constitution, who is rigorously controlled by other powers, jealous of his authority and who therefore obstruct his work,
and who is only able to exercise executive power. . . .
The public functionary is the agent of his countrymen
who consider themselves sovereign, a political concept
emerging historically out of eighteenth-century England
and France and which has been adopted by peoples all
over the globe. The caudillo is, on the other hand, both
governor and mandator who leads his people with their
consent.

---

[1] Probably a sly reference to the recent eclipse of Eva Perón as a
force in Argentine life. [ed.]

2. *The caudillo is not a tyrant.*   A tyrant is one who governs for his own benefit or for that of his clique, without justice and, therefore, violently. What in certain Spanish countries is called caciquismo is nothing more than a special brand of tyranny. . . . There is nothing more contrary to the rule of caudillaje in spite of having in common with caciquismo the mere *external forms* of rigid coercion of social conduct. Nothing . . . can justify the tyrant's invasion of justice.

3. *The caudillo is neither despot nor dictator.*   It is certainly not within the essence of caudillaje to govern without a council of state or a national representative legislature. Moreover, there ought to be active, vigorous, opposition groups operating within the caudillo's regime to inspire him to good government. Nevertheless, when a caudillo emerges to clean up an anarchic social and political state, he may feel that it does not suit his purpose to coexist with representatives in a national congress and that he must transform his government temporarily into a dictatorship. But never, not even in the most extreme cases, would he be within the spirit of caudillaje to dispense with the counsel of the wise.

4. *The caudillo is not a rightist ruler.*   Rightist politics and a government of the right are modern concepts . . . which, however, suggest the old conservative monarchies. Cautious in his attitude toward revolution and the left, the rightist leader is downright fearful before the masses. Surrounded by learned men of the elite, the rightist ruler oversees a social and political reality which is profoundly divided and which he restrains more than leads. . . . He conserves the existing social order rather than provides for the common welfare. . . .

5. *The caudillo is not a leftist demagogue.*   As a basic premise . . . I would say that a pure demagogue is incapable of ruling and that no government can be purely demagogic. . . . While it is tolerable for a leader to employ demagogic tactics in order to capture public support, it is impossible to imagine this as a permanent situation because once given over to the caprices and passions

of the masses there will be no acceptance of any form of normal public order.

CAUDILLAJE AS A SOCIOPOLITICAL INSTITUTION

The regime of caudillaje is an entity in what we recognize as that most complex reality, civil society. . . . In this situation the power of leadership is granted naturally to the caudillo by the consent of the community. This is what is called election, which can be either express or tacit. In the ultimate analysis, simple consent is not enough in caudillaje; rather, there must be total adherence, an adherence which is akin to the reciprocal attachment of lovers.

But what form of government or leadership is that of the caudillo? . . . In its essence, caudillaje is a *specific form of monarchy*. Its characteristics include: government by one man who possesses exceptional qualities of leadership and who governs righteously and virtuously, with love, and for life. . . . Above all else, the caudillo . . . is the veritable incarnation of authority. He enlivens those forms which are most conducive to order among his people according to the most cherished national values. The caudillo feels that he is heir to the men of the heroic age; he continues their work and achieves their goals. His successors in government should in turn see in him their inspiration and their teacher.

The caudillo loves his people and their customs; he rewards their services by an indestructible devotion. Celebrities and notables respect him, the humble folk love him, and he serves them both. . . . The caudillo is an authentic aristocrat who understands his social service mission. At the head of his people he laughs with them in their *fiestas* as he cries with them in their sorrows and defeats.

Magnanimous in the sight of all, true to his promises; chivalrous and splendid in so far as is necessary to display the magnificence of the dignity of authority; austere in his private life so as to be above the suspicions of public opinion; liberal and kind with the poor; capable and skillful in the business of government, aware of the force of human passions; a student of the psychological qualities of his subjects so that he may be their educator.

A soft word of understanding . . . a rough gesture of disapproval, a shout of indignation, an opportune speech, an *abrazo* for the faithful, a special ceremony for the learned, a show of manliness for the gathered military, a gift for the diplomat, a suave display of gallantry for the politician's wife, and, above all, a capacity for work bound up in and dedicated to the public welfare which he associates with his own: these are the multiple instruments which the caudillo must use to maintain his principate. For the caudillo is, indeed, the prince, who like the Roman emperors, the medieval monarchs, the leader of the modern Spanish state . . . enjoys an apotheosis for he is the first in work, the first in self-sacrifice, the first in glory. The last of these is, surely, the reward which the people owe in exchange for the first two. . . .

The roots of the caudillo's moral leadership and the ethical adherence of his people, which is the formal base of his regime, is without doubt based in psychology. In this regard . . . the prestige of the caudillo can only be maintained through a permanent and subtle vigilance. . . . He must always represent the incarnation of the dominant cultural principles of his society and of his times. . . .

CAUDILLAJE IN SPANISH AMERICA

In order to understand the caudillo in Spanish America we might recall the poetic and politic definition coined by the Spanish youth leader José Antonio Primo de Rivera[2] when he spoke of "The Hero as Father." The

---

[2] José Antonio Primo de Rivera was the son of Spain's dictator in the 1920's who founded the fascist Falange Party in 1933. He was tried and executed by the Republicans in November, 1936, and thus became a martyr for the Franco forces in the Spanish Civil War (1936-1939). [ed.]

phrase suggests a whole theory of sociology and politics . . . caudillaje is a new form of leadership which must surely be a reaction against the depersonalization of power associated with liberal rationalism; while there is much to adhere to in rationalist doctrine, we cannot agree with its impersonality but must affirm instead the charismatic personality of the leader.

It is almost impossible to explain the history of Spanish American social and political institutions without understanding something of what is meant by caudillaje. There has not been a Spanish American country which has not had her Artigas, her Portales, her Santa Cruz, her Sandino, or her Rosas. In the wise words of a great Spanish American leader, "The ideal of fortunate government should be that of the paternal autocrat who is intelligent, impartial, and indefatigable, who is energetically resolved to make his people happy. . . ."

In Spanish America nature, powerful, rich, and hostile, has imposed its norm on her governors. It has been useless for the liberal idealists to try to see social realities as they are not and as they cannot be; for Spanish America counts only among her eponymous heroes the great caudillos. They are her popular heroes, beloved by the humble people. . . . Whether we like it or not, our nations prefer and will only tolerate democratic monarchy as a form of government. . . . It was through the constant efforts of the caudillos that the political independence of our countries was secured against the will of those ideologists who sought enlightenment from foreign forces. . . .

The caudillo in our cultural world presents himself as *founder* or as *restorer* of a past splendor. Those who came first were those who set before us the collective goals and limitations. A prime example was Simón Bolívar, Liberator, Protector, Father of the Nation, and President . . . an authentic "natural monarch" and leader of the people. . . . In his message to the Bolivian congress, explaining the political constitution which he had drawn up for that nation, Bolívar sought, in effect, to legalize caudillaje when he said:

The President of the Republic shall come to be in our constitution like the sun, fixed in the center, giving life to the universe. This supreme authority ought to be perpetual, because in those systems without hierarchies there must be, more than in others, a fixed point around which the magistrates, the citizens, and all the elements may revolve. Give me a fixed point, says the ancient, and I will move the earth.

For Bolívar this fixed point was the life-term president; in him all our order was to be concentrated without fear that he would abuse it. . . .

Finally, in Argentina . . . caudillaje has become fact since it was legalized under the democratic forms of the Constitution of 1949. The caudillo . . . is the expression of what his country thinks and values. . . . Between caudillo and people . . . there is a mutual relationship. . . . And this has prevailed in Argentine history during the regimes of the three national caudillos: Rosas, Yrigoyen, and Perón. They, who are true reflections of the life of my people, drew close and bound themselves to us through their personal ideals, paternal power, and sense of mission in three different epochs. What has made them the more closely attached to us has been their attitudes in defense of national sovereignty, their consultation of the national will through elections, and their heartfelt attachment to the mass of citizens. . . .

Norman A. Bailey

THE UNITED STATES
AS CAUDILLO*

The role of the "Colossus of the North" in Hemispheric relations has long been the focus of much scholarly and polemical writing. Critics of the United States' role in Latin America have heaped blame on her for her use of Dollar Diplomacy, the Big Stick, the Marines, and other more subtle forms of intervention. Much has been made, for example, of the unwitting efforts of U. S. Marine Corps cadre to train such future caudillos as Anastasio Somoza and Rafael Trujillo in military science during the occupation of their respective countries. Furthermore, advocates of democracy on both sides of the Rio Grande have excoriated the tendency of the huge northern republic since World War II to "coddle dictators" provided that these strong men assume an ardent anti-Communist position. Whatever the extenuating circumstances in the past and the policy alterations in the future, the rising North American influence and, one must add, the fall of many Spanish American dictators cannot be denied.

In the following essay, the importance of the United States in Latin American relations is viewed

* Norman A. Bailey, "The United States as *Caudillo*," *Journal of Inter-American Studies*, Vol. V (July 1963), pp. 313-324. Excerpts given here come from pp. 313-316, 318-324. Reprinted by permission of the *Journal of Inter-American Studies*.

from quite a different, indeed unusual, perspective. It may be argued that a study of the personalist dictator should concentrate upon the phenomenon of the leaders themselves. However, Prof. Norman A. Bailey, who teaches Political Science at Queens College, offers an intriguing interpretation of Latin American responses to the United States which may enlarge one's understanding of the psychological atmosphere which has favored the caudillo, *qua* personalist ruler, in many parts of Spanish America for many years. His interpretation, also, suggests by comparison something of the benevolent and protective role which the individual caudillo is expected to play.

Latin American international behavior has always seemed puzzling to the policy-makers of Washington, but perhaps never quite as incomprehensible as in connection with the [1962] Cuban missile crisis. On various occasions, notably during the San José and Punta del Este Foreign Ministers' Conferences, the United States had attempted to obtain some concerted action against the aggressive and subversive activities of a Communist-dominated Cuba. The response of the Latin American nations ranged from lukewarm to frigid, and the maximum that the U.S. was able to obtain (and that by a bare two-thirds vote) in the way of anti-Cuban action, was the expulsion of Cuba from the Organization of American States, a step which one must assume was greeted by the Cuban leaders with something less than total consternation. Perhaps even more disturbing, the six nations which refused to vote in favor of even this feeble step included the largest and most important of the nations of Latin America: Brazil, Mexico, and Argentina. At the same time, anti-Yankee sentiment seemed on the rise among the populace at large, and almost weekly riots and demonstrations in support of Cuba took place in one city or another of the region.

Following President Kennedy's October 22, 1962, speech announcing that Russia had established missile bases in Cuba and that the United States would maintain a blockade of the island until the bases were dismantled, panicky directives went forth from Washington to U.S. embassies, consulates, United States Information Agency offices and other installations in Latin America, to prepare for severe rioting in response to the U.S. initiative. At the same time the Council of the OAS was convoked with the expectation that the abstentions of Punta del Este could be cut down to four, with Ecuador and Argentina joining the other nations in condemning the Soviet military moves and backing the blockade.

Whereupon surprises two and three of the Cuban affair occurred. The Council of the OAS voted unanimously and enthusiastically to back the American blockade and condemn Soviet aggression, and with the exception of La Paz, there was not a single important anti-U.S. demonstration or riot in any part of Latin America, whereas in some cities there were sizeable pro-U.S. manifestations. Even in La Paz, anti-Yankee rioters were vigorously opposed by a group of apparently equal size demonstrating in favor of the United States.

Despite their seeming contradiction, none of these events should have caused surprise in Washington. That they did, and that similar occurrences in the past have met with a similar incredulous and unprepared response indicate fundamental misconceptions concerning the political reactions of the Latin Americans.

THE PATRÓN-CAUDILLO MENTALITY

Since the 1930's, the approach of the sentimentalists in the field of Latin American affairs has been to advocate a program along the following lines: "In essence, this policy should be threefold: an abandonment of the attitude of taking Latin America for granted; a general

position favoring democracy against dictatorship in the
New World; and a program of real economic cooperation." Statements such as this are legion, and as far as
they go there is nothing wrong with them. They are,
however, woefully inadequate, because they totally ignore the power aspects of the relations between the
United States on the one hand and Latin America on
the other.

The "patrón" mentality, developed through centuries
of feudal economic relationships and paternalistic religious concepts, is a pervasive one throughout Latin
America. Although the processes of modernization and
industrialization have begun to make inroads into this
psychological tendency, they have not reached all of
Latin America, and even where they have been strong
their effect has been limited, and in some cases, through
social atomization, have in the short run simply intensified the frustrations of people used to the *patrón-peón*
relationship.

In provincial and national spheres, the *patrón* mentality of economic and social life is carried over into what
we may call the "caudillo" mentality. As with the local
patrón, the *caudillo* has not only authority but responsibilities, and is expected to be benevolent in his dis-
charge of those responsibilities, while at the same time
being firm and efficient in fulfilling them. "Strong" but
benevolent leadership is the ideal of the Latin American
in the national sphere. He is not, of course, a masochist,
and if the government or *caudillo* attacks his liberties or
what he considers his private concerns, he will resist. At
the same time a "weak" government, no matter how
benevolent and well-intentioned, is despised and ob-
structed, especially if it is not, in the individual's opinion, fulfilling its responsibilities.

This psychology is carried by the Latin American nations into the international sphere. They are perfectly
aware of their disabilities in the world arena and their
essential weakness. They expect to be benevolently protected and will as actively seek such protection as they
will fight back against their "protector" if they feel it is

interfering with their internal affairs. But precisely because they are preoccupied with their internal problems, which are manifold, they are not in the slightest interested in being asked to share in the responsibilities of the international "caudillo."

Why have these aspects of Latin American psychology been so largely ignored or misconceived? One reason may be the natural tendency to hypostatize the nation and to forget that it is an aggregate of individual wills. Thus many who are perfectly aware of the *patrón* and *caudillo* mentalities on the local and national levels do not carry this awareness over into the international sphere. Another reason may be simply a subconscious desire not to recognize the facts, since they clash so violently with the American ethic, causing deep feelings of guilt whenever the United States openly exerts its power in the international arena.

THE INTERNATIONAL CAUDILLOS

Latin America has had two international *caudillos* after the wars of independence from Spain and Portugal. During most of the nineteenth century, Great Britain fulfilled this role. After initial abortive attempts to grab portions of South America from the grasp of decadent Spain, and despite later depredations in the Caribbean, Great Britain was an almost perfect *caudillo*, protecting Latin America *in its own self-interest* from the other European powers, with a policy at once effective and highly predictable.

In 1895 this caudilloship passed from Britain to the United States. Although in power terms not inferior to Britain and later much more powerful, the *caudillo*-relationship has not been as satisfactory since 1895 as before. The United States is perhaps a little too close for comfort, and its power perhaps a bit too overwhelming. More important than this, however, is the extreme unpredictability of U.S. policy, seemingly eternally vacillating between direct intervention and absolute indifference, between power politics and idealism. It is for this reason that U.S. policy seems hypocritical to the

Latin Americans, and its vacillations puzzling and frustrating. . . .

An obscure boundary dispute between Venezuela and British Guiana led to the actual changeover of *caudillos* in the Western Hemisphere. By this time, Great Britain was heavily involved throughout the world and its position was being challenged everywhere. The United States, in contrast, was just beginning to flex its muscles and was about to embark on a new period of imperialism. President Cleveland demanded that Britain arbitrate and Salisbury refused. On July 20, 1895, Secretary of State Olney made his famous and flamboyant declaration: "Today the United States is practically sovereign on this continent, and its fiat is law upon the subjects to which it confines its interposition."

This could not have been a more perfect *pronunciamiento* had it been issued by Juan Vicente Gómez. For the next half-century, the only dispute concerning it would revolve about the questions of to *what* subjects the United States should properly confine its "interposition." After considerable hesitation and the possibility of war, the British yielded in 1896, and the United States replaced Britain as *Caudillo* of the Western Hemisphere. . . .

For a decade following the First World War, the United States seemed determined to follow the interpretations of the Monroe Doctrine and the Olney Declaration enunciated by President Theodore Roosevelt in 1905, in the so-called Roosevelt Corollary. This purported to give the United States the right to exercise an "international police power" in the Western Hemisphere, not as against outside incursion, but within the nations of the Hemisphere themselves. As a *caudillo*, the United States was proving by far too obstreperous, and was distinctly not confining itself to its international responsibilities. . . .

The Good Neighbor Policy, begun under Hoover and carried to fruition by Hull, Welles, and Franklin D. Roosevelt, restored the image of the United States as beneficent *caudillo* just in time to secure substantial

Latin American cooperation in the Second World War. Franklin Delano Roosevelt epitomized the benevolent *caudillo* for the Latin Americans, and the psychological basis of the sentiment can easily be ascertained by comparing the adulation of Roosevelt still practiced in Latin America with a recounting of what he actually did in inter-American relations. In 1960, Alfredo Vítolo, then Argentine Minister of the Interior, told William Benton that Roosevelt had won the confidence of the people of Latin America: "When he came here he was hailed as a world leader." Even avowed enemies of the United States, such as Guillermo Toriello, Arbenz's last Minister of Foreign Affairs, are lavish in their praise of Roosevelt:

> Among the horrors of the tragedy [World War II], the apostolic figure of Roosevelt had illuminated with hope the peoples of the world; hope of universal brotherhood, of freedom from oppression, misery and fear; that, particularly in America there will be no nations of first and second class, but that all will be equal. . . .

Roosevelt's qualities, which made him so perfect a *caudillo*, did not consist primarily in his inter-American policy as such, but rather in a combination, on the international sphere, of firm leadership, acceptance of the international responsibilities, interests, and limitations of the United States, and benevolence. This combination was rewarded with the allegiance of all classes of society in Latin America, and support for the war effort.

In the afterglow of the Roosevelt era and the successful conclusion of the Second World War, the *caudillo-* position of the United States was institutionalized in the Inter-American Treaty of Reciprocal Assistance (the Rio Treaty of 1947), and the Charter of the Organization of American States (1948). By these two instruments, the *Pax Americana* was legitimized, in effect unilaterally, in the international sphere, and through joint efforts and consultation in the sphere of intra-American relations. These instruments have worked remarkably well in settling those disputes with which they were established to deal. On nine separate occasions, from 1948 to 1960, the Rio Treaty has been formally invoked to deal with disputes within the American family. These disputes, involving, at various times, Costa Rica, Nicaragua, Honduras, Haiti, the Dominican Republic, Panama, Peru, Ecuador, Venezuela, and (pre-Castro) Cuba, or exactly half of the independent nations of Latin America, have all been successfully and rapidly settled by the inter-American system. Those cases which have involved the Cold War, however, Guatemala and Cuba, have not been settled through the machinery of the OAS, for the simple reason that that machinery is not designed to deal with such questions, nor could it be, given the psychology of the Latin American nations, a psychology demanding that the United States take care of its own responsibilities, and not try to fob them off on others. To keep Latin America free of the Cold War is one of the responsibilities of the United States, as the Latin Americans see it, and as far as they are concerned, the most important.

The Truman administration fulfilled its international duties adequately, but was not benevolent enough for the Latin American taste. A proper *caudillo* does not ignore you, but constantly has your interests at heart. The Eisenhower régime combined the evil qualities of being Republican (since Franklin Roosevelt, the Latin Americans have connected the Democratic Party with the proper caudillistic characteristic), having at its head a weak leader, and continuing to neglect Latin America. Coupled with the Dulles attempt to draw Latin America into the Cold War and his seeming intervention to halt a social revolution in Guatemala, U.S.–Latin American relations reached a new low. The Nixon trip symbolized the difficulties. To the Latins, Nixon was a malevolent, wishy-washy leader, the worst possible combination. Although greeted at first with enthusiasm, the Kennedy administration soon proved a disappointment in Latin America. Weak leadership seemed to continue, and deteriorate, in the Cold War. Extortion and bribery still seemed to be the only policies applied to

Latin America. The Bay of Pigs fiasco, perhaps the most damaging act the United States has ever been associated with in Latin America, gave the impression of senility and vacillation in American policy. U.S. setbacks elsewhere in the world, coupled with the frantic effort of the U.S. to get the Latin Americans to share responsibility for dealing with Cuba, set Latin America off on a frenzy of wondering if its international *caudillo* was about to abdicate. . . .

The *patrón* or *caudillo* psychology and its effects on the foreign policy of the Latin American countries are fairly straightforward and predictable. They do not want to become involved in the Cold War, except in a formal, ratificatory way. "They feel they have nothing to gain and much to lose from being sucked into the conflicts of the great powers, in which they will only be exploited." These matters are the responsibility of the United States, and it is precisely one of the functions of the international *caudillo* to keep them away from the hemisphere. Attempts to multilateralize this responsibility will be interpreted as signs of weakness. . . .

The United States cannot achieve the affection of the Latin American republics, and by striving for it we will lose their respect. Until October, 1962, it appeared that we were firmly set on a path of sentimentalism and bumbling interference, which led one acute observer of Latin American affairs to comment:

> . . . having discarded the whole body of experience and knowledge which the U.S. community possesses in the Latin American field, in favor of amateur seekers of dramatic effects, it is not likely that the United States now would be able to provide that leadership.

It may have taken Soviet intermediate-range missiles to prove the above observer wrong. It may be that not even that will in the long run produce a more nearly correct understanding of Latin American psychology.

Chester Lloyd Jones

IF I WERE DICTATOR*

No single reading can summarize the diverse materials presented in this volume nor can any article
provide a universally applicable panacea for the problem of dictatorship in Spanish America. This final
selection, written in 1940, has been included for its
provocative rather than its definitive qualities. In it,
Chester Lloyd Jones, an authority on Guatemala, asks
the reader to cast himself in the role of a benevolent
caudillo whose self-appointed and selfless task is to
transform Guatemala, or some similar country, into
a viable democracy. In a review of domestic conditions and attitudes, Jones points out the manifold
difficulties such a dictator would encounter in his attempt to create a government for Guatemala which
would be responsive to a democratic society of free
individuals.

With a quarter century's advantage, the reader may
go well beyond the doubts which Jones himself raises
about the appropriateness of his Anglo-Saxon model.
For instance, through improved communications, especially the transistor radio, the news of the revolution of rising expectations has complicated the task
of the benevolent caudillo far beyond that which
Professor Jones imagined in 1940. Because of the increased demand for rapid social change an essential

* Chester Lloyd Jones, *Guatemala: Past and Present* (Minneapolis: University of Minnesota Press, 1940), pp. 339, 343-350,
351-356. Copyright 1940 by the University of Minnesota Press.
Reprinted by permission of the University of Minnesota Press.

ingredient for democratization, ample time, may simply be absent in many Spanish American countries. Without it, the best of philosopher kings may well fail in his efforts to broaden the base of political power.

It has long been the custom among citizens of the more advanced democracies to decry dictators and all their works. Dictators and dictatorships are incompatible with that equality of political power with which citizens of democracies are assumed to be endowed and with that equality before the law which is accepted as one of the foundations of good government. It is not intended here to call into question the soundness of these convictions. . . .

Instead in the pages which follow it is proposed that the reader consider himself in the position of a dictator—a benevolent dictator—in one of the smaller states of the American tropics, and seek to map out . . . his governmental program. This task, it is assumed, looks toward the creation of conditions ultimately to make possible democratic government, an ideal all the governments of the region profess. It will call for consideration of the physical background of the area, the conditions social, economic, and political now to be met there, and the difficulties that must be overcome in these fields if popular government is to replace arbitrary rule. The reader will be presumed to ask himself "What would I do if I were dictator in Guatemala?" and the discussion will seek an answer to the question. . . .

Climate, national resources, and the composition of the population . . . are elements which the Guatemalan dictator has to accept practically as he finds them. There is [also] another set of factors which can be modified but little by any individual dictator. Though the influence of Spanish blood in the country has been small, the influence of Spanish culture and institutions has been far-reaching. For over four centuries they have set the norms of action, their vigor being but little modified by the rapid changes in other lines in recent years. Most important in the field of politics have been the Spanish concepts of the role of government and the Spanish ideals of liberty.

The adjustments between the two in Latin American countries are difficult for those reared in the democratic traditions of the British and North American democracies to understand. Government, as an Anglo-Saxon views it, is an instrument of the popular will, rising from authority delegated by action of the people, limited in powers, and subject to popular criticism of its acts and definition of its functions by legislatures and courts. In addition, at periodic elections formal judgments are passed on its personnel and performance.

But to the Spaniard, and perhaps even more to the Spanish American, government, especially the executive, is a thing apart with functions to perform which do not involve delegation of powers by the people and responsibility to them in the way that the Anglo-Saxon understands these terms. The powers of the central government in Spain at the time of the discovery and afterward had a proprietary basis and were not subsequently modified by adjustments to bring them toward the standards developed in British areas. Exercise of executive authority in the colonies depended on popular approval even less than in Spain. The New World territories were the patrimony of the king, and moreover there existed in them no "people" with opinions to be asserted as to their rights. Government stood apart with functions of its own; they were none of the people's business.

This concept of public authority is not borne out in the constitutions adopted in the republican period in Spanish America; in many of these the ideas and even the phrases of British, American, and French political philosophies of the time are espoused, reflecting the "delegated" character of the powers of the government and its "responsibility" to the people. Neither do the pronouncements of public men recognize the difference between their positions and those of the executives in democratic governments of the Anglo-Saxon type. Constitutions and public announcements both picture governments as rising from popular authority and as responsible to the people.

Nevertheless the fact that government does and is intended to take a different role in Latin American states crops out repeatedly in certain of the more specific clauses of the constitutions, especially in the articles detailing the wide powers and duties of the executive and in the grants to him of legislative power in crises and in periods when the regular lawmaking bodies are not in session. Nor is there any doubt, if theory be judged by actions rather than words, that the executive continues to act as an agency with powers enjoyed in its own right. It is of course easy for the executive to fall in with this philosophy since it accords with his own interests. Such a course of action interferes not at all with lip service to the other standard.

Nor is it to be supposed that there is among the people at large in Spanish American states a lack of tolerance and even acceptance of the philosophy which grants to governments and to the executive wide freedom of action. In many of the republics, including Guatemala, the indigenous population has never lived under any other system. Government for them has always been imposed. Those who share Spanish ancestry have also the inheritance of Spanish practice, from which they do not easily break away.

Spaniards have never been democrats to the extent of believing that all governments derive their authority from the consent of the governed. They have been individualists or at most sectionalists, ardently devoted to defense of their local rights but content to allow the central government to be controlled by those whose business it is to run it. In tropical America the circumstances of life, especially the diffusion of control over wide, sparsely settled areas, accentuated the acceptability of such a division of authority. If local problems were left to local solution the distant central government might do as it pleased. It was an arrangement giving the flexibility in government that was essential in the varied conditions of the New World.

Emphasis on executive authority fell in also with the Spanish and Spanish American enthusiasm for those who can get things done. If the caudillo, the head man, can do things—above all if he can keep peace within the locality—presumption is in his favor, and if incidental damages occur they may well be forgotten. Nothing succeeds like success and to him that hath shall be given. Ardent patriots who wish themselves to seize the reins of government and others less selfish in their aims may protest against violations of rights and privileges; but doubts, so far as they are shared by the people at large, will be resolved in favor of the government. Business interests both domestic and foreign, unless they fall out among themselves, will support the government if it protects public order. Dictators as a class do not rule cowed peoples but those who tolerate and often approve their acts. They rule by the prestige that comes to accomplishment and because change of rulers may, after all, be only change of rulers.

The Spanish concept of liberty itself is often an ally of dictatorship. No people are more jealous of individual rights than are Spaniards. Those who have been shaped by Spanish political ideals share this outstanding characteristic. The sectionalism which has been and still is characteristic of the mother country has sprung from the resistance of the Spaniard to forces which would press him into a common mold. In spite of his enthusiasm for leaders who can shape men to their wills he stands as one of the world's best examples of individualism. The inability to reconcile the conflict between the desire for freedom of individual expression and the longing for good government, especially good administration, largely explains the Spanish shortcomings in the larger political developments both in the Old World and the New.

Spanish individualism works out in a manner curiously in contrast to the result in countries of so-called Anglo-Saxon traditions. In the latter disregard by government of the inviolable rights is unthinkable. To the citizen maintenance of individual liberties is the first obligation of government, in comparison with which nothing else matters. If liberty and good government clash, government must yield. Failure to respect the citizens' rights results in prompt protest in association with others whose rights may still be untouched, and pressure upon the government to bring about its control or its overthrow—by peaceful means if possible; if not, by force. But Spanish individualism reacts differently though no less logically. If government interferes with freedom of speech or of the press, or with other rights of person or property, the reaction is personal or at most regional. The individual keeps for himself the decision whether it is best to suffer the abuses to which he is subjected or to defend his rights at the risk of more substantial losses. There is less impulse to appeal for support to classes who may later be affected, less urge to pass over local boundaries to appeal to the nation at large to defend itself against the oppression of government, and less response when the attempt is made to cross such boundaries. Only when the cumulation of grievances among large numbers of the population becomes intolerable does the resentment boil over, and then frequently in open revolt rather than in a loyal seeking for reform by lawful means.

This difference in reaction between Anglo-Saxon and Spanish individualism contributes to the contrast between opposition to government in states with one and the other background. In the former group opposition is constant, open, demonstrative, and generalized over the national territory, but in the long run less violent than in the second. In areas of Spanish inheritance it is personal or regional both in its base and in its leadership. It is frequently intermittent and undeclared until

the moment when it bursts out in the revolutions which
have been so frequent in Latin American countries and
often so hopeless.

On the whole this characteristic of the political opposition has left the executive in a stronger position than in
Anglo-Saxon communities. The government may lack the
forewarning which comes with freer airing of discontent
but up to the point when public authority is openly de-
fied a dictator acts as he pleases. Even then if grievances
are local and not too acute they can be crushed before
they become dangerous.

If this analysis be correct then here is another of the
factors confronting the dictator in which his policies cannot bring about quick changes. Geography, the classes
found within the population, and the political habits of
his cocitizens are not putty in his hands. The first element is practically completely beyond his control;
changes in the second, if they occur, will be brought
about by influences he cannot shape. The last he cannot greatly modify though he can support movements
which may in the long run bring significant changes.

The question may be raised whether such changes are
indeed desirable or even possible. It may be argued that
peoples develop the political ideologies suited to their
conditions and that dictatorships exist in Guatemala
and comparable states because they fit local conditions.
This question we pass to consider what plans the dictator may support if he is benevolent and convinced that
the constitutional declarations in favor of a government
on democratic foundations, representative of the popular will and under popular control, mean what the mak-
ers of the constitution declared them to mean and
what the dictator himself announces as his ambition to
make them mean.

What will be the dictator's program if he wishes to see
arise a democracy of the Anglo-Saxon sort? The first call
on his energies he will feel is for the maintenance of
public order. Its protection is the first function of all
governments and a constant and pressing obligation
upon any ruler of as ill-knit a political population as that

of Guatemala. He will be convinced that peace in crises is more important even than protection of the liberties of the citizen, to which no one more fulsomely avows devotion than he. If the choice must be between liberty and order there can be but one decision, and the government must be the judge of what is necessary for the public good. The army and police together must be the right arm of government. If the dictator is weak his program may go little farther than the maintenance of peace. Only the well-entrenched can afford the luxury of more far-reaching plans.

Once the benevolent dictator has established himself firmly in power he will find many other branches of activity subsidiary to keeping order which he would like to promote. Laws affecting public health, public education, transportation, elections, and public finance will all be in the list of his "must" measures. He will feel that theoretically there may be question as to their order of urgency. But under Guatemalan conditions he may conclude that one of the greatest needs is improvement of transportation facilities.

If they are bettered they will facilitate the maintenance of peace and allow already developed areas to market their products to better advantage and to undertake more intensive production. Inaccessible regions will be opened up to exploitation. The national wealth will be increased, and as a result the income of the treasury usable for public improvements will be greater. Indirectly too better communications will help make possible the advances in public health and education which are so sorely needed.

Expenditures to improve the physical well-being of the people the dictator will feel essential. The widespread prevalence of disease saps the national vigor, cuts down the spirit of enterprise, and contributes to the low standard of life upon which the people live.

Reform in education is also imperative, and not only for removal of the handicap of illiteracy, which weighs so heavily upon all but a small proportion of the Guatemalan population. Schools must be established, especially in the rural areas, which will also train the people in more diversified lines of economic endeavor, and thus increase their economic independence.

Greater variety in production will both help raise the standard of life and to some degree, possibly through the making of specialty products, help diversify exports and replace imports by production in lines to which the country is suited.

In the long run the better maintenance of order, better transportation, better health conditions, and better education may bring a social revolution in Guatemalan conditions by both incorporating the Indian in the active citizenry and increasing the opportunities open to the ladino. From them there may arise a better unified nationality, in which the rise of a social surplus above the minimum of subsistence may make possible increasing expenditures by individuals and private associations of cultural nature. These will help raise the standard of civilization in the republic.

When these things are won, or as they are won, there may arise a greater interest in public affairs. The neighborhood horizon which limits the economic and social activities of so large a part of the population will be broadened. Public interest in public affairs will be stimulated and bring more intelligent participation in them. Only by some such steps of progress can it be expected that popular control of government such as obtains in more advanced democracies may arise.

It is clear of course that the success of any such platform as is here given would break down the conditions by which dictators have held themselves in power and which perhaps have made them heretofore the normal instruments of government.

Guatemalan governments have not uniformly supported measures such as are outlined above. All have given them nominal support but frequently little more. When weaker governments have been in power programs have seldom gone farther than the paper stage.

None of even the stronger dictatorships has been in

all phases of its activity benevolent. None has escaped charges of violation of constitutional standards and of being guilty of heinous abuses. While these are regularly reported by the enemies of those in power and reach wide currency as a rule only after their alleged perpetrators are out of office or dead, they are so great in number and so often attested by such credible witnesses that their existence cannot be questioned. Assassinations having all the characteristics of murder, executions without trial or after trial before controlled courts, torture of political opponents and their relatives, the driving of political rivals into exile, and all manner of violations of person and property are reported in such number against both the earlier and more recent dictators that any unqualified defense of dictatorship as an institution of government in Guatemala is impossible.

The dictatorships are to be judged however not only by what they have or have not done but by keeping in mind what has occurred when they have not been in control. When that has been the case constitutional standards have not been observed and violations of person and property have been at least as flagrant as, if not more flagrant than, when strong men have been in power. Judged on the basis of the crimes they have committed there is little to choose between the dictatorial governments and those claiming to be otherwise. . . .

Review of developments shows, in spite of occasional backslidings, that especially in economic lines Guatemala is today far ahead of the Guatemala of 1870, and that progress has been fairly steady since the fall of Estrada Cabrera in 1920. Social advance in the period is less marked. If the reader were himself dictator, though he might prefer to go down in defeat rather than resort to the extremes the rulers have stooped to in treatment of the opposition, he would find little to condemn among the constructive measures for internal improvement which have been promised and in encouraging measure carried through. In the long run, to whatever degree they have failed to make their periods of rule examples of popular government, the dictators have, it seems clear, sought to create the conditions necessary before democracy in the tropics can be given a fair trial.

But it may well be asked, if that be the case, why democracy has not advanced further. . . . The answer is not simple. Some elements that have helped make the political progress much less marked than the economic may be stated. . . . Maintenance of public order still takes so large a part of public income that the support of constructive measures continues to be limited by lack of funds. . . .

The economic development so markedly reflected in foreign trade and public income has not become generalized in proportionately greater income for the mass of the people. The gains have gone chiefly to foreigners and a limited number of the ladinos. The national standard of life has continued to be extraordinarily low, lower even than in a number of comparable areas in the American tropics. . . .

If the more distinctively political features of Guatemalan life be examined, other features retarding progress present themselves. In Guatemala as in a number of other Hispanic American states only a very small proportion of the people have any interest in government. Overwhelmingly illiterate as all but a small fraction are, living on a low standard, consuming little beyond what they produce, almost untouched by government activities, they know little about who is in control and they care less. Only in the labor legislation and more recently in the exactions for road building has the Indian come into close contact with the demands of the central government. In public opinion he has no share; in elections he has no interest. If he were not, as is the case, counted out in the voting, he would count himself out.

It may be asked why the small class of Guatemalans whose standard of life is comparable to that of Europeans has not developed within itself a political consciousness which would bring about the use of democratic processes by a more restricted electorate through

excluding the great nonpolitical majority of the population from voting. Here also no easy answer is possible.

Those who have framed Guatemalan and other Central American constitutions and those who have passed
legislation under them have had an enthusiasm for
the standard of universal suffrage. It has appeared to
them a symbol of the democracy to which they aspired
and to many a means to secure it. However defensible
in theory, universal suffrage works badly or not at all in
Guatemala, since the Indian seldom wishes to vote and
the elections are practically never free. When they are
free the political factions struggle to record the Indian
vote in their favor. When they are not free those in
power vote the Indians as a part of political routine.
In any case Indian voting means the blind voting of
masses of electors who have no conception of the is-
sues espoused by the candidates. Manhood suffrage in
Guatemala has not stimulated the Indian population to
interest in politics, it does not result in division of opinion on policies, it has not fostered democracy. It has
made the Indian vote only a counterweight which the
ladino politicians feel they must control.

Universal suffrage has been accepted and continued
by the dictators though it is not clear that it has contributed to strengthen their hands. Possibly endeavor to
abandon it might be used by the opposition to question
the "democracy" of those in power. If it were abandoned the standard of voting would have greater reality
in that it would recognize the fact that government is actually a ladino function. The charge that Indian interests would not then have representation does not have
strength. They do not have representation now. There
is not however any movement in Guatemala toward mod-
ification of the basis on which elections rest.

It is not to be supposed that change in the electorate
would promptly bring conditions which would assure
popular government. Restriction of voting to the literate
or the enforcement of a property qualification would
make the number of voters smaller and increase its in-

telligence but might do little to cut down the personalism so strikingly characteristic of politics. Family connections and alliances are close among the ruling classes and the allegiances and rivalries arising therefrom would not be greatly modified under the changed system of voting. The efforts to control the voting in the larger electorate might only be concentrated on the smaller one.

One feature not itself political which may contribute to the instability of Guatemalan life lies in the economic organization of the country. Here as in all communities in comparable state of development the possible outlets for the ambitions of the more enterprising are severely limited. The wide variety of careers normally open for choice in a country of varied economic development does not exist. Energies which would normally be drawn off into business or the professions are turned into struggle for positions in the public service.

Development of the national resources might be expected to lessen this concentration of attention on politics but in Guatemala it has not done so. Upper-class Guatemalans as a rule have not gone into agriculture, have not shown strong predilections for industrial activity, and have not become the most active factors in commerce. The chief reason for this is allegedly the lack of local capital for financing new enterprises. In the case of larger undertakings such as the public utilities and more expensive plantation enterprises dependence upon foreigners who will make direct investments has been necessary or at least the practice. Even in smaller undertakings to supply the domestic market, in which capital has played a less important role, foreigners have taken the leading part.

As a result the economic life of the country has in the major enterprises come to be in large degree domestic neither in management nor ownership. Consequently, it is argued, while it has increased the development of the national resources and has indirectly increased the public income, it has not, at least as yet, lessened the desires of the more ambitious Guatemalans to secure government positions—on which, of course, they have a monopoly. . . .

Whether the public programs which have been followed and the extragovernmental changes in the interests of the Guatemalan people will build the bridge between dictatorship and popular government no one can say. If they do develop the national wealth, raise the standard of life, bring the Indian into the currents of the modern world, increase the income of the national treasury to be used for the common good, diversify the ambitions of the citizenship, and create a well-knit Guatemalan nationality, dictators may decline in power as the people insist on taking a greater measure of authority into their own hands. But developments may be irregular and of unexpected consequence and it is to be remembered that dictatorial power is not exercised only in undeveloped and nonindustrial states. The road from dictatorship to democracy for Latin American nations is a long one and a route on which many of them have seemed at times to start only to turn back. Possibly the apparent progress in Guatemala may be checked or reversed.

If the Indian population continues to play no real role in public affairs a higher standard of life for it, if it comes, may still leave the state divided against itself. . . .

Economic crises which affect so deeply and so frequently the prosperity of monoculture countries may continue to upset the economic bases of the national life and thereby delay the winning of political stability.

Unless the average citizen comes to be attracted by the more exacting duties which industrial responsibilities bring, the foreigner may keep the position he now holds in the economic activities of the country and thus divide the interests of those who develop its resources and of those who govern it.

If the traditional acceptance of the leadership of the executive continues, all the economic advance made by recent administrations and all that may come in the future may prove only to have given better weapons into the hands of those who find the maintenance of order justification for continuing their control. Better transportation facilities may strengthen their power to crush opposition. Increase of public wealth and revenue may have a similar result.

No one knows the formula for progress from dictatorship to popular government. How often have dictators been forced from power by democratic movements, with the result that order with sacrifice of liberty has been replaced by political chaos with no better guarantee of citizens' rights! How often, too, have hopes been aroused that dictators will show the necessary strength of character and the patriotism to permit the gradual lessening of their powers by peaceful means and how often have such hopes proved vain!

Neither the rulers nor the people of Guatemala can place all the blame upon the other for the failure to achieve that degree of popular government to which all profess to aspire. The dictators cannot through the economic measures they adopt create a bridge over which the country may promptly pass to the benefits of popular rule. The people cannot expect those who rule willingly to give up powers long enjoyed.

If Guatemala is to become a democracy in fact as well as in name, all factions must be willing to support governments which may gradually become more popular through a slow process of trial, error, and sacrifice. A survey of the experience of the republic does not indicate that such advance will be rapid, sustained, or free from disappointments. But the long task of creating the economic, cultural, and political conditions which may make such progress possible must be assumed by Guatemalans, both the dictators and those they rule, if the country is to win the goal they all declare for.

A Bibliographical Note

The literature on concentrations of power and strong man rule in an abstract or comparative sense is so vast that a mere handful of titles are suggested as provocative background for those interested in creating a broader frame of reference for studying the caudillo: Hannah Arendt, *The Origins of Totalitarianism* (New York: Meridian Books, 1958); J. O. Hertzler, "The Typical Life Cycle of Dictatorship," *Social Forces*, Vol. XVII (1938-1939); Sidney Hook, *The Hero in History: A Study in Limitation and Possibility* (Boston: Beacon Press, 1955); Seymour M. Lipset, *Political Man: The Social Base of Politics* (Garden City: Anchor, 1963); and Karl A. Wittfogel, *Oriental Despotism: A Comparative Study of Total Power* (New Haven: Yale University Press, 1957). Excellent annotated bibliographies which bear heavily on the problems of authoritarianism will be found in John J. Johnson's two works: *Political Change in Latin America: The Growth of the Middle Sectors* (Stanford: Stanford University Press, 1958) and *The Military and Society in Latin America* (Stanford: Stanford University Press, 1964).

Considering the importance of dictators and dictatorship in Latin America, it is remarkable how little has been done to organize bibliographies on the subject. The quarterly *Hispanic American Historical Review* (1918-   ) is the most valuable single source for information and contains the now dated "List of Books Referring to Caudillos in Hispanic America," Vol. XIII (1933), pp. 143-246, by Charles E. Chapman. Use of the *HAHR* will be facilitated by consulting Ruth Latham Butler (ed.), *Guide to the Hispanic American Historical Review, 1918-1945* (Durham: Duke Univ. Press, 1950) and the sequel covering 1946-1955 edited by Charles Gibson with the assistance of E. V. Niemeyer (Durham: Duke University Press, 1958). This same journal has published a distinguished series of historiographic essays for Spanish America which include the following: R. A. Humphreys, "The Historiography of the Spanish American Revolutions," Vol. XXXVI (1956), pp. 81-93; Robert Potash,

"The Historiography of Mexico Since 1821," Vol. XL (1960), pp. 383-424; William J. Griffith, "The Historiography of Central America Since 1830," Vol. XL (1960), pp. 548-569; Robert F. Smith, "Twentieth Century Cuban Historiography," Vol. XLIV (1964), pp. 44-73; Charles W. Arnade, "The Historiography of Colonial and Modern Bolivia," Vol. XLII (1962), pp. 333-384; and Joseph R. Barager, "The Historiography of the Río de la Plata Area since 1830," Vol. XXXIX (1959), pp. 588-642.

The standard history and political science textbooks on Latin America all bear more or less directly on the problem of the caudillo. Political analysis of Latin American societies is perhaps best developed in William S. Stokes, *Latin American Politics* (New York: Crowell, 1959). Likewise useful, especially for its exercise in the typology of dictatorships, is William W. Pierson and Federico G. Gil, *Governments of Latin America* (New York: McGraw-Hill, 1957). Two briefer paperback introductions should be noted: James L. Busey, *Latin America: Political Institutions and Processes* (New York: Random House, 1964) and R. A. Gómez, *Government and Politics in Latin America* (New York: Random House, 1960). See also Karl M. Schmitt and David D. Burks, *Evolution or Chaos: Dynamics of Latin American Government and Politics* (New York: F. A. Praeger, 1963). A provocative book of related essays by one of the most able scholars of Latin America is Frank Tannenbaum's *Ten Keys to Latin America* (New York: A. A. Knopf, 1962). Except for the particularly helpful "Political Dilemma in Latin America," which originally appeared in *Foreign Affairs* (April, 1960), most of these same essays will be found in slightly different form in Herbert L. Matthews (ed.), *The United States and Latin America*, 2nd ed. (Englewood Cliffs, N. J.: The American Assembly, Prentice-Hall, 1963).

Though somewhat dated, the fifty-five articles written by a host of scholars and collected into Asher N. Christensen's *The Evolution of Latin American Government* (New York: Holt, 1951) should be examined by the student of caudillismo. See also the relevant essays in A. Curtis Wilgus (ed.), *The Caribbean: Its Political Problems* (Gainesville: University of Florida Press, 1956). The crisp sketches of nineteenth- and early twentieth-century *pensadores* and critics by William Rex Crawford in his *A Century of Latin-American Thought*, 2nd ed. (Cambridge: Harvard University Press, 1961) are especially revealing studies of some of the foremost opponents of caudillismo among the intelligentsia. Many useful papers which explore the oppressive elements of dictatorship with respect to education, communications, religion, and the arts will be found in Ángel del Río (ed.), *Responsible Freedom in the Americas* (Garden City: Doubleday, 1955).

Expository and interpretative works which deal directly with the phenomenon of the dictator in Spanish America are often repetitious and lacking in novelty. Important contributions do exist, however. A sample which reveals divergent points of view might well begin with the oft cited article by Charles E. Chapman, "The Age of the Caudillos: A Chapter in Hispanic American History," *The Hispanic American Historical Review*, Vol. XII (1932), pp. 281-300. The cosmopolitan Peruvian Francisco García Calderón's *Latin America: Its Rise and Progress* (London: Fisher Unwin, 1913) should be consulted early in one's study of caudillismo as well as the same author's insightful essay "Dictatorship and Democracy in Latin America," *Foreign Affairs*, Vol. III (1925), 459-477. Cecil Jane's *Liberty and Despotism in Spanish America* (Oxford: Clarendon Press, 1929) is too tidy to be convincing but is still provocative and readable. With its pithy character sketches, J. Fred Rippy's thirty-year-old essay is worthy of attention: see "Dictatorship in Spanish America," in *Dictatorship in the Modern World*, Guy Stanton Ford (ed.), (Minneapolis: University of Minnesota Press, 1935). The English scholar R. A. Humphreys has written several pertinent interpretations. One is his fourth chapter in *The Evolution of Modern Latin America* (Oxford: Clarendon Press, 1946) and the other is entitled "Latin America: The Caudillo Tradition" and appears in Michael Howard (ed.), *Soldiers and Governments: Nine Studies in Civil–Military Relations* (Bloomington: Indiana University Press, 1959). The close association of dictators and the military has prompted many works. Notable among these are Edwin Lieuwen, *Arms and Politics in Latin America*, Rev. ed. (New York: F. A. Praeger, 1961); John Johnson's aforementioned *The Military and Society in Latin America* . . . ; the Swedish scholar Magnus Mörner's "Caudillos y militares en la evolución hispanoamericana," *Journal of Inter-American Studies*, Vol. II (1960), pp. 295-310; and Gino Germani and Kalman Silvert's important essay in typology "Politics, Social Structure and Military Intervention in Latin America," *Archives européennes de sociologie*, Vol. II (1961), pp. 62-81. Two efforts by Latin

Americans to explain the caudillo are José E. Iturriaga, "El tirano en la América Latina," *Jornadas* (El Colegio de México: Centro de Estudios Sociales), No. 15 (1944), and Domingo Alberto Rangel, "Una interpretación de las dictaduras latinoamericanas," *Cuadernos americanos.* Vol. LXXVII (September–October, 1954), No. 5, pp. 33-42. For a Spanish view which supports the thesis that life-term presidencies are appropriate in many parts of Latin America, see Antonio Carro Martínez, "El caudillismo americano," *Revista de estudios políticos* (Madrid: Instituto de Estudios Políticos), No. 93 (1957), pp. 139-163. A standard Communist interpretation will be found in William Z. Foster's *Outline Political History of the Americas* (New York: International Publishers, 1951), pp. 295-299.

The study of individual dictators may be approached through national histories and collective biographies. See Josefina del Toro (ed.), *A Bibliography of the Collective Biography of Spanish America* (Río Piedras, P.R., 1938). Collections which are useful include William S. Robertson, *Rise of the Spanish-American Republics: As Told in the Lives of Their Liberators,* Paper ed. (New York: Collier Books, 1961); A. Curtis Wilgus (ed.), *South American Dictators during the First Century of Independence,* 2nd ed. (New York: Russell and Russell, 1963); Harold E. Davis, *Latin American Leaders* (Washington: Inter-American Bibliographic and Library Association, 1949); Tad Szulc, *Twilight of the Tyrants* (New York: Henry Holt, 1959); and Robert J. Alexander, *Prophets of the Revolution: Profiles of the Latin American Leaders* (New York: Macmillan, 1962).

Recognizing that it is impossible to scan all the principal literature which bears on the individual caudillos of all eighteen Spanish American countries, a select concentration on some of the major works and bibliographic problems of a few countries will not be out of order. The Argentine dictators Juan Manuel Rosas and Juan Domingo Perón have been focal points for the study of caudillismo in the region of the Río de la Plata. Both a guide to the literature on Rosas and a fascinating study of the ways in which late nineteenth- and twentieth-century historians in Argentina have interpreted him will be found in Clifton B. Kroeber, "Rosas and the Revision of Argentine History, 1880-1955," *Inter-American Review of Bibliography,* Vol. X (1960), pp. 3-25. A sample of the revisionist writing which Kroeber discusses and which runs counter to Sarmiento's view of Rosas is Carlos

Ibarguren, *Juan Manuel de Rosas: su vida, su tiempo, su drama* (Buenos Aires, 1930). The Peronist decade, 1945-1955, and its aftermath are discussed with special attention to works published by Argentines in a bibliographic essay in two parts by Fritz L. Hoffmann, "Perón and After," Part I, *The Hispanic American Historical Review*, Vol. XXXVI (1956), pp. 510-528, and Part II (Conclusion), *Ibid*, Vol. XXXIX (1959), pp. 212-233. Three works in English which emerged before Perón's overthrow are useful points of departure for further study: Robert J. Alexander, *The Perón Era* (New York: Columbia University Press, 1951); George I. Blanksten, *Perón's Argentina* (Chicago: University of Chicago Press, 1953); and Arthur P. Whitaker, *The United States and Argentina* (Cambridge: Harvard University Press, 1954). For a caudillo-kinship study of Salta, 1815-1821, see Roger M. Haigh, "The Creation and Control of a Caudillo," *The Hispanic American Historical Review*, XLIV (1964), pp. 481-490.

The history of Gran Colombia and the nations which emerged from that confederation provides a wide canvas for works about caudillos. One might begin with the excellent biography of *Simón Bolívar* (Albuquerque: University of New Mexico Press, 1948) by Gerhard Masur and explore the wealth of material available on "The Liberator." Robert L. Gilmore's penetrating study of *Caudillism and Militarism in Venezuela, 1810-1910* (Athens, Ohio: Ohio University Press, 1964) examines prevailing conditions. A provocative study of one of the better known Venezuelan dictators of the later nineteenth century is George S. Wise, *Caudillo: A Portrait of Antonio Guzmán Blanco* (New York: Columbia University Press, 1951). Juan Vicente Gómez who dominated Venezuela during the first third of this century has been the subject of a polemical struggle which has ranged from the glowing defenses by Laureano Vallenilla Lanz, *Cesarismo democrático* (Caracas, 1929) and Pedro Manuel Arcaya, *The Gómez Régime in Venezuela and its Background* (Washington, D. C.: The Sun Printing Co., 1936) to the damning tale of atrocities by Thomas Rourke (Pseud. for D. J. Clinton), *Gómez: Tyrant of the Andes* (New York: Morrow, 1936) and the more measured critical study by John Lavin, *A Halo for Gómez* (New York: Pageant, 1954). In Ecuador the figure who has drawn the most attention is the theocratic dictator García Moreno. A generally favorable account is Richard Pattee, *Gabriel García Moreno y el Ecua-*

dor de su tiempo, 3rd ed. (México: Ed. Jus, 1962); while sharply critical views are expressed by Juan Montalvo in his famous essay "La dictadura perpetua," in Manuel Moreno Sánchez (ed.), *Montalvo* (México: Secretaría de Educación Pública, 1942), pp. 23-34, and by Benjamín Carrión, *García Moreno: el santo del patíbulo* (México: Fondo de Cultura, 1959). A pertinent examination of more recent history is George I. Blanksten, *Ecuador: Constitutions and Caudillos* (Berkeley and Los Angeles: University of California Press, 1951).

Chile, which has produced such a distinguished historiography during the last hundred years, is a fertile source for caudillo studies. Diego Portales, perhaps the most unusual of Chile's strong men, never assumed the presidency and remained influential long after his death in 1837. For a two volume study see Francisco A. Encina, *Portales: introducción a la historia de la época* . . . *1830-1894* (Santiago, 1934).

Mexico offers an exceptionally large laboratory for the study of individual caudillos, caciques, and the milieu which supported or tolerated them. A stimulating book which explores this range from Cortés to the present while offering an interpretation of Mexican history is Lesley B. Simpson, *Many Mexicos* (Berkeley: University of California Press, 1952). The decade of internecine fighting, 1810-1821, produced caudillos along with an uneasy independence. Useful studies include Hugh M. Hamill, Jr., *The Hidalgo Revolt: Prelude to Mexican Independence* (Gainesville: University of Florida Press, 1966); Wilbert H. Timmons, *Morelos of Mexico: Priest, Soldier, Statesman* (El Paso: Texas Western College Press, 1963); and William S. Robertson, *Iturbide of Mexico* (Durham: Duke University Press, 1952). For a good biography of Mexico's most cynical leader, see Wilfred H. Callcott, *Santa Anna: The Story of an Enigma Who Once Was Mexico*, 2nd ed. (Hamden, Conn.: Archon Books, 1964). Works on *La Reforma* include Walter V. Scholes, *Mexican Politics during the Juárez Regime*, 1855-1872 (Columbia: University of Missouri Press, 1957) and Charles Allen Smart, *Viva Juárez!* (New York: Lippincott, 1963). While there exists a readable biography in English of *Porfirio Díaz: Dictator of Mexico* (Philadelphia: Lippincott, 1932) by Carleton Beals, the most thorough analysis of the era called *El Porfiriato* (1876-1911) will be found in the distinguished multi-volume work of Daniel Cosío Villegas, *et al., Historia moderna de México* (México: Ed. Hermes,

1955-   ). On the ideology of the Díaz regime, see Leopoldo
Zea, "Positivism and Porfirism in Latin America," in F. S. C.
Northrop (ed.), *Ideological Differences and World Order*
(New Haven: Yale University Press, 1949), pp. 166-191.
The Mexican Revolution of 1910 and the emergent one-
party political system has given rise to a large literature
which touches both individual leaders and the presidency as
institution. For introductions, see Frank Tannenbaum, "Personal Government in Mexico," *Foreign Affairs*, Vol. XXVII
(1948), pp. 44-57, and the detailed study by Stephen S.
Goodspeed, "El papel del jefe del ejecutivo en México,"
Problemas industriales e agrícolas de México, Vol. VII
(1955), pp. 13-208.

Fidel Castro has been receiving closer scrutiny than any
other dictator in Latin American history. Robert F. Smith's
companion volume in this series entitled *Background to Revolution* explores essentials of the pre-Castro era. So charged
has been the political atmosphere surrounding Cuba that
most of the literature on Fidel is polemical. One exception,
which examines economic aspects between 1959 and 1962, is
Dudley Seers (ed.), *Cuba: The Economic and Social Revolution* (Chapel Hill: University of North Carolina Press, 1964).
A useful guide to the early years of the Cuban Revolution
is Margaret B. Mughisuddin and Bum-Joon Lee Park, *Cuba
since Castro: A Bibliography of Revolutionary Material*
(Washington, 1963).

Literary approaches to Spanish American dictatorship have
drawn foreign authors as diverse as Joseph Conrad, O. Henry,
and Ramón Valle-Inclán into print. Matched against the
famous interpretative essay on "Dr. Francia" by Thomas
Carlyle (1843) is the durable novel with the same subject
by Edward Lucas White, *El Supremo: A Romance of the
Great Dictator of Paraguay* (New York: Dutton, 1916). *The
Purple Land* (New York: The Modern Library, 1926),
W. H. Hudson's tale of the Banda Oriental (Uruguay) during the mid-nineteenth century, captures the nuances of the
fierce struggles among caciques for power. Spanish American
writers have, of course, found a principal theme in caudillismo. Among the major works of fiction which are representative are Mariano Azuela's novel of the Mexican Revolution *The Underdogs* (Los de abajo), trans. by E. Munguía, Jr.
(New York: New American Library, 1963); the Venezuelan
author-statesmen Rómulo Gallegos' *Doña Barbara* (Caracas,
1929) about the wild female cacique of the Llanos; and

Miguel Angel Asturias' terrifying novel of Central American
dictatorship, *El Señor Presidente*, trans. by Frances Partridge
(New York: Atheneum, 1964).

A NOTE ON THE TYPE

This book is set in Electra, a Linotype face designed by W. A. Dwiggins. This face cannot be classified as either modern or old-style. It is not based on any historical model, nor does it echo any particular period or style. It avoids the extreme contrasts between thick and thin elements that mark most modern faces, and attempts to give a feeling of fluidity, power, and speed.

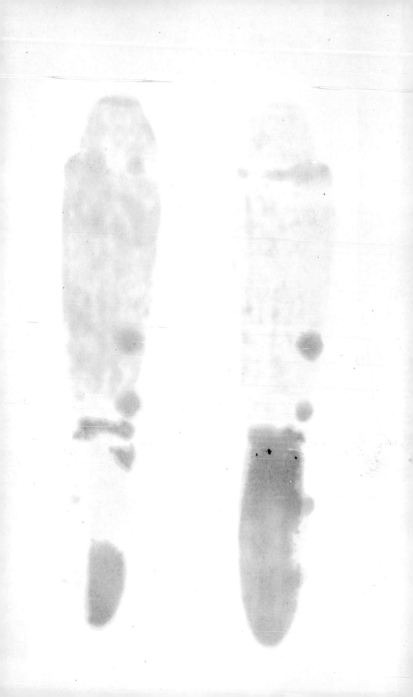

12/5/66